ART AND MORALITY

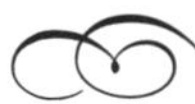

ART AND MORALITY

Essays in the Spirit of George Santayana

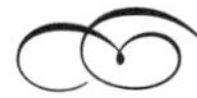

MORRIS GROSSMAN
Edited by Martin A. Coleman

FORDHAM UNIVERSITY PRESS   NEW YORK   2014

Fordham University Press has no responsibility for the persistence or accuracy of URLs for external or third-party Internet websites referred to in this publication and does not guarantee that any content on such websites is, or will remain, accurate or appropriate.

Fordham University Press also publishes its books in a variety of electronic formats. Some content that appears in print may not be available in electronic books.

Library of Congress Cataloging-in-Publication Data

Grossman, Morris, 1922–2012, author.
    [Essays. Selections]
    Art and morality : essays in the spirit of George Santayana / Morris Grossman ; edited by Martin A. Coleman.
        pages cm — (American philosophy)
    Includes bibliographical references and index.
    ISBN 978-0-8232-5722-5 (hardback) — ISBN 978-0-8232-5723-2 (paper)
  1. Art and morals.   I. Coleman, Martin A., editor of compilation.   II. Title.
    N72.E8G76 2014
    700.1—dc23

                                                                    2013046184

Printed in the United States of America

16 15 14   5 4 3 2 1

First edition

To the memory of my parents,
Dr. Isaac and Annie Grossman

Contents

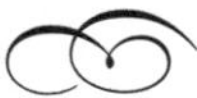

Part II. Artistic Philosophers and Philosophical Artists

Part III. Santayana

Acknowledgments

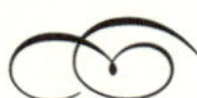

Thank you to Albert Hofstadter, Arthur C. Danto, and Justus Buchler; more recently, Carol Feldman and Alison Tannenbaum, not philosophers but helpful readers and correctors. Martin Coleman's help has been the most thorough and valuable. I am pleased to acknowledge David Spiech at the Santayana Edition, who worked on my texts. There are several others who have encouraged me over the years—including Herman Saatkamp, John Lachs, and Peter Hare.

MORRIS A. GROSSMAN

Editor's Preface

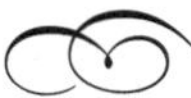

The majority of the essays included here have been published previously in journals and books. Previous publication is indicated by unnumbered endnotes that appear with (and precede) each essay's numbered endnotes at the back of the book. Each essay has been minimally revised by having typographical errors, misquotations, or formatting inconsistencies corrected. Some essays have been more extensively revised in order to improve readability, correct factual errors, or reflect changes in the author's preferred form of expression. More extensive revisions were made by the author or by the editor with the approval of the author.

MARTIN A. COLEMAN

ART AND MORALITY

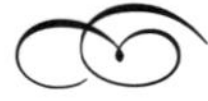

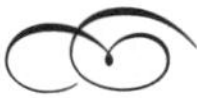

INTRODUCTION

In Macbeth, after Macduff learns of the murder of his wife and children, Malcolm says to him, "Dispute it like a man." In one of Shakespeare's great lines, almost lost in its brevity, Macduff replies, "I shall do so, but I must also feel it as a man" (*Macbeth*, Act 4, Scene 3). Many discussions about Macbeth deal with issues of manliness and gender. Even in this part of the play Macduff talks about the possibility of shedding womanly tears, and one might wonder whether "feel it as a man" has to do with gender. I suggest that it does not, and Macduff might just as well have said, "feel it like a person." The distinction that he draws attention to is what I call the art/morality distinction, not a gender one. The advice to "dispute it like a man" is a moral suggestion directed to outer action. The determination to "feel it as a man" is an aesthetic reminder, directed to the value of an immediate experience, to being human, despite its seeming irrelevance to pressing outer circumstances, and even despite the needless delay it might cause.

What makes the situation difficult and poignant (and, of course, intellectually challenging and ambiguous) is that the two choices are easily fused into one. They are not usually thought of as distinguishable or separate. The phrase "I shall do so" suggests futurity, even one action necessarily following upon another. But the choices occur together, or perhaps can more fully be brought together, by some effort and focus on Macduff's part. The "I shall do so" is already what he is thinking, but does it preclude the "feeling," the remembrances of his family, his wife, his little ones, along with the simultaneous anger and preparation for action? Anger itself is a most anomalous emotion. It can be self-contained, a body response, perhaps, as I elsewhere suggest, even an enjoyable one—like cursing the darkness. But it can and does notoriously look beyond itself, to action and revenge, and might see itself (as in Malcolm's urging and understanding of the matter) a wasted feeling and surely one that should not cause hesitation. It doesn't necessarily require a Shakespeare, or a noble soul like Macduff, to articulate comparable thoughts. I saw a tennis player interviewed after winning the semi-final of an important tournament. He was asked about his plans for the surely difficult final to be held two days later. He said, "I'll enjoy this one for the rest of the day. Tomorrow I'll regroup."

The intrigue of the art/morality distinction has occurred to me in various, sometimes strange and trivial, ways. I offer here a few other instances connected with very ordinary experiences. They might continue to serve as a prelude to later chapters and wider elaborations.

The Quorum Call. During C-SPAN telecasts of the live Senate in action, there are frequent moments (which might be seen as interruptions) when there is a Quorum Call. A senator declares the absence of a quorum. The Senate's deliberations, which might be about matters of great moment, are brought to a halt. The picture of the Senate persists on the TV screen, with two large blue-walled sections as background. There are three rows of desks where people sit quietly. Some move about, perhaps delivering papers. One hears no further discussion from the floor. Everything is in a waiting mode, waiting for something important.

But what one hears, as background to the interrupted and still visible Senate, might be a Mozart piano concerto or some other classical music. The juxtaposition is aesthetically and morally provocative. It is another variation on the double attentiveness that is the theme of this book. The experience focuses me as neither the Senate scene alone, nor the Mozart music alone, might have done. This is neither a derogation of the Senate, nor a praise of Mozart, or vice versa. There is simply a provocation to think about, to capture and spotlight, an elusive comparison.

During the quorum call the business of the Senate remains in mind and even remains, in part, on the TV screen. While one listens to the music, there is the knowledge that the Senate will soon resume its business. It is a concurrent, even a contrapuntal, experience. The welcome beauty of the Mozart piece is especially conspicuous, partly for the knowledge that it came as an interruption and is not done for its own sake, and partly because it will soon itself be interrupted by the end of the quorum call. At that point the serious business of the Senate will resume. The music will be halted, though the memory of the Mozart piece might remain.

The Senate, whatever the occasional failings of senators, embodies, in part, the legal and moral majesty of a State. Its deliberations, as Aristotle might explain, have to do with the proper defense of the State and the well-being of its people, and just possibly their creative potentials along with their opportunities to listen to Mozart.

The juxtaposition created by the quorum call involves us in two distinct awarenesses. It brings together what is not often so vividly brought together. But at the same time it makes one aware, despite the juxtaposition, of the enormous distances between the political efforts and actions needed to get things done and the rare flowerings of "Mozart moments," the things that are accomplished when the work of the State is finally fulfilled. Those moments do not usually juxtapose quickly and unexpectedly. They are usually the distant and dubitable outcome of those preliminary prosaic and political efforts. They are usually tragically far apart, as is the natural case with means and ends.

In life, the choice that this quorum call experience embodies and dramatizes is a relationship that is always with us. Even right now. Especially right now. Always right now. Art and morality may not usually be presented to us in just this artificial juxtaposition of music and politics. Yet any experience at any time has equivalent and searchable parts or moments. Shall I enjoy what I can now and stay here? Shall I think of where it leads and go there? In Macduff's terms, shall I now dispute what has to be disputed, or shall I feel what has to be felt?

How things begin and end—in life, music, whatever—is a continuous preoccupation in our art and morality survey. The quorum call, as we saw, begins when a senator proposes it, usually by suggesting the absence of a quorum. The business of the Senate, which got under way with its own purposes and procedures, is temporarily ended, or at least interrupted. No further official speaks, though there might be some stirring about and perhaps some private talk. The music begins, not at the appropriate beginning of a composition, but as a chance-like startup somewhere in its middle. As the music continues, it insinuates itself and holds our attention far more than the silent figures on the screen are able to do. We become involved in an essentially musical experience, with the Senate not entirely lost to thought but quite in the background. Such division of attention is familiar to us when we sit at a concert or at an opera, and when we perhaps take the sounds heard as far more important than the actions that are creating them. But there is usually a connection between the two. The music following the quorum call is fully disconnected from what goes on "on stage." It is probably supplied by a technician who likely does not even know what the Senate's concurrent business might have been. Naturally there is no link between the sounds, words, and actions, except for their forced proximity.

The quorum call is sometimes ended when a senator "vitiates" it. William Safire once did a column on "vitiation," which can range from mere termination to ending something with some opprobrium.[1] I have been annoyed at the stopping in the middle of, say, Mozart's "Piano Concerto No. 20" for the resumption of tiresome talk, and I saw such vitiation in the strong sense. But the stopping could be welcome.

The choice of attending to morality or art is itself morally duplicitous. Do we want sweet sounds interrupting and hovering over the Senate's urgent business? On the other hand, do we want Mozart interfering with the safety of the nation, a declaration of war, the building of its military, the restoration of its economy, the preservation of jobs, even the furtherance of that education and art that might make further Mozart moments possible? Whichever it is, only the mental leaps between the alternatives, between art and morality, can put us in a frame to make the creative judgment about how to proceed. Only those leaps can help us to know, or to leave us in ongoing ignorance, about where and who we are.

Lincoln Center and the Firehouse. When Lincoln Center was built I went to see it and in the process walked around the neighborhood it largely replaced. In the vicinity of the Center I saw a small firehouse, and as I went by saw firemen inside moving about and "working." My mind immediately juxtaposed, and compared, the respective institutions.

The firehouse is (to me) a dramatically simple embodiment of morality. It involves blue-collar effort and occasional heroics. Firemen save lives. To sacrifice and save a life or lives, as done by Sydney Carton in *A Tale of Two Cities*, or by a soldier on a battlefield, or by an Only Begotten Son in religion, is often thought of as the ultimate in morality. The firehouse is easily an illustrative icon of such ultimacy. The structure of a firehouse is about as close as one can get to the aesthetics of pure function. It is no larger than it has to be to house the engine and the firemen. Everything about it concerns ulterior purpose, nothing concerns appearance or pleasure to the eye. (Since writing this, inevitably, I've heard about firehouse architecture!)

And what is Lincoln Center? It too is an icon of sorts, a mighty and expensive series of structures dedicated to the conspicuous pleasure of great and lasting art! It displays symphonies, ballets, and operas. It required wealth to build and requires wealth to sustain. It could arguably be the world's greatest center devoted exclusively to art. The small firehouse is not part of Lincoln Center, not part of its architecture, but close enough to invite and press a comparison. Each is a kind of epitome of its own identity and purpose and each is, in the deepest sense, what the other is not. And if good definitions are by exclusion, what could be more exclusive than these separate structures, their separate identities and separate purposes? And what could better help us understand what each is than the other, and a willingness to weigh and encounter that otherness?

Candle in the Dark. Here is another example of, or early variation on, my theme. It has been said, "It is better to light a candle than to curse the darkness." I turn this around, by now almost inevitably, and consider whether it might not be better to curse the darkness than light a candle.

The case for the first claim is easy to make. Lighting a candle might be hopeful and useful. We might see what needs to be seen and accomplish what would otherwise not be accomplished. It might even help others;

that is, it might be more moral. The Talmud says, "One person's candle is light for many."

What case can be made for the phrase, "It is better to curse the darkness than to light a candle"? (Note that this is different from the mere dialectical countering phrase, "It is not the case that it is better . . . ," though there is some connection.) It could be argued that the candle doesn't extend much light, makes little difference with respect to how far we can see, and it is unlikely to help us to find or improve things. Its utility is doubtful and it gives little or no pleasure in itself. That's the crux—it's not much of an immediate joy. Though we may begin to set up the candle with slight stirrings of good feelings, it actually supplies little light and less warmth.

But can cursing the darkness ever be better? Cursing with fury and clever language is an old and honorable tradition. Skilled vituperation, as in Juvenalian satire, has enriched our literary enjoyment and is indeed one of those enjoyments. While cursing the darkness accomplishes little, and might be as morally futile as lighting the candle, it might have the greater terminal, or aesthetic, value—as just suggested.

I had a fleeting moment of "scholarly" joy, as can happen with a serendipitous "research" discovery, when I saw the following item in the *New York Times*:

> In Ashikaga, Japan, people participate in the Akutare Matsuri, or the Festival of Abusive Language. They climb a hill to the 1,200-year-old Saishoji temple while screaming curses and railing at employers, teachers or politicians. After that catharsis, they welcome the new year with ceremonies in the temple to allow happiness to flow in the coming months.[2]

Such findings, or confirming insights, are surely pleasing.

The obscurities remain, as with Macduff. Is the catharsis pleasing, or the later actions or ceremonies? Is it the "disputing" or the "feeling"? Just what is instrumental and what is terminal? What is morality and what is art?

The comparison of lighting a candle with cursing the darkness does not necessarily determine which is better. But making the comparison, a meta-action, might itself be more satisfying than engaging in either action. Comparisons do sway us, for better or worse, to move from action to contemplation, from deciding what to do to thinking about alternatives. Reflecting on a choice, to be sure, might help us to make a choice. But it gives us, inevitably, *as a performative choice itself,* another matter to reflect upon. It is a further hidden, and ongoing, move from the moral to the aesthetic, from the practical to the theoretical.

My challenge to lighting the candle—to wit, cursing the darkness—is not, need I say, what the creator of the original aphorism intended or wanted. He did not expect that a case could be made against lighting the candle. He would surely think of the cursing as a moral failure, even if perversely enjoyed. Along with what he saw, with or without candles, it did not occur to him that there could be any argument for the cursing.

Yet my repeated interest (perhaps it occurs bellicosely) is in the non-thought-about or neglected alternative.

My challenge also reveals something further to me that I could not see before I did my comparison, the gained insight that my reversal accomplishes. It is the kind of reflexivity dear to art, and that I later look at in literary, theatrical, and mirroring terms. Whether A is better than B, or vice versa, is unknown and possibly unknowable. But to reflect on why either is better than the other is thoughtful activity. It might be a wiser or more satisfying thing to do than to dwell or suggest or act on either one. Ergo, it might be better, more insightful, more useful, more joyful, to compare the two opposing aphorisms than to utter either one, or do what either one suggests as a worldly action. Such intellectual comparing, or thinking, is aesthetic or terminal, and arguably worthwhile. It is a move to *theoria,* to understanding. It feigns the motivation of a practical concern but moves beyond it.

These superadded reflexivities always inhere in the art/morality distinction. To sum up, it might be better to disparage or contradict the precept, "It is better to light a candle than to curse the darkness," than to utter or enjoy it. Of course, this is a new, a different, moral precept, a meta-precept, with different aesthetic overtones. Uttering a precept is not the same as referring to it or suggesting it, let alone acting on it, and the art-morality distribution is altered, so to speak, as soon as we start making and contextualizing a distinction. This suggests the ambiguities of moral utterance, how such utterance easily veers to the aesthetic. Any move to the intellectual, to *theoria*, to seeing things comprehensively rather than *doing* anything, is also unwittingly a move to the aesthetic.

But of course—to compromise what was just written—seeing is another way of doing.

The following is perhaps a simpler example of the regress of hidden contextualizing. Santayana somewhere wrote that when Peter tells you something about Paul you learn more about Peter than about Paul.[3] The point is clear enough, whether or not we know the textual origins of what Peter said about Paul or what his words actually were. We have all encountered in social situations this kind of duplicity of revelation— sometimes attending more carefully to the speaker, sometimes about whom he speaks. Santayana invites us to think about the ambiguity of deciding from whom we learn more, and perhaps also suggests that the answer is by no means obvious.

But does he not invite us to do, or can he prevent us from doing, something else? And was it obvious? When Santayana says what he has said, do we not, perhaps, learn more about Santayana than we do about Peter or Paul? Such reflexivity always awaits us; that is, it awaits us pervasively or endlessly. To press the obvious (also to risk some failure of humility), when I report what Santayana has written, the reader might learn more about me than he does about Santayana. And if the reader were to quote or merely think about what I have just written, he would be moving the process one step further. I have here belabored the regress—but wasn't the infinity of it implicit when Santayana said what he said in the first place? And isn't this regression implicit in many, in all, human moments?

Gettysburg Address. "The world will little note nor long remember what we say here," Lincoln said. Then he paid succinct tribute to what was done there, the battle that was the reason and occasion for his address. Lincoln was wrong, many have observed; what he said has been much noted, remembered, reread, and repeated. The address endures as an astonishing occasional piece, a prose poem, a rare instance of brief literary art become larger than the place where it was spoken. It surely is more widely known than the battlefield.

That Lincoln was wrong is not to the point. He may have been modest, unaware of his own poetic talents, uncertain of history's unpredictable judgments. He might even have expressed himself with a touch of irony, of negative exaggeration. He certainly did not want to presume that what he said and felt on that occasion could be remotely commensurate with what had been righteously and sacrificially done by others before he spoke, and what still needed to be done after he finished.

But that is the point, at least my point now. (That *now* is forever elusive; it challenges both the measure of great moments and of trivial ones.) What was more important, the battle or the address, the national "dispute" or Lincoln's "feelings"? The Trojan War or Homer's *Iliad*? The Peloponnesian War or Thucydides' *History*?

They are honored together, and interchangeably. But they are never entirely together or entirely apart. If we can no longer distinguish them, let us remember that Lincoln, without the benefit of hindsight, felt the need to distinguish the battle from his account of it. And like him we still might be wrong in our judgments. My general point is that we usually think we are sure about what is important, and this turns frequently on the art/morality distinction. But the times when we are wrong, or might be wrong, are momentous and should keep us alert and contrarian. If this book were to have a moral point, clearly at its permanent peril, it would be to always remember its aesthetic alternative.

Don Giovanni. Mozart's great opera enormously straddles the art/ morality distinction. It is a work of joyous art, a gigantic musical masterpiece. But it has, at least nominally, a moral point or focus. It is about the proper punishment of evil (as confirmed by its subtitle, *Il Dissoluto Punito*) after a fairly detailed depiction of much evil behavior.

What if we deliberately pay attention to its avowed theme, drop our musical sophistication, or at least ask ourselves why we (mostly) give the work's "morality," that is, its message, minimal attention in favor of the work's "artistry," that is, its musical glory?

I once discovered, to my pleasing consternation (an art/morality moment!), that this is not always the case. I learned about a woman who refused ever to see the opera because (she had heard) of the enormous amount of misbehavior and misogyny that it contained. She knew that the Don was a scoundrel, and I suppose she did not want to encounter such distasteful behavior directly, or encourage it obliquely, by supporting the opera. I confess to an elitist contempt for her condemnation, though now I need to qualify it. I must be forever unsure about possibly misplaced aestheticism and possibly misplaced righteousness!

One might say that there is irony, or even irrelevance, in the judgment of the non-attending woman. After all, Don Giovanni is punished for the very misdeeds she so much dislikes. If she saw the opera there could be some moral satisfaction on her part, as there could be, just possibly, with some listeners who attend more to the libretto than to the music. But a subtle counterpoint to this analysis might continue to justify her disapproval. The depiction of the Don's attitudes, the glorification of his behavior, the maliciousness of his tallied seductions, far exceeds in volume and importance his perfunctory punishment. So even what the opera is morally about is hardly entirely transparent. At the end of it there is no recognition or regret on the Don's part, the kind of thing that usually redeems a tragic hero and makes him worthy of our sympathy and our sorrow. The morality of the opera is commingled with the music's artistry, but remains dubious and at least as inaccessible.

I do not know whether the boycotting woman was aware that the Don, the immoralist, was punished, and that the work had some kind of a moral message. Maybe she indeed knew something about the libretto and chose to understand the matter quite otherwise! As we can readily conclude, the opera celebrates, even glorifies, the Don's behavior more than it perfunctorily disparages it. The devil is in the details, and the details are on the side of wickedness. The last scene of the opera, in which the survivors recall the Don's just punishment, has sometimes been omitted from a performance. This was the suggestion of Donald Francis Tovey, but surely on musical and not on moral grounds. Even if not omitted it could be seen as morally inadequate to the larger thrust of the libretto, and not compensatory.

There is an art/morality tension here that cannot be teased away. Though the art, we might say, is ultimate and dazzling, and the morality of refusing to attend the opera is silly and superficial, the issue of the relationship is pressingly present. Is not the libretto of the opera (*pace* Lorenzo Da Ponte) an essential part of the total work? Is not the plot, the proper punishment of a dissolute person, to be taken seriously? The person who refuses to see *Don Giovanni* on moral grounds does indeed take it seriously. More seriously, I have to acknowledge with some reluctance, than one who merely enjoys it enormously for the sake of an evening's respite. Seriousness is what morality is essentially about. Enjoyment is what art is essentially about. Unless one reverses the matter!

In lieu of the anonymous woman I have alluded to, I might have linked this matter to that consummate artist-moralist, Ludwig van Beethoven. (How could anyone find an earthly wife whose model of marital perfection was Leonora?) A very unreliable person, Seyfried, has Beethoven say of *Don Giovanni*: "The sacred arts should never demean themselves to the folly of such a scandalous subject."[4] Beethoven did in fact say that he could not have composed on such a subject, however that might have been meant. Comparing the moral statures of Mozart and Beethoven— say, via the libretti of *Don Giovanni* and *Fidelio*—is as fascinating a subject as it is probably a philosophically useless one. The art/morality distinction has met its masters.

Tosca. I used to argue, with deliberate perversity (before I realized that there could be a different kind of argument), that the opera did not end as it seemed. Cavaradossi really shot? Tosca in a death leap over the ramparts of the Castel Sant'Angelo? But (I feigned to claim) I saw them take curtain calls! They are alive and well!

The child (though not the country bumpkin; we will meet him later) would know better. They died in the story, but not really. Yet "really" is but another story, and we can choose among stories. It takes long effort to "realize" this, and this book is a necessarily failed effort to animate this other story.

The dogmatic conviction that one can always distinguish the real from the unreal is treacherous, mischievous, and dangerous. What we see as obvious, sure, self-evident, and solid generates religious fundamentalism, philosophical blindness, and political fanaticism, along with a slew of milder ills—like possible misreadings (misprisions?) of literature and art. The notion of ontological parity (see Chapter 18, "Ontology and Morality")—gently advising us to think further about the real and the unreal—has entered philosophical parlance. But it hardly prevails in philosophical thinking and remains alien even to sophisticated minds.

For example, "The Bible as Literature" is a standardized college course. It avoids the possible danger, or accusation, of indoctrination (i.e., proclaiming as real what is not real, or what might not be true) while presumably honoring what needs to be honored, such as art. But there are no courses (so far as I know) of "Literature as Religion" or "Art as Religion" or, indeed, "Art as Truth," though these have come up as subjects in aesthetics. Perhaps a study of Walter Pater would suggest such a centrality of art, in what many would see as a misplaced aestheticism, that is, a moral mistake. The mistake, of course, is the absence of a moral equivalency or parity with respect to the above courses. The mistake is philosophical. It is a prior assured notion, or dogma, about what is "really real." It is my theme.

More about the real. There are other reflexivities that are obvious, but perhaps not all that obvious. Does the viewer of Hamlet, when he sees the play within the play, remember that he too, like Claudius out there, is watching a play? Does he wonder whether his predicament, and identity, are the same as, or different from, Claudius's? What mirror is being held up to nature for him, and by whom? If these issues seem philosophically settled to some, so be it. But they can quickly be unsettled by a flick of attention, or attitude, or emphasis . . . which is the constant theme of this study.

We are all familiar with the anecdote about the country bumpkin who does not know that he is at a play and who jumps up on the stage to pick up the actress's fallen handkerchief. Unlike the rest of us, he has to be told that he is at a play and should remain seated. But that hardly ends the philosophical matter. Aren't we, in some deeper sense, country bumpkins all? Was Prince Myshkin "really" an idiot? Don't we, who are watching Hamlet, need to be reminded, or to remember that we were reminded, that all the world's a stage? And that we too are players in some larger mind or some equivalent scheme of things? Don't we see that there may be no privileged stage, neither Hamlet's players, nor Hamlet himself, talking and fretting, nor the rest of us sitting in the pit and thinking we are the ones who are part of a privileged stage, the "real world," Shakespeare's world rather than Hamlet's? Aren't we on this larger stage, which is only a stage among stages, a stage not as different from the others as we first thought? (This might be the "theater" effect; see Chapter 13, "Lessing as Philosophical Dramatist.") Hamlet told the visiting players what to say. Hold the mirror up to Claudius's nature and catch the conscience of the king. Shakespeare told Hamlet what to say, or helped him. Who told Shakespeare, or tells the rest of us, what to say? Foolish questions? Only if we have chosen one metaworld over another, without accepting the possibility that all the world is, indeed, one stage. Hamlet is Shakespeare's voice, we assure ourselves, while we are free and "real." Shakespeare was once free and real, but no longer, as we, too, soon will be unreal. Finally, what the bumpkin doesn't know, and what we might not know until we are transformed, is that the real-unreal, the distinction between Claudius, and Hamlet, and Shakespeare, and us, is part of a play, one and the same play.

In a deeper and possibly wiser sense we are country bumpkins all, with no stage so privileged or real as to make other stages fanciful and unreal. This is what the move from urgent morality to wistful and halting art can always remind us. This is what Macduff momentarily does. When Macduff says he must first feel it as a man he is doing more than merely making a moral choice and acting on it. He is revealing a larger self, a different kind of reality, a different way of being, than Malcolm can encompass. His doing so accomplishes nothing, is nonevidential, and is not part of a world that Malcolm can care about or see. The country bumpkin clearly misses something that the rest of us are sure we know. But don't we all miss something when we are incapable of missing what he misses?

If I seem to be belaboring the obvious it is because I am. It is also because the obvious is profoundly elusive and vice versa. It depends how, at the moment, we are teased, or flicker, or allow ourselves to acquire or lose a mental identity.

The idea that we are on a basic parity with Shakespeare, that his world and stage are the same ones we occupy, and that the real and unreal are the same for him as they are for us, is a pure conceit, or it is at best (what is the same thing) a philosophical position. It is in much need of the kind of suspension of disbelief that I characterize as the move between the moral and the aesthetic.

The bumpkin, in a word, might not be a bumpkin at all, but someone who dislikes theater and prosceniums. He does not want to occupy a world with two stages, especially one for smart people and one for dumb people. He resents righteousness, obedience, and, above all, to be told where, or in whose imagination, he belongs. He does not want to be taught what is real and what he should do. The rest of us, us learned people, need to learn (at times!) to bring learning to a halt, to relinquish righteousness, to praise folly, to allow the future to forgive our neglect of it, to bring time to a stop, to feel and momentarily enjoy the omnipresent real—the only glimpse of eternity that might ever come our way. This, if it is not too far back to recall, was Macduff's move.

Art and Morality is my title, and I have ventured some initial approaches to the distinction. One of my first publications was "Art and Morality: On the Ambiguity of a Distinction." It appears here as Chapter 1, so my interest has persisted over many years. Something like the art/morality distinction appears widely in philosophical literature, under various nomenclatures. For example, the distinction is developed as "work" and "play" in Santayana's *The Sense of Beauty.* There is the activity, the experience, the language, whatever, that is ulterior and whose purport is beyond itself, and there is the experience, the language, that is final, consummatory, for its own sake. It is a frequent distinction, almost too simplistic in itself. But its richness is in its subtlety, its elusiveness, its complications, and what further reflections it gives rise to. Like a simple theme in music—perhaps the simpler the better—the variations on Art and Morality can be long, remote, and possibly of greater interest than the crude distinction, or theme, upon which it is based. What follows is a venture into such a set of such variations.

The juxtaposition for me of art and morality, the fascination with it, has become something of an *idée fixe.* It probably originated in the first aesthetics course that I took. The distinction is at once naive and grandiose and has the virtue, as I conceive it, of leaving out nothing and hence the vice of covering everything. It has a gloriousness to it and a madness. It is what is now called the "hedgehog" approach, a "unified field theory" for everything. I am reminded of a remark by C. S. Peirce, which I quote in Chapter 9 ("Interpreting Peirce"):

> Many a man has cherished for years as his hobby some vague shadow
> of an idea, too meaningless to be positively false; he has, nevertheless,
> passionately loved it, has made it his companion by day and by night,
> and has given to it his strength and his life, leaving all other occupa-

tions for its sake, and in short has lived with it and for it, until it has become, as it were flesh of his flesh and bone of his bone; and then he has waked up some bright morning to find it gone, clean vanished away like the beautiful Melusina of the fable, and the essence of his life gone with it. I have myself known such a man; and who can tell how many histories of circle-squarers, metaphysicians, astrologers, and what not, may not be told in the old German [French!] story?[5]

I will not admit *a priori* to that much madness, but only as much as can be properly extracted from the texts that follow. And extracted only by others, not by me. My Melusina is partly ironic and illusory, but she is surely not yet vanished. Her ongoing presence and absence is my very theme. And it is now too early for her to appear permanently and too late for her to disappear entirely.

Like my *Macbeth* example at the outset, I will offer others illustrative of my theme—the rival claims of art and morality. They seem to involve a willingness to take a contrarian stance, even as Macduff seems to do when he challenges Malcolm, and it is always a self-contrarian stance.

PART ONE

ART AND MORALITY

ONE

ART AND MORALITY

On the Ambiguity of a Distinction

1973

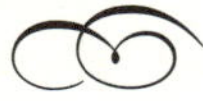

There is a tension between art and its seemingly anti-aesthetic moral thrust that prompts inquiry into the relation of art and life. Life lacks the organization and direction of art, and art is born when the waste and distraction of life are discarded. Reconciliation with these inartistic moments gives rise to tragedy and shows that humans prefer to give "pain aesthetic and moral dimensions [rather] than be . . . alienated from what counts." Some thinkers have suggested that art transcends life while others have seen aesthetic experience as continuous with other life experience. To separate art and life in a clear and definite way leads to "a morally negligent life spiced by aesthetic kicks. . . . mak[ing] art vicious and . . . life hypocritical." To see art as continuous with life can add to the glory of being alive, and the moral thrust of art can be a reminder of this and indicate the larger context of human life lying beyond the artwork.

What is the full import of the moral thrust of art? This thrust is found in much art, yet it is sometimes held to be unaesthetic; righteous indignation may be a culminating satisfaction for some, yet its function is to undeliver us from the "consummatory" contentment of actual art works, and from our isolation in those works. What, in brief, is the larger relationship between art and life that the morality of art presses us to examine?

Let us approach this theme by way of the idea of treating life itself, total life, as an aesthetic project or work of art. It is an old idea, as old as

{ *19* }

the Greeks, but fallen into disrepute. We still occasionally acknowledge that some people live more artfully than others, and when we are enthusiastic we might refer to a singularly successful career—some man's life—as a work of art. But we feel the metaphorical exaggeration of such talk and on more prosaic occasions flinch from it. Art may heighten life and elevate some of its many moments but, just as surely, life eludes art and refuses to turn into an experiential unity or a singular accomplishment. Life cannot be art and, in its totality, is not even good material for art. As Aristotle and others have argued, any life is too full of irrelevancy to make a good story. Its beginning is chance-like and not of our making; its middle is likely a muddle; its end is often curtailed, more like a preposition than a noun. Abrupt, codaless exits leave us unreconciled. Put simply, life is too disorganized, random, and miscellaneous to admit of overarching direction and control.

We might even press the distinction between life and art to the point of coming up with definitional criteria that would guarantee their separateness. Is it not the case that aesthetic creation always seems to involve a pruning, a separation of art from life so that art will be art *by virtue of the separation*? Do we not excise those aspects of life that cannot be brought into aesthetic purview and remove them from the canvas or the story? Is not art essentially such selection and excision?

Consider the painter's workshop when his masterpiece is completed. Around the painting, separated from it, are the messy palette, the dirty smock, the dingy garret, the unpaid rent, the vulgar liaisons—and everything else that is material waste or spiritual distraction. The painting is perfect, better than life, and set off against it like a flawless gem in a tawdry case. And it is perfect because it is less than all of life; indeed, it is said to redeem life (strange redemption) by making part of life better than all of it and by vaunting the aloofness of that moment of separation.

But what kind of predicament are we describing? The part and the whole that we are here dealing with remain fundamentally estranged and violently disconnected. The awareness of this makes the moralist, the artist of life, discontent. (There is nothing that brings things together so much as the poignancy of their separation, suitably sensed.) The moralist is pressed to question the nature of the artistic achievement, the masterpiece, which heightens disconnectedness, and the definition and conception of art that gives intellectual fortification to that disconnectedness.

Just what are we about when we turn parts of life into art, separate art and life practically, and distinguish between them theoretically? Are we sacrificing man for his art or saving man from his life? In choosing to perfect art at the expense of life, does it perfect man to make this choice, or only his art? Though we can conceal the clutter of the workshop from others, can we conceal it from ourselves? Where are the parings we omit from our purview, the unorganized residue that does not get into our art? What remains of the large substance of an artist's, or any man's, life that never hangs in a museum or sounds in a concert hall or gets into a novel, or is simply never an occasion for worthwhile remembrances?

These are difficult questions, but once we know the agony of the quandary the answers will come forth of themselves. If an artist is an artist by virtue of what he can discard, a man remains a man by virtue of what he cannot discard, and this is always the bulkier, the more challenging, the more problematic part of himself. What remains is the hair and the dirt and the ugliness of existence, the rubbish he knows is under the rug, the bugs in hiding, the guilts that burgeon from buried places, the boredom and the pain, the waste and the claptrap of life, and its oppressive and random and sheer *et ceteras*. Here is what waits to be reckoned with, not colors to be squeezed from tubes, not tones to be plectrumed and plucked, not words to be rhymed and cadenced. There is a vale of soul-making that is beyond all media, that symphonies and canvases and poems barely touch. It is a vale in which we are pressed beyond mere arts to where art and life fuse in a single strategy and a total task.

In plainer language we can say that the materials discarded in fashioning art are no loss to the art, and yet they remain a continuing burden. With respect to life there is no context, no place for waste, no way of getting rid of what might metaphorically be called the radioactive debris and the black oil slicks. Man's condition is like Earth's condition—limited, closed in, contaminable. There can only be arrangements and rearrangements of what there is, total manipulations of total accumulations, a voluminous burden that must be carried and projected to an uncertain end.

Life apart from art—and there would be no apartness apart from the following considerations—consists of opposites unseen and conflicts unreconciled. It consists of moments that are not reflected upon and assimilated, that intrude on us when we do not want them to, that randomly distract and oppress. They are our accumulating but unaccumulated selves. We cannot shed them; because we cannot use them positively, they weigh on us negatively. Life apart from art, inartistic life, is the negative weight, the tiresome burden, the existential stress of being, the tragic sense of the unencompassed.

The tragic sense, tragedy understood this way, is not, as it is so often taken to be, a reconciliation with death, or a reconciliation of specific moral claims. Tragedy, rather, is a reconciliation with those moments of life that resist a coming together in some organizing purpose. Tragedy is the sense of, and the ideal victory over, the living dissolution that continuously pervades us, not victory over the actual extinction that eventually terminates us. Termination and extinction are no great loss when they come in due time. The silence at the end of a symphony is as necessary as any other part of it; indeed, it is sometimes the best part of it and a great relief. Dissolution and disconnectedness are the real tragic losses. The tragic sense reaches out to those intransigent elements of our being that otherwise resist containment, and they become contaminated morally and ideally in the pathos of the awareness of failure.

Tragedy binds wounds but cannot perforce heal them. They remain bound wounds, the more painful because the more conspicuous. But bound and comprehended pain is preferred to the deeper pain, that is, anxiety, of anaesthetized and purposeless moments. It is astonishing how much sadness and suffering a man will embrace unto himself to avoid disconnectedness, and to satisfy his organizing and time-binding self. Even the words of a popular song tell us that "Loneliness remembers what happiness forgets."[1] Movement without direction, process without contour, suffering without redemption, are all there is to ugliness and hell.

Tragedy and the tragic sense are the evidence that man refuses to be the patient etherized on the table. He would rather give his pain aesthetic and moral dimension than be sundered in his being and alienated from what counts. The search for wholeness and completion is a formidable principle. Organizing around some biological purpose from the start, we remain organizational to the end. And every accomplishment, sweet as it may be, must partly sour on itself as it looks to the task of some larger project.

Our view then has been that aesthetic experience is not, and ought not to be, separated from other life experience. In the tradition of aesthetic theory some writers (e.g., Dewey) have defended this view, and other writers (e.g., Pater) have defended the view that art is something special, distinctive, exalted, and different in kind from the life experience out of which it emerges and departs.

These alternatives hardly admit of theoretical resolution. Like most distinctions based on a high order of metaphysical generality, the distinction between life and art can be seen as a difference of degree or as a difference of kind. Like many other such distinctions, there is a "sense" in which it is warranted and a "sense" in which it is not. Any difference in degree can be converted into a difference in kind by a philosopher with appropriate, or inappropriate, labels to hand.

But the making of philosophical distinctions is not without practical consequences, and what concerns us here is the moral effect of each of the alternatives. The effect of separating art and life, definitively rather than tentatively, clearly rather than ambiguously, is to give to art a premature elevation. This ultra-laudatory conception of art, which sees it as so many nodules of perfection, so many gemlike inflammatory moments, in a life that is otherwise dull, drab and dubious—this conception turns our thoughts away from the larger task of composing life, and of bringing to that larger task and art a modicum of order and sequence and contoured joy. It is a conception that leads toward aestheticism (in the worst sense of that word)—a morally negligent life spiced by aesthetic kicks. To view art and life thus, to separate them in contentment and to be content in their separation, is to make art vicious and to make life hypocritical. At its worst it is to enjoy without reference to consequences, to be righteous without reference to joy, to fiddle while Rome burns, and to raise flowers alongside crematoria.

The purpose in seeing art as continuous with other life activities is not to debunk or degrade art but hopefully to glorify and elevate life. The moral aspect of art, insofar as it overflows art, is a reminder of this and points to needs and predicaments beyond the obvious confines of the art work. It is a reminder that the perfection of art is purchased at a price, that a gain here is a neglect there, and that there is inadequacy in the life in which the art work is embedded. It is a reminder that much needs to be done, that a larger project waits, and that to rest in temporary conditions of seeming permanence is a permanent condition of unrecognized failure.

There are certain artists we might call upon who strongly and specifically convey the tragic sense of the unfinished and unfinishable quality of works of art. They refuse, by repeated shows of reluctance, to make that separation of art and life which tends to be manifested in the *fait accompli* of the finished and presented art work. For them the art work is never an isolable thing but always a work in progress, always in need of revision, always modifiable in the direction of an unrealized and unrealizable goal. These men invite the force of life, with its raging fires and its unshored fragments, to overwhelm the temporary ramparts of the art medium. They are writers like Proust, for whom a proof sheet was simply an occasion for ever-renewed correction and expansion. They are sculptors like Giacometti, who was always "failing" and destroying what he did, and for whom it was apparent agony to face the false finality of allowing a work to be exhibited. "There is no hope of achieving what I want, of expressing my vision of reality," said Giacometti. "I go on painting and sculpting because I am curious to know why I fail."[2]

For these artists, the separation of art and life is "performatively" denied by virtue of the way in which ongoing artistic activity (not a mere series of art works) is a conscious grappling with life. All glimpses of reality are repudiated for being glimpses, discrete perspectives: for being less than unitary visions and unitary accomplishments. The various pieces Giacometti produced, the fragments of his life, will make their way into various hands, never to be shored up or united. And yet this knowledge of failure, this tragic sense constantly alive, is success beyond all art. The best art, the best artists are pervaded by the tragic sense, which is awareness of the sort of defeat and recalcitrance that life itself has always imposed upon the living of it. And so artists love to leave loose ends, ambiguities, elements of randomness, as a tribute and echo and reminder of what life is like and what needs to be done.

Art is better than life, and should be; but not so much better that it neglects life's challenges or departs life's memories. The task of great art has always been to transcend life but to remain relevant to it, to focus enjoyment but not to forget sorrow, to surmount the futility of blind righteousness but not to be blind to prevailing evil. This too has been the task of the good life, which is a self-regenerative process in which art is that part which is also the ongoing measure of the whole. Yeats's poem "The Choice" sets out two alternatives: "Perfection of the life, or of the work."[3] To care about the choice and to sense its poignancy is all the response that it needs.

TWO

MORALITY BOUND AND UNBOUND
Some Parameters of Literary Art

1972

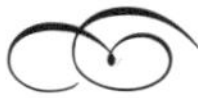

Moral claims in an artwork might be of two kinds: bound and unbound. When moral claims in an artwork serve a certain aesthetic effect, morality may be said to be bound to that artwork. When moral claims in an artwork are identified with the purposes of the artist in shaping actual living, such morality escapes the confines of the art form and may be said to be unbound. Here "the moral thrust breaks all bonds of aesthetic constraint and propriety, at least as these have sometimes been known." The categories of morality bound and unbound do not define artworks absolutely. An artwork may oscillate between them or fall into them ambiguously. "These perspectives are shiftable and almost compresent—as in those pictures of adjacent cubes, or duck-rabbits, which can be seen in one way or suddenly in another way." Art, in maintaining these contrary perspectives, exhibits "the ulterior drama of art;" that is, the "very rivalry between art and life" in which the desire to rest in contemplation of the ideal contends with the desire for involvement with the larger living context and the tasks at hand.

Art, especially literary art, has traditionally dealt with moral matters. Dramatic literature is essentially about choice and conflict, characters placed in situations in which they reveal—and perhaps even recommend—the values for which they are willing to live, to suffer, and to die. Whether what the character reveals is the same as what the author recommends is of course problematic. Whatever else we encounter in literature, we meet up with modes of righteousness that touch our feelings and engage our thoughts.

But is the morality of or in art a true morality? A widely held view would deny that it is, or would assert that the extent to which a moral message protrudes from a work simply marks its failure as art. (The slogan of the MGM motion picture company is "Ars Gratia Artis" and Mr. Goldwyn was once reputed to have said, "If I want to send a message I go to Western Union."[1]) In this view, a moral theme is not morality *per se*; it is not a writer's unequivocal expression of what he regards as right, nor an exhortation to the reader to behave in a certain way. Rather, it is an attitude that is contained, usually by virtue of its juxtaposition with alternative attitudes. A moral claim, along with its contenders, is part of a fabric of claims and counterclaims designed to create a certain aesthetic effect. On this theory, for example, Sophocles reveals how Antigone acts out of loyalty to her brother and to her religious conscience, while Creon acts out of his sense of civil and kingly prerogative. Sophocles doesn't opt for any of his characters or for any of their predilections. He has no axe to grind and his artistry is realized in his rendering of the conflict and by the tragic vision that ensues. In this conception of art we have a situation, or an interpretation, which I characterize as "morality bound." The artist is himself ethically aloof and messageless, and the moral ingredients in his art are indeed ingredients, part of a pattern of relationships that remains internal to, and constitutive of, an aesthetic achievement. Art is art, disconnected from the exigencies of life and containing no recommendations for the living of it.

However, in some instances of art the element of exhortation, of proclaimed righteousness, is so clear-cut and so obviously to be identified with the passion and the purpose of the artist, that such morality can hardly be said to be contained within the framework of the art form. Morality plays might have served as diversionary entertainments, but they also taught lessons about Christian piety and virtue. In modern dramas by Genet and Brecht, the moral thrust breaks all bonds of aesthetic constraint and propriety, at least as these have sometimes been known. The decorum of their art is shattered by the terror of their wrath. Works like *The Blacks* and *The Exception and the Rule* expend much of their energy defying the proscenium, in splashing off the stage and onto the audience and out of the theater. The playwrights use every device known to theater, and then some, to hurl their vituperations and scoldings at their spectators and at their world. It is as though the thrust of morality has become the very measure of their art, and the traditional constraints and decencies are themselves seen as indecent. Edward Bond, the British dramatist, said, "Critics annoy me. If a house is on fire and I shout 'Fire! Fire!' I don't want people to commend my shouting ability, I want them to join in the fire fighting."[2] Everything is done to keep the plays in question from canceling and offsetting their moral urgencies and from being terminal aesthetic experiences. We have, in brief, a situation of "morality unbound."

Despite the examples given here, I do not propose that "boundness" and "unboundness" are definitive categories into which works of art neatly and separately fit. I would suggest, rather, that these categories are the parameters within which literary art oscillates, and that this oscillation or ambiguity is one of the ulterior achievements of the artistic vision. Boundness and unboundness, except in the most extreme and obvious of cases, are not simply there as unequivocal qualities of a work in question. Rather, what is there is the conflict between them, the dramatic tension between art experienced as immediate and terminal, as over, against art experienced as mediate and instrumental.

Consider a satire by Juvenal. It reads in a measure like a tract by a fuming, reforming moralist who hates hatable things in order to change them. On this supposition the morality of Juvenal's art is unbound, calculated to improve Rome by influencing his readers. But Juvenal also reads like a writer who enjoys hatable things for the literary ridicule that they lend themselves to, and for the mocking cleverness and exasperation they so effectively encourage. In this view the bitter laughter and broad caricature are terminal and self-justifying effects, and the moral interests are bound, subsidiary to the enjoyment of their artful expression.

Other examples might help us to fix the rich ambiguity and pertinence of the bound-unbound distinction. Marlowe's *Doctor Faustus* presents two conflicting moralities: the overt morality of the chorus (particularly in the opening and closing lines), which harks back to the Christian message of older morality plays; and the covert and implicit morality, as exhibited by Faustus's yearning, defiant, knowledge-thirsty, and power-seeking spirit. Is there a balance between these moralities—are they locked into quiescence like contesting elks—or is one of them Marlowe's unmistakable message and "unbounded" recommendation?

Beethoven's *Ninth Symphony* musically fuses with, and bolsters, a poem that is a paean to universal brotherhood. Surely we have here an artistic vehicle for unbound morality. Beethoven meant to communicate a message, a message that has to do with brotherly behavior in extra-artistic situations—what one does, for example, when one is not listening to Beethoven. But again, as with our changing perspectives of Juvenal, the morality of the symphony can be experienced as bound and brotherhood encountered as something expressed and felt. The praise of brotherhood will then be dissociated from brotherly behavior, and the experience of the symphony will be irrelevant to what people do as a consequence of listening to it.

The same work, then, can be seen as a container for moral attitudes that never get beyond the framework in which these *attitudes* are embedded, as by contrast it can be seen as an occasion for moral urgency, a device for pointing beyond itself to the larger life context in which the entire work is embedded. These perspectives are shiftable and almost compresent—as in those pictures of adjacent cubes, or duck-rabbits, which can be seen in one way or suddenly in another way.

An adequate and appropriate largeness of view requires that we sustain and keep alive in our apprehensions of art these contrary alternatives. Boundness and unboundness coexist as persistent options, even though they seem to be mutually exclusive. Of course, contrariety is always difficult to maintain, and the attempt at it can sometimes make for dialectical malfeasance and critical confusion. But art itself suggests the way out of the dilemma. Just as different moral claims within a work of art can be balanced by a suitable juxtaposition and presentation of them, so can the claim for the simultaneous presence of both boundness and unboundness.

The tension between boundness and unboundness, their pull in opposite directions, is the ulterior drama of art. It is implicitly present in the experience of art, hovering over the specific characters with their clashes and contestations. It has to do with the very rivalry between art and life, between the desire to rest content in an ideal and self-sufficient attainment, and the desire to wrench loose from temporary contentments in order to revert to the larger context in which art always functions and in which there are still worthwhile tasks to be performed.

A searching and ongoing ambiguity with respect to boundness and unboundness is desirable. Art not only balances, and leaves unbalanced, specific moral claims—it also balances, and leaves unbalanced, the bound and unbound nature of its moral status. In doing so, in allowing us to experience it as doing so, art enables us to elevate our vision from the drama of this or that specific issue to the larger drama of life itself, in which the temptations of art and the stirrings of morality are frozen in an unsettled condition of dynamic conflict.

I have variously suggested the ambiguities of the art-morality distinction. (Recall discussions of Don Giovanni, Lincoln Center, and the Gettysburg Address.) This chapter proposes that the morality of artworks inheres in them in two somewhat distinctive ways. H. Osborne, editor of the *British Journal of Aesthetics*, commented on the various papers of the conference at which mine was also delivered. I was pleased that he had this to say about my paper, which perhaps expresses the point more clearly than I said it myself:

> Related also to the problem of truth in art is a paper by Dr. Morris Grossman entitled "Morality Bound and Unbound." The writer divides works of literary art into those where the contained moral message has an urgency which demands acceptance and those in which it sits more loosely so that the reader may embrace it provisionally and imaginatively only for the purpose of appreciating the particular work. He uses the word "bound" for the latter and "unbound" for the former case. In the latter case moral issues and statements contribute to the aesthetic effect merely by being part of the pattern of internal relationship presented for contemplation. In the other case the moral themes are "unbound" to the work in that the writer or dramatist is involved in pleas or exhortations designed to cause the artwork to function as an instrument of social change. In this case the aesthetic adequacy of the work is at least in part inseparable from its moral urgency. The paper is exceptionally open-minded and sensible on a

matter which often has caused heated argument. It suggests that the two classes are not mutually exclusive but that "bound" and "unbound" characteristics may exist to different degrees even in the same work and that the tension between them may on occasion give to the art work its singularity, its relevance and its superiority to the life experiences from which it is extracted.[3]

THREE

MUSIC, MODULATION, AND METAPHOR

1980

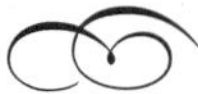

The difficulties of writing about musical modulation—variations in musical key—result from the inadequacy of technical analysis to capture the phenomenological experience of music, namely, "its pushes and pulls, its durational ambiguities, and . . . its uncanny connections with life itself." In such a context, metaphor is unavoidable: modulation is a kind of travel, and experiences of both modulation and travel depend on memory and time elapsed. But time and distance impose limits on human memory, "and they cut short the possible unities both of our musical experiences and of our comprehended lives." The common lack of unity suggests that "the uncertainties of a musical home key partake of . . . the uncertainties of any other notion of home." Such uncertainties and human limitations make it impossible to "have fully clear goals or fully clear enjoyments, which is another way of saying that we straddle the art/morality distinction." Transitions in art and life are both made and discovered, and music both reveals this and makes it possible. "Music could not exist without a life in which it is echoed, embedded and accompanied. Life could not have discovered its lasting value and its deepest enjoyment without music."

I

To write about modulation—unless one is prematurely metaphorical and vaguely anticipates that one might be writing about something else—is to write about music. And to write about music usually requires musical literacy and the expectation of such literacy in readers.

Musical literacy is harder to define than ordinary literacy, though easier to come by. It is so native to us, so ingrained, that it needs far less education to acquire, if any at all. The infant responds to sounds and can replicate them before he knows words. If we are literate in English, and this might well go beyond literacy, we had to have learned to read, understand, and write the language, perhaps even to know something about its structural components. Whereas educated people can talk in some detail about sonnets, tragedy, alliteration, rhyme, recognition scenes, and other concepts describing literary art, many a musical person lacks that kind of knowledge. He listens to and likes some music though he might not sing or perform on an instrument. (To make a possible distinction, he might have musical literacy without being musically literate.) His enjoyment, even his musical sophistication, could be genuine even though he could not define words used to describe music, such as C major, D minor, dominant seventh, canon, bass clef, fugue, tonal structure . . . or *modulation*.

In a conversation I had with Leonard Meyer many years ago, he deplored what he saw as a general absence of musical literacy. He wasn't talking about the enjoyment of music. He meant the lack of a rudimentary ability to refer to the technical elements of music, even by people who listened to and "liked" music. What clearly annoyed Meyer was the musically knowledgeable person, that is, the sophisticated lover of music, who was ignorant of its basic grammar and nomenclature.

Musical illiteracy might mean such ignorance but, as suggested, it could hardly mean lack of musical response. Such responsiveness is widespread, as evidenced by the ubiquitous enthusiasms, excitements, bodily motions, and physical effects it engenders. This responsiveness would not seem to require technical knowledge, and yet it surely is a literacy of sorts. One might not know how to read music, or what words like "recapitulation," and "modulation" mean, and still genuinely enjoy the music to which those words refer.

This listening and enjoying aspect of music is capable of much description and discussion, apart from, or at least supplemental to, any technical discussion. Non-technical writing, descriptive in its way, is probably the bulk of writing on music. It ranges from program notes, reviews of concerts, glowing biographies of composers, and even a great deal of what passes for musical aesthetics. This kind of writing certainly has its merits and insights, but it demands or expects little or no technical literacy and usually ignores it.

Absent the technically precise, will other words, even if insufficient and inadequate, describe what happens in music? Even when available and used well, technical language must somehow be conjoined to other ways of writing and thinking about music, and this sometimes takes us to the extravagant, the fanciful, the metaphorical, and indeed to non-musical life experiences.

Hence our predicament and our dilemma. Whereas only technical musical analysis can define modulation, non-technical words are needed for larger comprehension. Adequate writing about music, if it is to have any probity, requires a relationship between technical musical analysis and what might loosely be called the phenomenological experience of music. Combining these two is a straddling challenge that regularly faces those who write about "aesthetics" or the philosophy of art. It creates a kind of necessary, sometimes dubious, duplicity.

What I propose here is not dismissive of the value of technical analysis, nor is it based, I trust, on ignorance. It requires some technical skill and the ability to do or follow such analysis. It also requires a willingness to go beyond the technical and to recognize its limitations. It requires, perhaps, an unusual kind of writing, with a kind of leaping between, or a juxtaposition of, musical and ordinary literacy.

Specifically, I develop here an analogy between musical motion (i.e., modulation) and other kinds of travel, and seek to show how the homing instinct animates both life and art. Every attempt at metaphor goes from what we know to what we don't know, or know less well, and the primary direction of a good metaphor is moot.

Metaphors both extend what we know and depend on what we know, in mixtures that can be individual and uncertain. They can be multidirectional. "A camel is the ship of the desert" is good for seafaring and well-traveled Englishmen. "A ship is a camel of the sea" might work for a sand-bound Arab who has at least heard of the ocean.

Metaphors can be reversed, vehicle can change with tenor, albeit usually with some loss. The moon is queen of the night, to be sure; but a queen is the moon of her realm? Not as good, but possible.

II

Before turning more directly to musical modulation, and to prepare for the metaphor that seeks to animate this study, I look at some of the vagaries of other areas of "explanation," that is, of intrusions of metaphor. They might have both parallel helpfulness and inadequacy. Pervading our efforts to understand, metaphors are sometimes imaginative and ingenious, sometimes fantastic and far-fetched.

(A) The night sky has a structure. Santayana calls it multiplicity in uniformity.[1] Such a structure is challenging, even unsettling. There seems to be an infinity of stars—their numbers overwhelm—yet they show bits of regularity here and there even to the untutored eye. How to understand? "Look at and gaze in awe" is one recommendation. One might even say of music—"listen, be overwhelmed, and leave it alone." But the impulse to understand, to follow, to imagine, whatever that eventually means by way of creation and intrusion, is irresistible.

The ancients, of Greece in particular but also peoples of many other cultures, saw patterns in the sky. They looked at the "same" sky we do, but not in the same way. What exists apart from "interpretation," indeed apart from metaphor, remains obscure. They saw structure and detail. They saw constellations, configurations of stars that presumably resemble Taurus, or Andromeda, or Draco, or Hercules. There are stars that make up Orion's Belt, the Twins, the Sisters, and so on. The ancients not only saw those figures but provided many narratives about who they were and how they got into the sky. As with any religious belief, it could have been genuine enough, even observationally credible. It seems that more than any other constellation, Scorpius resembles its given name! Resembles indeed! We now are likely to see such structures with poetic sympathy, but also as arbitrary, superimposed, and fantastic.

The Greek Constellations, embedded in their ancient religion and myth, surely became more and more suspect with the advance of science. We now "know" that the pattern of stars, bright and dim, on the planar surface of the sky involves stars of incredibly different distances away from us. The Belt of Orion, indeed!

The stars seem fairly randomly distributed, with a few regularities and patterns here and there that allow us to find some groups again and again even without naming them. But to recognize and recall, as with a tune or a bird call, is an incipient naming and begins a process that can become elaborate and full of references. What is first merely found, a slight regularity, becomes a metaphor richly created, with various degrees of credibility or persuasiveness.

Do the constellations explain anything? Do they exist side by side with the "actual" sky as separate entities, or do they fuse as actual metaphors, each for the other, so that they help us to bring sky and pictures together in a unitary and worthwhile experience? I hope to avoid an either/or answer to this question. Metaphors are like that, ranging from the insightful to irrelevant to supererogatory. Metaphors are mysterious in their hold on us. But they surely depend in part on what we know and how we know.

(B) In one of my first courses in music theory, I studied Heinrich Schenker. He is very complicated and has elicited much learned theoretical commentary. He provides unitary structures, explanations, "constellations" dare I say, that are mapped over the musical score. They go well beyond the "mere" aural experience of music. Or do they? A theory of anything, even what might come to be regarded as a "wrong" theory, enriches what it ventures to deal with. Hence the creativity of Schenker and his followers. Their musical diagrams are as rich and extensive as those pictures made by the ancient cartographers of the night sky. They are metaphors, which sometimes work wonderfully and sometimes seem labored and arbitrary.

The Schenker system, and the constellations, are both of them subtle, perceptive, and . . . fantastic. They are not radically different from each other, in kind or in value. A metaphor has to earn its way, as and when it is properly appreciated. It cannot be guaranteed in advance.

III

Modulation has its origins in tonality, which has been central to Western music (my only concern here) for a long time. Such music has been produced in various keys, but particular compositions are usually in one tonality, the tonic key, which begins and ends the work and prevails in it during its sounding in ways we will examine and qualify. A Sonata in D minor, or Variations in C minor, is in the named key and that defines and determines its tonality.

The tonal key has many steps or chords on different notes of the scale. These chords typically harmonize melodies and bring variety to what would otherwise be a tiresome repetition of the tonic chord. Some chords, the subdominant IVth and the dominant Vth, have a special relation to the tonic. The sounding of them impels a return to the tonic. The dominant especially, seventh or ninth, pulls both away from home and toward home.

The phrase "impels a return to the tonic" brings us almost too quickly to the other kind of language that goes beyond analysis of keys and chords. Technical analysis cannot explain the impulsion, nor can it fathom the reason for the existence of such an impulsion. What "impels" a return to the tonic, or even a departure from it, is a mystery that musical analysis cannot even begin to address.

This might seem to belie a long history of musical analysis, from Pythagoras to modern studies in the physics and psychology of music. In such analysis, one musical place, say, a dominant chord, might be shown to be musically similar, or even adjacent, to a tonic chord. But still the *impulse* to move away, or to return, is only metaphorically musical and has extra-, or non-musical origins. Similarities repel and attract, suggesting motion, to be sure, but that is hardly a musical claim or insight.

Musicians, then, can define a move (e.g., by its termini), but they cannot account for it. Indeed, movement is as mysterious in music as movements of arrows in space were for Zeno. When C stops sounding and D starts, why do we talk about "going" from C to D? We are perhaps involved in the proto-metaphors of experience, which are too embedded in us to be accessible either to understanding or denial. If a physical object appeared successively in different, even adjacent, positions in front of us we might not think of it as moving. We might think, up to a certain point, in terms of appearance and disappearance and no more. A sense of motion requires a special contiguity, perhaps a certain speed, in its successive moments. We know we are psychologically "deceived" by motion pictures because we know that the separate frames of the pictures do not move. For Zeno even the arrow couldn't move.

Space is a natural metaphor for the "distance" between keys. We can't seem to refer to tones without reference to movement, yet there is no movement (it could be argued), only succession (before and after) between tones, more or less acceptable for various reasons.

Just why changes in tone are seen (or heard) as spatial, as motion, is mysterious to a critical, or to a metaphor-resistant, mind. Why indeed is space the prevailing, the inevitable, the unavoidable, metaphor for what we call the "ups and downs" of music? Sounds precede and follow each other, but why up and down? Does it connect with holes in a flute, fingers on a string, the way an instrument is held? The piano is always "flat," so to speak, and could have been built right to left.

There are other conventions in musical nomenclature that seem inevitable, but that need not be. They seem to involve unavoidable, or secure, or hard to resist, metaphors. Why is the octave thought of as a return to the same note, with the same lettering, as in C to C? The notes of the piano could have had eighty-eight different names and it would have been arguably truer to the uniqueness of each of them than how we in fact name them. "Register," indeed, has a stronger effect on some musicians and listeners than on others.

Since bodies do move, Zeno's paradoxes notwithstanding, is there any connection between the perceived movement of a body and the perceived movement of a sound? In music, though the sounds of C and D are different, we think in terms of a move when they are successively heard. When C and G are successively heard, it is a bit more problematic. A sudden move from C to G is a leap, but leaps are readily perceived as occurring through intervening space, as when dancing. So sound leaps are not like magical rabbits that just appear unexpectedly or like electrons that move between orbits (they tell us) without a sense of intervening steps.

The persisting sameness of an object, to some extent, works against our seeing (or hearing) it as appearing and disappearing. If I hear C and then see red there is no sense of motion although there is a relation between the note and the color that can be used in art. (We might even talk of "going" from one to the other.) However, we don't sense a move from sound to color even if they appear successively. Where there is a commonality of sound that persists as *sound* even if we proceed, say, from the piccolo to the radically different tuba, we perceive motion. Though D is not the same tone as C, or G, the fact of ongoing sound is the equivalent of a persistent physical object and is the constant with respect to the idea of motion.

How we perceive persistence and motion remains puzzling. Recall that Alice, in Wonderland, could credibly and rapidly change in size and move in space, while still remaining (she thought) the "same" girl.

But none of this gets at the impulse to move, or to return. Alice chose to go down the rabbit hole (how otherwise have adventures?) but she also had doubts about changing size, preferred a return to her true size, and probably wanted to be back with the Liddells. She might even, after long hours of too many stories, have had enough of the delightful Mr. Dodgson. This fact, which isn't a fact but a Carrollian leap through inner space, might help to lead us later, with some literary straining, to a sought-after connection between tonality and a homing instinct.

IV

Musicians define modulation as the move from one key to another, say, C major to G major, perhaps with the use of a dominant seventh. Modulations require greater or lesser preparation, with specific steps involved in their creation.

Because of the usual requirements of steps or of preparation, there is a technical uncertainty about the definition of modulation. If leaps are great and if there are no preparations, there is a loss of a sense of proper motion and of credibility. What is heard then is not an accepted change but a trick or a deception. Analyses of musical modulations show a great attention to steps, proper moves from here to there. Musical leaps without preparations are like prestidigitation, where objects appear and disappear without credibility or justification. Thus (it could be argued) you cannot have three different keys juxtaposed in one measure of music; two of the keys could not have been properly established.

This is, at least, problematic. A borderline case, a possible exception with respect to whether we can say that a modulation has occurred, is an extreme jump from one key to another, without steps or preparation. Whether this should be defined as modulation is arguable, as are so many problems of definition. What is not arguable—and won't be argued here but simply claimed—is that when we hear such a leap it has a musical effect on us. The new key is not created *ex nihilo*. The old key is not entirely lost or forgotten, however far away, when the new key is suggested. (Suggested, but not yet established!) We are still in the realm of sound. Remembrance persists, whether we get to the new key carefully or arbitrarily, by the subtlest preparation (i.e., by *modulation* proper), or by a huge leap. Such a leap might be deemed unmusical, unpleasant, incoherent, and unacceptable, and not by definition a modulation. Yet it can have a strong effect.

Such leaps do occur, and in many cases seem fitting and right. (My favorite example is the move in Beethoven's Third Piano Concerto from the C minor of the first movement to the E major of the second.) Any shift, however remote, will be heard differently from any other shift. When the new is juxtaposed with the old, however far away the old is, the old stays with us, though for how long is a question that needs to be pursued, and I will pursue it later . . . if I remember! The persistence of the old in experience, and the anticipation of the new before it has occurred, is clearly not uniquely musical. But the manner of the persistence (perhaps the compression of it) and the joy of the anticipation (perhaps the emotion of it) might be unique to music and other temporal arts like writing.

In music, the tonic key, the home key, has to be established and is usually established quickly when the work begins. Was it lurking in the composer's psyche before he established it? He starts in a given key, usually not by way of another key but after silence, long silence, non-musical silence.

Silences, musical and non-musical, are in fact not as distinct as musical analysis would sometimes suggest. Silences, brief moments or long intervals of them, are often parts of a musical structure. Furthermore, the silences before and after music, *pace* John Cage, are not as void of remembered sounds (and other things) as we sometimes think. Although the silences, the musical silences that precede and follow the sound of music, are usually not connected with what we think of as modulation, they well might be. Indeed, the silences between the movements of a composition (as in the Beethoven Third Piano Concerto mentioned above, after which there is a sudden change of key, but not a conventional modulation) and the silences between different works on a musical program (which might or might not be deliberate) have not been given much attention. They are too varied, informal, unpredictable, and possibly unremembered in the listening. They are silences possibly related to hovering, prior, distant, or semi-lost sounds, and possibly not. The time factor is critical, as it surely is in different ways, with all remembrance in life or art. Novels, we have been told, are often long and understandably require several sittings, whereas the short story, aiming for a single effect (they are each, as it were, in one key and never leave home), should be read in one sitting.

I have been suggesting that keys are not established as clearly and quickly as formal analysis might suggest. Nor are they departed from as quickly and clearly as that same analysis is inclined to imply. Many of us might think that the works we know well begin clearly in a given key, with a specific tonality. But this could not have been the case when we heard them for the first time. For example, it might be thought that the first four notes of Beethoven's Fifth Symphony establish the key of C minor. They don't. Not even the first eight notes. It would be easy to turn that beginning into a solid E♭ major (albeit not as quickly or solidly as Beethoven does with the two loud chords that open the *Eroica*). If those first four notes of Beethoven's Fifth put us, in fact, into the feel of C minor, it is because *we have heard them before*, with their giveaway beat, and we remember them as "in" that symphony. But we should remind ourselves that at our very first hearing of the Symphony we learned what happens *after* the first four or eight notes; it was then that the tonality was "securely" established by a C minor chord, as securely or as insecurely as such things are ever established—again, might I say, in music as in life.

The establishment of a key, or a tonality, can be deliberately ambiguous, much more so than the brief opening four notes of Beethoven's Fifth. That ambiguity was exceedingly brief. But consider the opening of Beethoven's First Symphony. It is famous for surprising and "deceiving" us, of suggesting a tonality that is different from the one that is only established after several slow measures. Does Beethoven begin in F major and then modulate to C major? Are we *on* the dominant or *in* the dominant, or in this case, more exactly, on the fourth or in the fourth? Fixing such an analysis clearly, deciding dogmatically where we are at any moment, is precisely how technical analysis ignores, misses, or removes us from the felt ambiguity of modulation. Indeed, what different persons experience, or even what we might experience at different times when there has been a growth of remembrance, is not a good subject for technical or formal analysis of anything.

Thus, the first hearing of Beethoven's First (or Fifth) Symphony will be different from later hearings. We might even say that a later hearing is different from what Beethoven wanted, for as soon as we hear the first chord of the *previously* familiar Beethoven First, we know we are hearing it in connection with an awaited C major. Likewise, on subsequent hearings of Beethoven's Fifth, we immediately assume the remembered tonality, before it needs to be experienced or established properly. Tonality—and this is my main theme—has a pervasive life in our heads that has some important independence of what can be clearly pointed to in a musical score.

There are countless examples of ambiguous opening tonalities. Beethoven's Tempest Sonata, Op. 31, No. 2, does not immediately reveal D minor, but begins, close enough, with an arpeggio chord on the dominant. Many, many minutes later, more for the mind than for the ear, there is a subtle remembrance at the end of the Sonata. Beethoven's closing notes, in a final affirmation of D minor, move down into the same register where his opening dominant chord had begun.

The formal study of modulation, the syntactical analyses that musicians richly provide, can hardly be based on, or be made to vary with, how well a work is known. That is not part of the score! Yet how well it is known is profoundly connected with the nature, quality, and extent of its appreciation or enjoyment.

Analysis employs a time structure, since music, as they say, is a temporal art, whatever else we might philosophically argue about time and motion. In such analysis, "A comes before B" means that B comes after A. But listening is rife with anticipations and remembrances. They vary with the talents of listeners, the numbers of repetitions, and the distance between them. The clear sequencing of musical analysis, like the helpful logic of explanatory narrative, is a betrayal of what goes on in our experiencing heads. Keys cannot be clocked, or accounted for, in strictly temporal or technical terms. The musical remembrance of A does not await the sounding of B, and the anticipation of, or impulsion to, B can come during the sounding of A. And there's the rub: the elusiveness. There can be a mixing (as the poet suggests) of memory and desire in a temporal no-man's-land.[2] That might even be a metaphorical definition of modulation.

This is not a claim that has a natural appeal to composers and musicians. As persons, like the rest of us, they have the usual troubles deciphering what goes on in their heads, apart from what they can name. But as musicians, and hence as anti-aestheticians and non-philosophers, they need to be precise. They have to find out clearly what happens in a musical score rather than what might happen pre-musically or extra-musically, or what might be said to constitute, or what I here claim constitutes, the non-temporal, impulse-rich, memory-laden experience of music.

V

Let us look further at this temporal elusiveness. The composer somehow establishes his key, tentatively or firmly. And then? He might stay in that key, and in much simple music there is no modulation. (Think *The Battle Hymn of the Republic*, or some other simple favorite.) The key is established and persists to the firm conclusion.

It probably persists for some time after the conclusion and one proof would be how it affected the hearing of the beginning of a subsequent song. The duration (i.e., influence) of tonality, as I have been insisting, cannot be formally marked by the beginnings and endings of musical passages or compositions and cannot be confirmed by such limits.

The persistence of tonality, beyond its formal boundaries, has no surer evidence than when a composer does, in fact, modulate. Can you modulate without remembering where you came from, and if you didn't remember, would there be any reason to modulate? (I threaten my metaphor here, since I might want to travel to forget where I have been!) In sophisticated Western music the composer does modulate, as he doesn't in *The Battle Hymn of the Republic*. Even then, he probably doesn't modulate immediately but uses the different chords of his key, like the subdominant and the dominant, before he gets to the dominant *key*!

And here I get to my main theme, reaffirm my tonality, from which I will not modulate. The most provocative, and hence most revealing, remark I ever read about modulation is Donald Francis Tovey's observation that we must distinguish between being *on* the dominant and *in* the dominant. Like all great distinctions, it tantalizingly brings together what it separates and undermines its own precision. It is when we are neither *on* nor *in* the dominant, I choose to argue, that the modulation significantly takes place. The modulation is the feel of the transition and obliterates the distinction that is used in explaining what happens. If I travel from A to B, then the places A and B, the outposts, in one sense, define the trip. But they are hardly the experiential substance of it or convey its profound ongoing ambiguity when we are neither here nor there.

Tovey's distinction between being *on* the dominant and *in* the dominant must have some clarity, otherwise how could the distinction be made? Indeed, when *on* the dominant, the homing instinct is short and swift. The tonic call, or pull, is the powerful determinative ambience. The composer, so to speak, has never left home. *The Battle Hymn of the Republic* and other simple songs use different chords, here typically I, IV, I, V, and I, but the tonic is strongly felt for the entire brief duration of that powerful tune.

But suppose we modulate to the dominant *key*. Then we are in a new place, and it is what Tovey means by being *in* the dominant rather than *on* it. Yet the only difference between the dominant chord / tonic chord relationship, and dominant key / tonic key relationships is in the duration, the distance between them, the remembrance. The pull is the same, or almost the same, since there will be an attenuation of that pull only because of a time lapse. The pull must be there and it must persist, at least for a while, or we could not refer to a larger tonal structure. After all, the composer's last movement of a long symphony, perhaps an hour after the work began, is usually in the tonic key!

Tonality, in a word, is only partly objective and it cannot simply be found in the score. It is not circumscribed, or adequately characterized, by technical analysis. It hovers around us, establishes itself in us, vaguely leaves us, we know not exactly how and when. The tonality that musicians like to point to in a musical score, *in* the dominant or *on* the dominant, the fixed location and boundaries of modulation, are not how we experience them. The clearest orthography cannot contain them or limit them. A purely musical and formal analysis of modulation does not get at something that might be called, perhaps pretentiously, the phenomenological feel of a transition, its pushes and pulls, its durational ambiguities, and, I dare to say, its uncanny connections with life itself.

What is musically significant about a modulation (to repeat for emphasis) is the transition, one might even say the feel of the transition, the impulse behind it. It is the time when we are neither securely *in* the dominant nor *on* the dominant. The radiations go back and forth and there is no permanent resting place, neither an old home nor new one.

Whether we are *in* the dominant or *on* the dominant can be radically indeterminate. To repeat (as musicians do to confirm or stress a theme), a dominant chord points quickly and decisively to the tonic, to which it "needs" to return, as surely as the second shoe needs to drop. This obtains within a short time frame, as when a tune has a simple sequence of chords. But it does not apply over greater distances, and when a work modulates to the dominant key, or to any other key, there is a homing influence that has uncertain duration and force. We may be in the dominant, but not quite on it, or in a new place. There is a wandering, a traveling, a modulating influence that prepares us to end up elsewhere—and eventually to stay there. But do we ever blissfully forget from whence we came, or ever escape a nostalgic desire to return? Or do we agonizingly remember our origins and become grateful that we don't have to go back? At any given musical moment we don't know exactly how much we remember (where home was, as it were) and how much we are resettled, regretfully or contentedly.

To recapitulate my previous point (and to ensure that it is remembered!), the dominant chord is related to the tonic chord the way the dominant key is related to the tonic key. The difference is not only the distance in time but also the strength of memory (connected often with distance in time) that affects how much, or whether, we want to get back. This difference is at once crucial and obscure, and probably of enormous importance with respect to how, or even whether, we enjoy music. (Without primitive awareness of structure, music can be listened to without being heard.) How stretched out in time can there be a perceived working relationship between keys? How long does the homing instinct endure, if it endures? When does it cease to exist, if it ceases? Can we ever be permanently resettled, with home fully forgotten?

Writers recapitulate for the same reasons musicians do: to remember, to reconfirm with useful purpose, and sometimes to reestablish with unnecessary redundancy. Even Beethoven, who apparently lived in more places in Vienna than anyone else, sometimes reminds us more than is necessary (as at the end of the Fifth Symphony, tonic chord after tonic chord) that he has gotten home!

VI

What is home? The place you start from or the place you find?

Home, Homeland, *Heimat, Pays*—and I am sure the word in any other language, whatever its particular associations—is often the sentimental place one started from and the place to which one wants to return. Be it ever so humble, we have been told, there's no place like it.

But not all starting places, whatever hardwiring they might have produced in individual psyches, are places to which we necessarily want to return. Home, in life or music, is either the place from which you started, or the place that you never left, or the place to which you sort of wish to return after you sort of left it, or the place you never want to see again! The strong homing, or tonal, instinct of classical music has not prevented drifts toward the atonal, and we cannot know what the distant outcome will be.

I venture the extravagant claim that the uncertainties of a musical home key partake of, and are similar to, the uncertainties of any other notion of home.

I further suggest—though I perhaps have been doing the opposite—that the human notions of home should not be taken as a metaphor for the musical notions of tonality. They are metaphors for each other, and there is no primacy. It is only their connection that is the relevant interest, or that possibly intrigues. They have samenesses and differences, but neither is surely prior nor original.

Mozart, daring classical composer that he was, had a strong tonal instinct. How did he take to his travels, sometimes absent from Salzburg for years, from which he variously wanted to get away and to which he occasionally wanted to return, and which he eventually left permanently?

As a metaphor for modulation, if not a mocking variation of it, I might describe travel from home city A to city F with the following "technical" analysis. Fly from A to B. Take a bus to C and catch another plane. Stay over until the next morning (don't get too used to the stopover or change your mind about going on!) and then catch a train to D (St. Paul, let us say), and then leave from E (Minneapolis—an enharmonic change!). And then fly quickly to F, your destination. There might be other ways of going from A to F, shorter or longer, more restful or more taxing, more pleasing or more displeasing. We take such journeys—we do modulations— because there is some distance between A and F and we either want to get to F or away from A. Geographically, one way or another, we have to go over some intervening spaces, nonstop or stepwise. But the goal of a journey is not the exclusive reason for it nor is it the impulse behind it. And the geographical (read *technical*) explanation of it, though true enough, does not do it justice. If you just wanted to get from A to F, and could do it nonstop, while asleep, why not?

There are famous people who never traveled, for lack of opportunity or desire. Immanuel Kant never left Koenigsberg. Would an excursion to Paris have enhanced him or his impressive identity? Or interested him? Or enlarged his "horizons"? He traveled in other realms and surely had his own departures and arrivals.

Music and space are not the only places we can travel, for all these present preoccupations with them. It might be the case that imaginary space, in which we take real trips without moving, has a close connection with real music, in which we take imaginary trips while actually moving. Kant walked around Koenigsberg with great clock-setting precision, we are told. The rest of the time he traveled among strained and difficult arguments, with nary a literary flourish to alter his momentum or his direction. He did at least once glance at the starry sky above and the moral law within and saw a connection. For that we can be grateful.

VII

The lastingness of a tone, or even a chord, might be a personally variable and unknowable experience and not register on us equally. Mahler's *Das Lied von der Erde* has the line, in the first movement, "Dunkel ist das Leben, ist der Tod." It appears three times and moves up a half step the second and third time. I did not know this before seeing the score, which is evidence of the limitation of my memory. Absent this cognizance, did the ascent have a musical effect on me? I assume that it did. Detailed knowledge of the technical ingredients of a score can be a joy unto itself. It is separable, but not entirely distinguishable, from how things are heard. I once read an incredibly detailed Schenkerian analysis of the first movement of *Das Lied*. It put the Greek constellations to shame in its thoroughness. There were modulations galore to be accounted for, or to leave unaccounted. The movement begins and ends somehow in the same key, though I am not sure why. We do not always remember what we remember. (One writer, John Murdoch Tarrh, wrote, "Many different areas of tonality are expressed, but one seldom feels the existence of a stable key area."[3])

Did Mozart know, or deliberately see to it, or remember, or care, that the key in which "Non più andrai" appears in *Figaro* is different from the key in which it is quoted in *Don Giovanni*? Does any composer know whether the phrase "D minor" refers to a tonality, or whether it is a reference to, or a connotation of, all the works he knows (remembers) in that key? "D minor" was not the same pitch several centuries ago as it is now.

How long does the memory and influence of a key last even with the best musician or composer? I don't know and very likely the composer doesn't know. His score doesn't tell us.

It is not an evidentiary matter. If a composer returns to his tonic key at the end of a symphonic movement, or a symphony, or a long opera (Wagner's *Ring des Nibelungen*), is it because of an enduring homing instinct—that is, an ongoing musical remembrance of what was past and long ago? Or is it because he is operating within the framework or a rule that was musically (emotionally?) coercive in a shorter song or composition and that he now chooses to continue?

Perhaps every moment of musical originality (and this can be extended to all the arts) involves a feelingful or impulsive departure from an established way of doing something, that is, a breaking of some rule or custom.

Maybe that is how modulation started, or how travel away from home started. A prevailing way, or place, no longer seemed right, or interesting (or safe!), just as staying in the tonic, at some point in music history, must not have seemed right. The practice of modulation itself, looked at historically, was a new impulse or habit of breaking away from a fixed key or tonality. Of course, the new impulse or habit gave rise to the very idea of tonality. As regularly happens, the breaking of a rule becomes part of a new system of rules and creates a new theoretical category.

In fact, the habit of modulation eventually acquired its own rules and ways, with its own complications and novelties. The variety of those rules and procedures, as we saw, is endlessly fascinating to musicologists and theoreticians. They become a closed study, full of intriguing combinations and permutations, perhaps very helpful to students but only mildly helpful, if helpful at all, to composers. Such studies of modulation are perhaps like the Greek theories of the modes. They are heavily intellectual and subtle, but no longer generative (as perhaps was the case even in ancient times) of creative originality or novelty. They were about as useful in explaining or creating music as the "constellations" were in explaining or understanding the stars. Or to be more fair, useful for a limited time.

I have alluded to the evidence for the pull of tonality. There is also much evidence for how it can be, and has been, blatantly ignored. While much classical music adheres to fairly formal and tonal structures, we know that the performance habits of musicians were sometimes extremely casual, even tonally indifferent. In public concerts the movements of a symphony were frequently divided up and other works performed during the interval. We know that an aria might be transposed for the convenience of an ageing soprano, playing havoc with any claim to tonal structure. In such cases, it might seem, memory does not matter at all.

VIII

I have already suggested that the endings of music are not followed by a context of toneless silence. The same applies to beginnings. Beginnings are preceded by vague ambiences, sometimes music heard some time back, perhaps uncertainly remembered, and sometimes by mechanical and electronic sounds that are nowadays ubiquitous. There were always the birds, however their talents and tessituras might have varied. I have heard a bird do the beginning, the first four notes, of the last movement of Beethoven's Tempest Sonata. (We know, from the Pastoral Symphony, how intrigued Beethoven was with bird song.) One biographical report (from Ignaz Schuppanzigh) has it that the Tempest tones were suggested to Beethoven by the sounds of a galloping horse. Poor horse. Poor rider.

All they wanted to do was get from town A to town B, to home or away from it, without intending either to bother Beethoven or inspire him. And all Beethoven wanted to do was start in D minor (via a dominant chord), end in D minor, and have some interesting moves and sounds in the interim.

The ultimate surrounding of music is silence, we might think, but the silence before music starts is at least somewhat obscure, and the silence that follows music is certainly not empty of some sense of hovering or lingering tonality.

The sense of tonality, as we saw, persists in various ways and degrees. It persists to the start of the next movement of a composition, it persists in the organization of pieces in a program, and it persists over an uncertain length of time. The rest is silence, the poet said.[4] But until life ends there is no absolute terminal silence, and before life ends there can be imaginings and anticipations, even of heavenly choirs. And while the beginnings of sound are largely lost in our memories, newer speculations suggest that they might even be prenatal, as in musical families like the Mozarts.

Tonality and modulation are certainly not all of music, but a contemporary sense of their considerable role is seen in the current speculations about whether atonal music can escape the tradition and pull of tonality or whether tonal music will indeed survive. Mahler at one time thought that the end of tonality would be the end of music.

Perhaps the rise of tonality was an historical event, beginning at a certain time in Western music and possibly now facing its prolonged but sure extinction. Looked at this way, one might say that the several hundred years of prevailing tonality in music was a "modulation" (loosely or metaphorically speaking) from something that preceded it to something that will follow it. But such audacious historical speculations are beyond our time spanning capacities' (i.e., our memories') ability to grasp. We have enough trouble with shorter time spans (e.g., a Mahler symphony, a Wagner opera), let alone our own lives. We can only know or feel or express more ultimate historical spans as metaphorical or conceptual indulgences.

Schenker, to whom I have several times referred, was strongly interested in Western music of a given, limited period. His sense of the force of tonality was so strong that he seemed of the opinion that modulations did not occur. (In Tovey's terms, you might be *on* the dominant but never *in* the dominant.) In my more general language, whatever the distance away from home, home persists as a reference point. His view serves my own uncertainty about the persistence of tonality, in myself and I presume in others.

IX

In music, as we saw, the tonic key, the home key, has to be somehow established. We are not quite sure what was lurking in our psyches before the composer starts out. He usually (but not always) establishes his tonality quickly as his composition begins. His chosen key usually begins not by way of another key but after silence. Silences, moments of them, are often part of a musical structure—and we need to consider these silences with respect to modulation. But the silences, the musical silences that precede and follow the sound of music, are usually not connected with what we think of as modulation. Indeed, the silences between the movements of a composition, and the silences (say) between the works on a musical program, have not been given much attention. They are too informal and indefinable. They are silences possibly related to hidden but perhaps hovering sounds, but uncertainly or vaguely remembered.

Attempts to describe art straddle the ambiguities of the creative process. Is the artist or musician following a form or creating one, does his decision flow from a new feel of what is right, or is he repeating a structure because it is habitual, familiar, and time-tested? Is he acting in accord with his own fresh judgment, or is he doing what an honored predecessor, or perhaps he himself, repeatedly did?

The distinction between a newly felt appropriateness, on the one hand, and convention or established form, on the other hand, is at the confusing heart and origin of creativity. All moments of originality, so much pointed to and honored by critics, *are* such moments because they depart from the conventional or the expected. Modulation is not only a departure from what has been fixed and established, a key or tonality, but is itself a procedure that has acquired its own conventions and, to some extent, even its own rules and fixities. It is now an expected departure from what once was fixed and once did not change. Perhaps the varieties of modulation in a tonal system are perceived as exhausted, hence the invention of atonality.

Modulations, if nothing else, are departures and returns. There are novel ways of doing them and already established ones. Historically, the very practice of modulation was a departure from mono-tonality, or whatever there was and still occasionally is, that precedes tonal variety.

Since fully mature Western tonality depends on modulation, atonality can be viewed historically (and of course metaphorically) as a daring modulation away from modulation! We are culturally in the throes of that historical move. Atonality hasn't always worked; some composers have tried it and have reverted to tonality and others have sought to juxtapose the old and the new.

At the outset I said I would return to a point if I remembered it. I thought it was a good point at the time and I thought that I should remember it. I don't. I would have remembered it if I were simply recalling my previous paragraph. But now it is long ago and many paragraphs have intervened. This forgetfulness—whether genuine or artful—supports my theme. The remembered, in music and in life, is absolutely essential for a full and proper appreciation of either. But time and distance have human limits, and they cut short the possible unities both of our musical experiences and of our comprehended lives. We cannot have fully clear purposes or fully clear enjoyments, which is another way of saying that we straddle the art/morality distinction. To recall *Macbeth*, if it is not too long ago, to feel and to dispute persist as alternatives. To see life steady and to see it whole is a noble ambition. But it is for another time and place.

X Coda

There is a musical work, actually part of one, to which I have now travelled and almost succeeded in reaching. In its poignancy and exalted simplicity it is emblematic of what I have said about tonality and modulation. It is *Der Leiermann*, the concluding section of Schubert's great song-cycle *Die Winterreise*. It can be thought of as both a life journey and a musical journey, each commenting on and mirroring the other, each the metaphor for the other.

The *Leiermann*, the organ grinder, might be the last song that Schubert ever wrote, a fittingly final effort. The text, by Wilhelm Mueller, describes the organ grinder as a frozen, suffering shadow of a musician, who cannot really create music but can only repeat what he has sounded before, in nearly silent desperation. With dogs gnarling at him, he grinds away in the cold, alone and barefoot, his cup empty. Nobody sees him, nobody hears him. His situation does not change—it is essentially static and final; his life hangs by a thread; his journey and his song's journey are over and he accepts his fate.

In the last part of the text, in the very last measures of the song, somewhat unexpectedly and even startlingly, there is an outside intrusion and the organ grinder is addressed. "Wunderlich Alter," begins the questioning. (*Wunderlich* can mean strange, singular, odd, curious, eccentric; it can even touch on the miraculous and supernatural.) "Strange old man, can I go with you? Will you sing my songs?" The voice here briefly reaches its highest point in the contour of the song, the dominant ninth, which can be said to pressure to the tonic even more strongly than does the dominant seventh.

Wunderlicher Alter is what Schubert might have thought of himself—despite his comparative youth—in the penultimate moments of his life. In asking the organ grinder to sing his music, the music he has created and is finally finishing, what has been *by* the composer is now also *about* him. Schubert has become united with the organ grinder in the shared recognition of their predicaments. The organ grinder is no longer merely the composer's "objective correlative." They are metaphors for each other. Singer and song are simultaneous, and one. They are at their journey's end, creating and perceiving, judging and enduring, focusing and finishing in the stark simplicity of an art/morality moment.

Der Leiermann starts in a tonality from which it never departs, a tonality that has been arrived at after a long, bitter winter journey. It is a tonality that might be said never to have been completely found nor completely abandoned.

The music, which I have been hearing or thinking of concurrently with the writing of this piece, moves with a vengeance in its tonal repetition, uninterrupted for sixty-two measures. The I–V bass chord never varies, staying the same in every measure—which in any other composition would be mono-tonous! In the upper registers there is only a bare move away, but never completely away, to the dominant chord. The dominant never leaves the tonic completely. The tonic never stops sounding. There is even less chordal variety here—in this sophisticated art song—than we saw earlier in the simple I–IV–I–V–I chords in *The Battle Hymn of the Republic*. The dominant chord is sounded in *Der Leiermann* but never stands alone. We are never really *in* the dominant (recalling Tovey's distinction), let alone *on* the dominant.

The tonic (to repeat) sounds throughout in the repeated base, from beginning to end, even when the dominant chord sounds above or alongside it. This juxtaposition of tonic and dominant is quite remarkable, though not entirely unusual. It gives the total effect, with the repeated simplicity of the melody, not of a tonal movement, back and forth, to and fro, but of a sustained, non-temporal, tonic-dominant simultaneity. Home and exile are no longer different places; time and travel have come to a halt.

This repetition, along with some slight arc and variety in the voice, continues to the end. Almost to the end, since in the very last measure Schubert returns to a full tonic minor chord. The dominant chord is abandoned, as it needs to be in a conventional, proper, and expected closing in the tonal tradition.

It is arrogant of me to attempt to modify a master and to suggest an ending that Schubert did not use. But it would have been true to the spirit of his work (i.e., to my preferred way of hearing it) if he had concluded on the tonic and dominant together and allowed them to fade out simultaneously. I would like to think that a thorough search of manuscripts would reveal that he had at least entertained that possibility.

My metaphor of home and tonality, in either direction, like all metaphor, is created-discovered. Metaphor is at the heart of all art. It is humanly fashioned and externally found in the selfsame moment, mixing memory of what is known with a desire to reach something beyond. It sometimes seems right and sometimes does not, depending on who does the "seeming." It can fall apart, like a faulty contraption sloppily constructed, or it can soar like a skylark, as though assembled by a higher and alien power. Good metaphors both extend what we know and also depend on what we know. Recall the ship and the camel, with the help of which and from which we traveled some ways back if not a long time ago.

Music could not exist without a life in which it is echoed, embedded, and accompanied. Life could not have discovered its lasting value and its deepest enjoyment without music. The two came to us, luckily or miraculously, at the same time and will surely end together.

PERFORMANCE AND OBLIGATION
Musical Variations on Art and Morality

1987

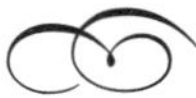

The tension between the obligations a performing musical artist has to a musical score and to him- or herself as a creative artist varies with time and circumstance. Considering this varying tension between obligations to constraint and freedom suggests that an artist cannot choose one obligation over the other, and this further obligation to maintain the tension is as much moral as artistic. Rigid aesthetic theory can obscure both the tension and its moral import, while attention to this tension reveals the variety of a performer's obligations in relation to notation, instruments, tonality, tempo, and virtuosity. Further inquiry reveals how a performer's obligations quickly exceed the realm of art, as when, for example, the obligation to perform leads to choices significant for a performer's health. This essay contends that the object of a performer's obligation is twofold: it is both a prior existence that serves as an independent standard and an ideal that the individual performer articulates and pursues. Hence, the performer's obligation, "as with ethical obligation in general, is to something both internal and external." And the variety of a performer's obligations "are not uniquely aesthetic; they are complicated ethical tasks in a particular interpersonal setting."

Performance is an elusive category, epistemologically and morally. I largely avoid epistemology and focus on the specifics of musical performance and its obligations. However, there are connections between making music and obligations: (A) in the other performing arts, (B) in the non-performing arts, and (C) in the general urgencies of life, with which even music obligations are connected. I draw on examples from (A) and (B) and dwell at some length on (C).

My theoretical contribution, if any, is minimal. I assume that the performer has a double obligation, to the music he performs (score or prior performance) and to himself as a creative artist. What is perhaps not so obvious is the complicated and precarious way in which the performer functions within the framework of these contrasting obligations and how these obligations can vary with time and circumstance. Francis Sparshott says that the "score does not command but merely specifies and thus provides opportunities."[1] Quite so. My ongoing elaborations are a gloss, or a set of variations, on what is meant by "specifies" and "provides opportunities," and on the scope and complication of what lies between. Finally, the score has a meta-obligation. The fact of its existence invites us to honor the tension between the score's specific obligations to constraint and to freedom, and not just to choose between them. Appreciation of this larger obligation is as much a moral as it is a musical demand.

Musical experience requires active encounter with the creation and/or appreciation of music—with performance lodged somewhere between the two. I stay close to that experience for the few conclusions I draw. I move more among the challenges to the rigidities of theory than among the theories themselves.

If Sparshott and others are right, it took centuries to move from Pythagorean and cognitive interest in how the universe works musically to greater interest in how music works humanly. It is nice to speculate about the music of the spheres and the kind of performance (or happening?) it might be, or whether there is some obligation on the Creator's part to make it the best of all possible performances. The nearest I get to that kind of problem is the special situation of the composer-performer, who might be thought to have Prospero- or God-like powers, and I give one fictional example of musical intelligence at work in outer space.

First, I speculate (*a priori* fashion) on the origins of performance obligations, relating them to law and contract. Next, I turn to the requirements of scores, with comment on Sparshott's remarks on notation and performance. I also deal with musical instruments and persons as embodiments of obligation. Sections on tonality and key explore unusual difficulties with respect to what they seem to demand and allow. Lastly, I consider the effect on obligation of risk-taking—the risk of live performance, virtuoso display, and playing from memory.

Largely, I show that distinctions employed in musical aesthetics, while seemingly secure and fixed, tend to be underdetermined. They enshrine some favored theory as to what ought to happen but do not readily stand up when confronted with what does happen, and to the contradictory "oughts" that actually prevail.[2]

Nelson Goodman's "all notes right" criterion for the definition of a performance is an example of this. Aware of usual practice, he says, perhaps plaintively, "Could we not bring our theoretical vocabulary into better agreement with common practice . . . by allowing some limited degree of deviation in performances admitted as instances of a work?" His intellectual scheme requires him to answer with a firm "no."[3] Theoretical, like musical, performances are wide-ranging and make obligations to self as well as to truth, to virtuoso display as well as to anything as simple or straightforward as "agreement with common practice." When I recapitulate my themes I touch on extreme contemporary notions about such self-obligation. Nowadays, performances of all kinds—musical, literary, theoretical—verge on the *sui generis*.

Origins

Performance is a highly generic concept; Sparshott has even defined works of art in terms of performance; there is performance in nonperforming as well as in performing arts, and pervasively in life itself.

In the early history of storytelling and music-making, performing must have been an untendentious remembering of earlier performances, a primal way of enjoying and preserving that must have worked for a long time. The story or music heard was the story or music retold or sung. Any sense of obligation and responsibility could only have come about belatedly.

That songs and stories underwent changes (now we would say interpretations) in the resinging and the retelling must have occurred to people fairly early; but the changes were not likely to be perceived as bothersome, let alone as betrayals. New remembrances replaced old ones, and so long as the latest remembrances satisfied, there would not have been much sense of loss. To modify Santayana's famous remark—but, of course, without betraying it—we might say that those who cannot remember the past are condemned to change it and not be bothered by the change.

The first concerns about notation for purposes of preservation surely had to do with words rather than with music and particularly with words that fixed agreements and contracts. It is in the area of contract and law that forgetting what has been spoken and agreed upon can become an affront, a threat, and what we would now call an injustice. Early surviving texts, so many papyri and clay tablets, are economic obligations. They would prevent "bad performances"; accidental, deliberate, and creative lapses; or a reluctance to act out agreements in the manner stated.

The notion of good and bad performance had its origins in the moral and economic sphere rather than in the aesthetic one, though these spheres are related. The persistence into our own day of improvisational traditions in music, without use of notation, attests to a certain kind of moral indifference to performance obligations. Now, as in the very beginnings of music, a prior performance can be the basis of a performance as surely as a score can be such a basis. Sparshott makes this point; I plan to play upon it and will return to it.

Eventually the early bards and psalmists must have perceived that the retelling of a heard story or the resinging of a heard song produced variants of the original. But in the absence of texts and scores—that is, before the peculiar invariants of the written word or notation—one cannot guess how the retelling or the performance would have been perceived in relation to its originals. Any original was a performance, not different in kind from the performance of which it was the further occasion. With performances and performances of performances constituting the tradition, the very idea of performance could only have half-emerged and been quite inarticulate. The concept of performance obligation, if not the fact of the performances themselves, requires some sense of a fixed, known, or remembered original. Differences could not have been discerned with the same surety as became possible with notation.

Notation

Sparshott criticizes the view "that the introduction of musical notation changes . . . music into a new sort of art" and objects to the notion that "what identifies the work is that in it which is notated, and whatever complies with that is a correct performance of the work."[4] I agree that "there is no musical need that identity be preservable in any one way."[5] A performance remains a performance, whether of a score or of a performance, and Sparshott properly suggests that there is an arbitrary element in what counts as a work and what counts as a performance of a work.

However, without changing music, or defining it with respect to its performances, notation modifies performance considerably and alters its responsibilities. It becomes important both in terms of what it energetically and forcefully prescribes and what it cannot, and indeed, refuses to prescribe. It has a special kind of egalitarian neutrality and makes a generalized demand upon all who use it. Composers want to create scores, and performers want to work from scores even when other originals (live performances, recordings) are available. The score is desired neither because it prescribes performances with exactness, nor because it allows for endless freedoms, leeways, and departures. The score is valued by composer and performer alike because it establishes standard and persistent parameters for certain kinds of obedience and certain kinds of originality. It is a vehicle for creating the possibility of varied performances within a particular framework of strictures and of freedoms.

These strictures and freedoms are partly accidental in their origins. Thus, notation can more easily name and fix pitch than indicate dynamic relations between tones. Contrariwise, the live performance fixes dynamics more readily, and fixes pitch less readily, than does the written score. Crudely put, the score fixes a syntactical structure whereas the performance fixes dynamics and emotion. What each fixes, and what each allows to remain free, needs to be differentially explored and specified.

The encouragement to freedom, to specific "opportunities," is a crucial part of a score. It differs from performance-as-model—whether in degree or kind, I scrutinize more carefully later. We know teachers and composers sometimes perform in order to reveal to students how something "should be done." But this guidance might well be undertaken with some hesitation, and though absolute authority is sometimes assumed by or attributed to him, the composer-performer ought to be reluctant to indicate anything like one "right" performance.

Some clarifying evidence for the existence of this attitude—of wanting to preserve but in an egalitarian and open way—is seen in labanotation. This dance notation is fairly recent in origin and does not antedate the filming of dance as a preservation device the way music notation antedates audio recording. Choreographers use this dance notation despite the fact that filming a performance from several angles offers surer preservation of a particular performance. Such notation remains neutral with respect to dancers, gestures, nuances, styles, and charismas, which are an inevitable part of any performance; it avoids preserving too much of the uniquely personal and idiosyncratic and gives all performers the same base.

According to Sparshott, a score understood in a certain way "correspond[s] to a class of musical performances."[6] Does this include as yet unperformed performances? What is gained by this terminology? A score gives rise to performances when it will, or when performers will, and that is about it.

Sparshott further says: "There is . . . one way in which playing from a score does differ in principle from playing on the basis of what one has heard played. What one has heard was one or more individual performances; a score answers to a class of performances."[7] I made a similar point: a score has about it an egalitarian neutrality that not only allows but invites interpretation. A performance is specific (now I am inclined to say relatively specific) and does not allow the same kind of openness to interpretation that a score allows.

But there is a problem here: Sparshott's analysis is possibly incomplete and mine possibly inconsistent. As is often the case in such matters, a difference in degree may or may not be seen as a difference in kind, or a difference "in principle."

In the tradition of "playing on the basis of what one has heard played," and it is a live tradition, the new performance is not a precise replica, usually not even an intended replica, of what was heard. If a number of performers played on the basis of hearing a particular performance, the original performance could be said to correspond, in Sparshott's words, to a class of new performances. The new performances would vary among themselves in differing ways. They would retain something of the original and also depart from it—which is what makes them performances.

What, then, is the *theoretical* difference between playing from a score and playing from performance? Are they "in principle" different, as suggested? The score has standardized, but not absolute, fixities and freedoms. The score sets up parameters and habitual ways between which the fixed and the free can operate. But this also happens when one "plays what one hears." Performances of performances are likely to be more about what is fixed and what is free, more influenced by the vicissitudes of memory, less governed by an enduring tradition. Each of the two ways of performing fixes and frees different aspects of music—pitch, dynamics, tempo, and so on—and the score, for better or worse, preserves these over longer periods of time. So whether performing from a score and performing from performance are in principle different is a quibble, an intellectual grace note; likewise is the claim that one way gives rise to a nameable "class" of performances and the other does not.

Let us look a bit further at the range of what notation fixes and frees. Sparshott is rather permissive (elfin? as he says of Nelson Goodman[8]) with respect to what can be done with a score. "It can be played straight, but that is not the only thing that can be done with it. It can form the basis of improvisations or alternative works, used as a source of ideas or transformations, as one will, and such uses are not necessarily any less musically worthwhile than the 'normal' use of it by a performer who has nothing in head or hand beyond the intention of producing a performance in which nothing fails to comply with the score."[9] Yes, indeed, and one might even extend this permissiveness to the kind of radical happenings that nowadays occur in art. For the score can be used to light a fire (or whatever) either (A) as a critical or moral comment on it, or (B) as a one-time aesthetic-cum-moral treat in the form of a sensuous sizzle of singeing sound. Would it be out of place here, out of respect for our scholarly activities and in a spirit of extreme permissiveness, to suggest that scores can be used to try to unravel not their sounds but their uses?

Scores can be performed in many ways, and playing them philosophically, with silent cerebral attention, is a bit of night music that differs from the other kind just in degree!

If there is no theoretical solidity or limit at the extreme of permissiveness, neither is there much solidity at the extreme of specificity. What is it "to play a score straight?" A synthesizer might do this, get the notes without dynamics, or maybe with just the dynamics that can be dealt with in a rule-governed, computerized way. But a performer is incapable of having "nothing in head or hand . . . ," despite much seeming evidence to the contrary. It might surprise non-performers to learn that a performer could not for the life of him play a score straight—if straight means avoiding nuances, dynamics, subtle tempo changes, and so on, that are no longer consciously chosen but are built into mind and fingers, body and breath. The only reasonably straight way to play a score is to study it without sounding it, to turn its unheard melodies into thoughts. So the extreme of permissiveness nicely merges with the extreme of severity, and freedom (as we knew in principle all along) is the recognition of necessity.

The perennial vagaries in all obligation, between the specified and the unspecified, the fixed and the free, are astonishing. I once saw a sign in front of a church[10] that said if God had meant to be permissive (i.e., if He had wanted us to interpret His words and not merely to obey them), He would have given us Ten Suggestions. As we know, the Ten Commandments have been open to various readings and deconstructions; some Commandments are honored more in the breach than in the observance; they all have been given amazing interpretations as though *"a piacere"* were written after them. Is it any wonder that the performance range in music, where there are only critics and the public to fear, is comparably wide?

One moves, understandably, in musical as in moral life, between severity and permissiveness. The question, always, is whether one has explored the parameters, understood the reason for their range, and has made some particular choice well, and with reference to some understanding of the problem of choice. I turn to those problems as they apply to some of the specifics of music.

Instruments and Performers

Except for singers, in whom performer and instrument coincide, performers use physical instruments and have to make decisions about them. Concern about instrumental authenticity is a recurrent, tired theme. At one extreme of obligation, the purist says that only the clavichord or fortepiano will do. At the other extreme, the piano is seen as the natural entelechy toward which all keyboard instruments have striven; it should be used for all keyboard works; it represents nontemporal perfection and is never anachronistic. In the case of the violin, it was Stradivarius who a long time ago masterfully coaxed it into *its* natural entelechy.

The structures of instruments largely determine what music is made with them. Musical detectives have come up with remarkable guesses about what ancient instruments did. Handling any instrument, ancient or modern, suggests its performance parameters, though virtuosos (like children with toys) will always do more with an instrument than the inventor intended, or than previous virtuosos did. Tuning is a loose element in instrument structure and makes for uncertainties.

Some structures are so taken for granted that we easily forget that they provide performance limitations as well as performance opportunities. Consider the keyboard with its specific positional relationships of "black" and "white" keys. This construction certainly allows for enormous dexterity but it is not the only way of assembling a keyboard; other ways might have been better, and might have produced a different performing tradition. QWERTY persists on the typewriter keyboard though it is not the best way to place the letters: the original choice was designed to limit finger speed, which the early typewriters could not handle. The point is that what has become fixed—whether in instruments or notational systems, or even in the habits of performing fingers or voices or bodies—good or bad, becomes, willy-nilly, a secondary obligation.

The modification of persons as performing instruments has received less attention than changes in other instruments. The human body (and its possibilities) has been both respected for its natural limitations and coerced beyond its natural powers. In at least one instance it was violently altered for aesthetic reasons and, later, kept from being altered for moral ones. The castrati by all accounts had beautiful voices, but it was decided by the end of the eighteenth century to stop producing them. Where a score calls for castrati, the performance or aesthetic obligation now yields to the moral one. Perhaps there are purists who object to this, but their voices are not too shrill.

While this example may seem extreme, in many cases virtuoso demands, written implicitly into scores, have had inordinately bad effects on performers. These performers, successful or otherwise, were forced, or chose, to succumb to the hours, days, and years of work needed to perfect their skills. The transformations that resulted, while not as dramatic as to the castrati, were nevertheless devastating. My point, again, is that performing obligations are embedded in other obligations. Many great performers, among them Gould, Van Cliburn, and Horowitz, have stopped performing or modified their ways of performing for moral, psychological, and health reasons. Are performers obligated to acquire the skills necessary to perform (say) Liszt's *Transcendental Etudes* or Balakirev's *Islamey*? There are now specialists in "Performing Arts Medicine" who deal with the effects of wind instruments on mouth and teeth, who recognize a Satchmo syndrome, and who treat hearing loss, fainting spells, and high blood pressure.

Kafka's "A Hunger Artist" is a wonderful paradigm of the predicament of the virtuoso performer who does well, with sustained and dazzling destructiveness, what he should not be doing at all. The castrati's physical deformation is often mirrored by the fanatical obligation, self-imposed or otherwise, of those who are determined to assume performance obligations that are inherently harmful, absurd, or immoral (cf. Plato and Tolstoy for details). The obligation to perform is inevitably connected with the obligation to choose to perform, to prepare for performance, and to know when to stop performing.

Tonality and Key

Tonality and key are among the more opaque structures of music that impinge on obligation. Tonality has its mysteries and Sparshott details them. I elaborate Sparshott's suggestion that the tone implies the world of music and the world of music implies the tone. Neither is properly part of or prior to the other and each can be analyzed in terms of the other. When a tone is experienced, even a very "isolated" tone, it is not heard in some kind of pristine purity. The world of music crowds in. The tone (for the Western listener) will intimate a key, a tonality a series of tonal relationships. It cannot he heard otherwise.

Sparshott suggests a kind of birth of music when we begin to hear sounds as tones. I suggest that sounds are always heard as tones because of both our biological and our musical histories. But whether sounds will be heard as tones of different registers, or of a D minor scale, or of a Schoenbergian tone row will, of course, depend upon context and circumstance.

We are never free of tone, even when sound is without very clear pitch identification. But tonal perception is partly a matter of attention and context. Strike a piece of wood and we don't hear the pitch for the noise. But should a series of graduated pieces of wood be struck, the noise factor would dwindle and the pitch factor become conspicuous. Even ordinary speech, sans music, hovers around tones and tonality.

Sparshott says that "the original importance of pitch was derived from the contrast between the singing and the speaking voice. This suggests that music is, originally, song. . . ."[11] The original importance? Isn't this a blindness, or should I say deafness, to the importance of register? For surely the awareness of pitch difference between the male and female voice, with its biological implications, antedated the distinction between speech and song.

Or else we have to minimize the distinction between speech and song and say that the speech song of men and women was always different. The speaking voice, male or female, is laden with pitch inflections that are readily discriminated. We still have, after all, those conspicuous in-between uses of voice, heard in certain kinds of prayer, *sprechstimme*, etc., that straddle speaking and singing. And there are individual and ethnic differences in singsong or pitch, variations. Anglo-Saxons, with stiff lower larynxes, might not notice the natural singsongness of Russian and other languages and so be inclined to exaggerate the theoretical difference between speech and song.

It is indeed likely, as Sparshott suggests, that more formal music began with song rather than with instruments. Precisely pitched bird song (if they are precise) and other ordered sounds in nature would have served as early models for voice imitation. But the invention and making of crude instruments, with fixed pitches of one kind or another, is so easy that one can speculate that instruments were coterminous with the singing voice. Some instruments are practically found objects.

Sparshott makes a great deal of what might be called the "institutional" status of tone. "Properly speaking, a tone is such a sound segment as is regularly assigned to a music. It must then belong to a system of such sounds and must be recognizable as occupying a determinate place in the system."[12] Perhaps "properly" here means "theoretically." Experientially, tones are no such things. We have a feel for tones and discriminate among them, recognizing registers before such regular assignings, just as we enjoy art objects before they receive the blessings of the art world. Everything empirical, biological, and historical suggests that we had capacities for tonal discrimination and appreciation (and hence for performance and enjoyment of music) in advance of systems and without their sanctions or validations. But we are forever caught between the innocence of what we hear and what theory and tradition tell us we ought to hear.

Sparshott also says that "a tone is treated as functionally identical with a tone of double or half its frequency. . . ."[13] "Functionally" is the arguable word here. It is true that we go from A to G and then back to A, the octave, rather than to H, I, J, and onward. But to what extent are these recurrent As "functionally" the same, heard as identical or even as similar, and to what extent is the sameness an arbitrary fact about nomenclature and theory? (Piano keys could have had eighty-eight different names!)

Experience and theory influence and tug at each other. There is some experiential sameness in the two As an octave apart, but there is also an experiential and functional difference. Play middle A on your piano, then B eight notes higher, then C six notes lower; then D eight notes higher, then E six notes lower, etc., and you will hear (I hear!) an ascending scale (in the Aeolian mode?) along with strange leaps and bounds. Of course such sequences can be performed in different ways to secure different emphases. Performers are constantly deciding between hiding the obvious and accentuating the hidden. In any case, contemporary composers and performers appreciate the aforementioned jumps and have directed much effort at differentiating the As, Bs, and Cs of different registers. Did Pythagoreanism, or whatever it was that caused halved and doubled tones to be given the same name, discover something about our hearing or victimize us by closing us off to finer aural distinctions? Perhaps it did both and guaranteed our musical quandaries.

A word about the merits of tonalities and about how theory might improperly descry them. Sparshott says that "our major and minor tonalities are the impoverished descendants of 'modes'. . . ."[14] Why impoverished? Does Sparshott merely mean that they are fewer? Is our language with its twenty-six letters rich or impoverished? It suffices for *Hamlet*. The major and minor keys suffice for *Don Giovanni*. Ancient Greek music, with its many modes, was probably over-intellectualized, offering structure at the expense of musical inventiveness, perfect for Plato's *Republic*, where, as we know, heard music mostly gave way to better things. Freedom always has to function within fixities, but too many initial structural fixities can cut down on the playful and creative choices possible within those fixities. Suppose that there were two dozen, and not two, standard forms for the sonnet, and suppose that each one had its learned glosses and commentaries. Such a situation might steer the natural poet from the writing of sonnets to the study of sonnetology. If Sparshott is right about the history of music, it took a long time to break free from intellectualized and cognitive concerns. Such concerns, of course, always have to be reckoned with. Much musical aesthetics remains persistently scholastic, piping its learned obbligatos, its unheard music, in occasional defiance of actual music practices.

There is nothing sacrosanct about the major and minor tonalities. Nor do they preclude or exclude other modes that persist in and are occasionally "written into" Western music (cf. Beethoven's *Heiliger Dankgesang*, Mozart's *Requiem*). The major and the minor modes allow for closeness and distance, "harmony" (in the very broad sense) between them, and tension. Twoness (as we know from social relationships) suffices wonderfully for all kinds of consonance and dissonance, great and small. Threeness and fourness and multiple musical modes could work, too, as perhaps they did for the Greeks, but not as neatly and as economically. Would we call dialogue impoverished colloquy?[15]

We always hear and must always have heard tones in terms of a context. Like the social contract, the first shepherd piping or singing a pure tone is a fiction. He would have heard birds, and at least the first intimations of some kind of tonality, or scale or relationship between tones. If birds produce different tones, as they do, we can presume that other birds hear them in their relationships. Man could never have existed with his exquisite faculty for deciphering tones and his repeated occasion to hear them, without a fairly complicated and persistently present, albeit untheoretical, sense of tonal structure. What the structures must have been elude us until they become standardized into musical scales and modes.

Here and now, and always, we are pervaded by musical structures, which seize us as much as we seize them. The world of music is our permanent ambience, within us and outside us, and it readily reverberates to the slightest of musical suggestion. The very notion of hearing a tone, that tone, is to separate it from the tones that it is not, and of which we are thereupon wittingly or unwittingly reminded. Western tonality is one such context, and for those of us immersed in it, it pervades our silences; it surrounds us always ready to intrude.

Whatever the mysteries of tonality and the ways in which we are under its grip, it might be assumed that staying in the key of a piece is basic obligation. Yet conductors and composers have changed keys to accommodate the voice range of singers or to make the "same" song (confirming Pythagoras!) available to both baritone and soprano. Is the transposition a lot of wrong notes for Nelson Goodman?

But there is a subtler point about key obligation sometimes neglected even by purists who are intent upon all kinds of authenticity. We talk of key "signature," but do we mean pitch, so many vibrations per second, or do we mean (as I shall suggest) the cluster of classical works written in, and associated with, the key in question?

The historical evidence is that absolute keys have changed, standard pitch has gone up, and our D minor is not the key (insofar as it is identified by pitch) in which Mozart wrote and heard his Twentieth Piano Concerto. Nonetheless, even if key has no absolute physical meaning and has changed by a tone or more over the centuries, phrases like "C minor" and "D minor" have a kind of reference and involve an obligation, albeit not the one usually assumed. Such key labels bear the connotations of the totality of works written in them. They have highly generic meanings, not because of the pitches they denote but because of the various works they comprehend and connote. It does not matter that our D minor is not, literally, Mozart's. What does matter is that the works we associate with D minor overlap those that he associated with D minor. The performing obligation is more to this common label and to its musical associations (the "class" of works identified with that signature) than to anything more precisely definable. Because of these associations, C minor and D minor would have a different performance "feel"—entirely apart from pitch—than E minor or B minor.

The common notion that keys (e.g., C minor, D minor, B minor) have "inherent" emotional qualities that need to be respected may be a misguided and nonsensical carryover of the exegesis of modes, which at least differed from each other tonally. My explanation attempts to give rationale to claims about keys showing how those claims could have developed in time. (Of course, there is a difference in key quality that is connected with instrument structure. Some keys employed on the violin, for instance, will use more of the open strings than other keys. The vocal structure of a singer might make it possible for her to do a song in C major but challenge her if transposed to A major. Later I take up the value and disvalue of such straining and effort.)

The rest is tonal mysticism, misguided Pythagoreanism, or forgivable discovery of the *a priori* after the fact. But people will continue to say that an orchestra tuned to an A of 448 vibrations per second is more "brilliant" than an orchestra tuned to an A of 440. A credible claim of inherent emotional difference between, say, C minor and D minor (let alone C minor and C sharp minor) could be made only if someone's hearing acuity were so great that he heard them the way the rest of us hear register difference.

In this electronic age we live among more tonal constants than people did in the past. There were always the birds, but they, too, might have *tessituras*, like people. Has anyone checked Beethoven's *Pastoral Symphony* with real birds, for pitch and tempo? As I type this on a word processor I hear the pitch and hum of my PC. It confirms everything I have said about pitch. It suggests key, and while my mind's ear can play around with its position on a scale, it sets my options. What is the psychic effect of the B flat of the telephone dial tone? Do people in 50-cycle-per-second countries differ musically from 60-cycle-per-second people? Pitch standards used to lack constancy. Is that inconstancy now at an end? Will being permanently plugged into acoustical absolutes, numerically defined, have a musical effect upon us? Tempos and pitches are now assigned to us, instilled into our being by the gadgetries we have created, and our fixities and our freedoms—including musical ones—will never be the same.

Tempo

In both life and art, slowing down and speeding up can be funny or serious, can produce laughter or sorrow. There are right times for "faster" and "slower." There is also, perhaps, something like a good basic tempo, an essential speed around which changes should occur. The proper pacing of life has to do with, among other things, one's age, and both the comic and tragic are connected with departures from some vague norms appropriate to youthfulness and elderliness. The pacing of music, too— going faster and slower—revolves around different essential and proper speeds. The movements of a given (Western classical) work will differ among themselves, but each will have a more or less constant, basic speed. Last movements do not parallel life, for they are rarely slow.

There are some hidden meanings in performance tempos. Great speed can indicate obvious skill, as well as the condition of being helpless and lost; playing slowly and well can be more difficult than playing quickly, though slowness is often associated with a performer's incompetence or unfamiliarity with a score. We delight in tempo changes and so they are sometimes built into scores locally as strettos, augmentations, and the like.

What about the correct starting speed, the essential tempo, around which the changes occur? Is it important? One can "transpose" tempo like key, indeed along with key, by speeding up or slowing down the playback rate of a recording. As with key, small changes of basic tempo do not matter much, but big changes, to what might be called a different tempo "register," leave us listless or frenetic, unattentive or amused, with a sense that we are hearing a different work or a work badly played.

A variety of starting tempos is acceptable if they remain within a conventional "register." We can normally expect the differing temperaments of performers to result in different tempos, but the acceptable ranges are elusive.

Initially, there were no tempo indications in notation; markings like "gigue," "minuet," and "courante" associated tempos with dance, with the natural determinations and limitations of human movement. But how reliable are these references? People can do the same ("same"?) dance quickly and slowly. Later words like "allegro" (not actually a description of speed) and "presto" were vaguely informative, but not demanding. These words, like the keys I spoke of earlier, acquired their musical meanings from the works or movements with which they were associated. If we encounter one hundred scores marked "allegro," we infer from those scores, after the fact, the tempo of "allegro."

Tempo is now easily specified. Surely the performer has some obligation to original tempo—intended, implied, or notated. Does it help to give that intention mathematically, as by a metronome? That device—invented in the clock-crazy century of ultimate reasonableness—made tempo designations precise. But it also forced the hands of composers and performers, as gadgetry sometimes will, in uncongenial ways.

Tempo is very dependent upon a performer's mood and personality, on internal rhythms like heartbeats and brain waves, on emotions and excitements. It cannot be safely, neutrally, and universally prescribed.

The range of the "acceptable" is amazing. There are recorded performances of a Bach work, by Toscanini and Casals, in which the ratio of the respective pacing is two to one. Despite this extraordinary difference, each conductor was doubtlessly satisfying a stern sense of performing obligation. Not infrequently, the performer varies his own tempo when playing the same work on different occasions.

David Carrier has asked us to do this:

> Imagine Mozart's K. 331 performed *very* slowly; the concert takes a week. Such a playing of his notes could not be heard as a performance, for as many accounts of performing emphasize there is a difference in kind between hearing notes related to one another, as the sounds of the clock striking eleven are related, and hearing separate,

phenomenologically unconnected notes, as when the clock strikes once and then in an hour strikes again.[16]

This argument is not entirely convincing since the "phenomenologically connected" can range over years, as we see in Proustian experiences. The one hour for the clock is particularly doubtful. It would seem to be possible to focus aural attention for longer than that. What if we hear Wagner's *Ring* over a week, or four days? Are the themes sounded the last day "phenomenologically unconnected" with the themes sounded the first day?

It could be argued that themes—and even the clock sound heard an hour ago—can be remembered but that consciousness has lost its ongoing stream, its "phenomenological connections." Consciousness is always interrupting its streaming continuity, even in listening to or performing short works. It is one of the standard obligations of good performance to sustain attention; exaggerated slowness and speed can help to interrupt attention. But attention, as William James said, is always perching and flying.[17] I do not know how an "attention span" can be linked with musically experienced time or what it would mean to measure it. Phenomenologically, can we say what persists in consciousness as over against what is brought back from memory? If I hear a song in a simple ABA format, is the recurrence of the second A "phenomenologically connected" to the first, or recalled and thought about? What would it mean to confirm or deny either claim? If a theme is a retrograde version of another, is it mind and memory that note it, or is it sustained consciousness that keeps everything in its purview? Thought names what experience grasps in the absence of naming and labeling. But how can we talk about what experience grasps? Tovey makes a case for attention span, measured in so many minutes, in connection with the experience of modulation. It is a topic that founders, or leaves me foundering, in unsettled or unsettling issues of epistemology.

I am certainly not arguing against Carrier in favor of an ultra-*schleppend* performance of Mozart, though some musical Warhol might want to try it. I merely suggest that we can apprehend wider tempo ranges than he suggests and that we would be hard put with respect to tempo variation to separate difference of degree from difference of kind. If Toscanini and

Casals can vary from one to two, how about one to three, or one to four? We are caught on a slippery slope or on a decelerating time warp. Principles cannot apply, except for the unformulable meta-principle of using circumspect good sense.

Tempo obligations have ranged between extremely loose and tight. Composers since Beethoven have on occasion used metronome markings. Performers have had to reckon with them and to decide how much to respect them. Performers have given tempo interpolations for later performers. Schnabel, in his edition of Beethoven's Sonatas, specifies changing tempos for the various portions of a single sonata movement. To be accurate to Schnabel would require extraordinary and almost mechanical constraints on the pianist's spontaneous impulses. The result would not be a performance of a composition by Beethoven but a performance of a designated performance by Beethoven-Schnabel. Schnabel's markings could be seen merely as a report on how he played Beethoven and not as prescriptive. But existing in score (like Hans von Bülow's gratuitous editings) and not merely in performance or recording gives them added panache and authority.

Leonard Bernstein, in a rehearsal (videotaped, of course, as a performance in itself!) of his *West Side Story*, said that other conductors had not done a particular section in the tempo he had intended. Does this new advice, and Bernstein's performance (his first of *West Side Story*), now become part of the score, even "peripherally"? Not necessarily. The openness to tempo variation might remain a most desirable part of the original score. Some composers incorporate wide ranges of choice, as though to underline the performer's autonomy. Some do not.

In Fred Hoyle's science fiction novel, *The Black Cloud*, a superintelligent cloud establishes communication with the earth. It absorbs and understands, more completely than humans can, whatever information it receives. The earthlings transmit a sampling of music to it and the recording chosen happens to be Beethoven's Opus 106, the *Hammerklavier Sonata*. This Sonata, with the tempo given as (half-note = 138), has always been somewhat puzzling. A lady in the Hoyle novel remarks: "The first movement of the B Flat Sonata bears a metronome marking requiring a quite fantastic pace, far faster than any normal pianist can achieve, certainly far faster than I can manage."[18] After the superintelligent being "receives" the recording, it responds: "Very interesting. Please repeat the first part at a speed increased by thirty percent."[19] When this is done— and I fear Hoyle did not consider that the key would be changed in the process of speeding up the phonograph—the Cloud says: "Better. Very good. I intend to think this over."[20] So much for extraterrestrial care about accuracy of tempo and the willingness to weigh alternatives.

Are "allegro" and "presto" and "half-note = 138" integral or supplementary parts of a score? Nelson Goodman says, "The tempo words cannot be integral parts of a score insofar as the score serves the function of identifying a work from performance to performance." Right notes are defining, but "No departure from the indicated tempo disqualifies a performance as an instance—however wretched—of the work defined by the score."[21] Separating notes and tempo in this sharp way is an intellectual performance of which music making is but the bare occasion, just as for some musical performers the score is but the slimmest excuse for display and originality. Intellectual virtuosity, like musical virtuosity (which I discuss later), is a morally ambiguous display of itself, sometimes entertaining, sometimes (for me, in this case) exasperating. There is an obligation to remove from aesthetics neat and irrelevant pairings like "integral and supplementary," "essential and peripheral." But the spirit of permissiveness might recognize and even share in the joy that people find in making conspicuous and dazzling distinctions. The obligations of theorists are as duplicitous and complicated as the obligations of performing artists.

My concluding and repeated refrain is this: the performer has an obligation to the right tempo, both to what the composer suggests and to how the performer inclines. The composer (who also has some obligations) probably does better to suggest than to command, even though the precise metronome specification is available to him. Good composers will "oblige" performers to exercise their freedoms and good performers will recognize and practice their freedoms, appreciating, but not abusing, the liberties that composers allow.

A word here about still other directions on scores that can create dilemmas for performers: Sometimes there are prose comments (as in the Mahler manuscripts) of the strangest intensity, variety, vagueness, and apparent irrelevance. Before "performing" them, one has to decide what they mean and whether they deserve attention. Like the programs of program music, they are a kind of separable verbal obbligato to the music, to be attended to, or not, as one pleases.

Some markings (*nicht schleppend* is a favorite of mine) are not so much indications of what to do as suggestions to avoid a tendency the composer thinks a performer will have in the absence of such instruction. What is the performer to do when he sees "not too loud" at a point in the score where he had no inclination to play too loud? He might be resentful. Such markings may be supererogatory. The implied obligation in every score is that it is never to be played too loudly, too slowly, or too anything that might be wrong.

Sometimes a composer's directions are linked with a score, whether written on it or not. Gershwin (and now his estate) insisted that *Porgy and Bess* be performed only with black singers. Is such a direction integral or supplementary? Would refusal to follow it, as times change, be a bad performance like singing wrong notes, or even a non-performance? I can imagine arguments running to both extremes: (A) that it is a direction that is not even supplementary, that has nothing to do with the score; and (B) that it is the most central and urgent performing demand.

We cannot say in general what is accidental or essential to a score because nothing (in general!) is absolutely accidental or absolutely essential. We can point to a needed tension between greater or lesser demands, and greater or lesser freedoms—and indeed to the need to assess, as part of any performance, which are the greater and which are the lesser. Part of this obligation, as in all ethical matters, is a sense of openness, even a sense of play; fixing what is free, and freeing what is fixed, is a delicate and ongoing matter, beyond rule and definition. The discovery of theoretical principles, of rules, is itself not a rule-governed gathering of facts but a creative activity with its own ambiguous obligations.

Risk Taking: Virtuosity, Memory, Recording

Much has been said about performance as risk taking and the excitement conveyed by the live performance because something may go wrong. Virtuosity is presumably appreciated because of risk and risk is supposed to be enhanced when playing from memory. What are the performer's obligations? Sparshott says that "risk and the sense of it are an overwhelmingly important factor in all art. . . ."[22]

No doubt, virtuosity and risk are displayed together, and the greater the technical challenges, the greater the risks. But whether a show of virtuosity adds to or detracts from a performance is itself to some extent a performance decision. I say "to some extent" because while some risk and difficulty will always obtain in some compositions, one of the functions of virtuosity (when it is not a display of itself) is to reduce or minimize the sense of difficulty and to show an effortless adequacy whatever the challenges.

Some ideals of performance (and even such ideals as enter into its decisions) will emphasize ease, control, and sureness rather than a display of difficulty, uncertainty, and an anything-at-the-moment-can-happen ambience. So virtuosity, general technical prowess, can have several artistic functions and can meet different obligations. Virtuosity can have (A) the essentially musical virtue of rendering all the notes in the manner in which they should be sounded, without attention to conspicuous show; and (B) the derivatively musical function of displaying itself as masterful, physically acrobatic, and risky.

If I have loaded the dice by the phrases "essentially musical" and "derivatively musical," so be it. They have critical, but no theoretical status. The point is that these tendencies counter each other, and theory cannot hone in on one or the other as the absolutely proper function. Some people sit glued to their opera seats, breathlessly awaiting the soprano's high E, rooting for or against her, as at a sporting event. Let them enjoy the risk, the excitement, and the tenterhooks. Aficionados, persons with greater musicianship, are more interested in what the singer accomplishes before she gets to, and runs the risk of, the high E.

There is nothing simple about virtuosity and the contrary uses to which it can be put. Glenn Gould, by all accounts, conveyed the ambiguity. Edward Strickland called him a paradoxical moralist, a virtuoso performer, with "a peculiarly Canadian revulsion to flamboyance or exhibitionism."[23] Of Gould on the concerto, Strickland wrote, "The very concept of [it] is attacked for the immorality of its inherent grandstanding and the competition it sets up between soloist and orchestra."[24] Gould's later career is certainly a moralistic statement against the risk taking of live performances. The performer's obligation, as I have elsewhere said, includes whether, as well as how, he shall perform.

It is easy, and not unusual, for a performer to make a performance seem more difficult, more risky, than it really is; it is done by suitable (or unsuitable) body jerkings and facial expressions. Good taste should rule this out, but the Romantic tradition, with its notion of performer as adventure hero, has its devotees. Mozart understandably disliked such grimacing. He compared the faces of overly expressive performers to that of a child alongside its shitpile. In both cases you see by the expression what is being or what has been produced. The performer has to search for his own meaning between the conspicuous, effortful grimace (Rubinstein) and the Greek mask-like deadpan (Schnabel).

There is a famous photograph of the conductor Toscanini with his finger to his lips in a "shushing" gesture. If this were taken during a rehearsal and he wanted the orchestra to play more softly at that moment it would be understandable and appropriate. It would constitute behind-the-scenes preparation for a later performance. But if this kind of demand for *pianissimo* occurs during a performance, and it often does, there is something wrong and irrational about it. The orchestra must be playing louder than the conductor thinks it should at that juncture. He hasn't prepared it properly!

There is a palpable absurdity in a performer or a conductor overtly indicating, as part of his performance, that something is going wrong, even a little bit wrong. But this kind of thing happens all the time. What is conveyed by such effort is not so much an obligation to the music or to the performer's interpretation of it; what is conveyed is his obligation to obligation and effort. The performer is a moral person; he cares; he scolds and tries to improve himself and others—and he wants you to know that he is trying. Such obligation to obligation—the need for the performer to reveal his Kantian good will—has crept into music, just as it is part of other ethical performances.

Consider the histrionics of teaching. One plays on old thoughts and old notes—with feigned ignorance, risk, discovery, effort, and excitement. The ultimate performers are the charismatic religious and political rabble-rousers, whose deliveries are nearly devoid of rational content or significant reference, but full of unction. Performance of music, on its ultra-virtuoso side, has some of this wicked power, and Paganini's violin was said to have been possessed by the devil. Plato may have known the corruptions of emotion, but even Socrates performed, feigned ignorance, and displayed intellectual and verbal virtuosity. Performance partakes of the ironies of the human condition; it should not surprise us that thoughtful musicians, like Glenn Gould, have been sensitive to the inherent moral dilemmas.

What is the relationship between using a score and playing from memory? The latter, it has been said, adds to the sense of risk and conveys how hard the performer has practiced and prepared. But this is largely a mistake; memorization is readily accomplished, particularly by the young; it is not much of a gamble or a feat. What might really produce risk, ironically, is too much dependence upon a score. In a composition of moderate difficulty there is no way in which the pianist (the existence of blind ones notwithstanding—there are certain works they cannot learn) can avoid glancing at the keyboard to get certain notes right. In any case, the pianist reading from a score memorizes intermittently, and at least briefly. Even sight reading (the phenomenology of which is worth exploring) involves jumping ahead, learning, and remembering so that the pianist can anticipate the notes he is striking. The better he is as a sight reader, the further ahead he is in the score, and the bigger the ongoing chunks of memorized music. There is a limiting case, a kind of overlap of sight reading and memorization; it is when the pianist looks at the whole score, memorizes it, sets it aside, and then plays it. While most memorization is muscular and bodily—in the fingers, as it were—some pianists can memorize scores in the above fashion. These are rare cases but they occur—performances that are also memorizations. Even when scores are used at concerts (by soloists and chamber musicians—orchestras almost never play from memory) they are mostly memorized and serve as security blankets. So much, then, for memory and its connections with risk taking.

The live performance is supposed to have that peculiar and titillating risk factor that is absent when we listen to recordings. There is a difference between live and recorded performances, but this is another distinction that is not as clear as it seems, or whose conclusions are obvious. The live performance is not always that risky; there are pianists with steely fingers and iron nerves, as well as those with prodigious memories. The accuracy of what they are in the process of doing is more or less a foregone conclusion and has greater technical, or technological, reliability than a recording.

Recordings and broadcasts of recordings and "live on tape" telecasts have failed or been interrupted. There are simply all kinds of risk out there, personal, technical, and social. Somebody might shoot the piano player; he can have a memory lapse; a string on the piano or violin can break; the hi-fi can fail; the electricity can stop; the live broadcast can be interrupted with "We bring you a special news bulletin," or "Another plane has been hijacked," or "World War Three has begun."

The problem with performance risks is twofold: we cannot readily assess their aesthetic desirability, and we do not know when they will occur, indeed, how risky a particular risk is. Life's larger risks and excitements make the risks of both live and recorded performance, and their fine differentiae, puny by comparison.

Recapitulation

Recapitulations are parts of performances, performances turning in on themselves, and self-remembering. Such restatements, appropriate to music and other texts, will be repetitions with differences. Here is my recapitulation.

The performer has obligations and they are connected with other obligations in art and life, and with ethical considerations of the widest scope. The portrait painter usually has an obligation to produce a likeness, but as artist he can also create his idealization, his distortion, his commentary. There is a conspicuous twoness here, the person imitated on the one hand, and the contribution of the artist on the other. The performing artist is a commentator of sorts who holds the mirror up to the score (if not to nature) and separates himself to some extent from the work he performs.

Apart from such external mirrorings, there does not seem to be the possibility of deception and of performance evaluation; indeed, the very concept of performance might be called into question in the absence of such references and standards.

And yet, in our post-Romantic, postmodernist age, issues of deception and performance have taken a new turn. In the contemporary novel, for example, the very distinction between fact and fiction is being deliberately challenged, if not obliterated. We have various nonfiction novels and E. L. Doctorow, the author of *Ragtime*, said that "there is no longer any such thing as fiction or nonfiction; there's only narrative."[25] Susan Sontag refers to the "tradition inaugurated by Rilke's *The Notebooks of Malte Laurids Brigge*, which crossbreeds fiction, essayist speculation and autobiography in a linear-notebook rather than a linear-narrative form."[26] Max Frisch's *Man in the Holocene* includes many quotations from actual identified works that become absorbed in the text. "But they are so sinister in context, so grimly comic, so ironically appropriate, that they feel as though Frisch had written them. They comprise about one-quarter of the text, but they lend their objective quality to the rest."[27]

The impulse to want to get away from the distinction between fact and fiction is culturally deep-seated, arising in its modern form with the Romantics. It is connected with the view, shot through with paradoxes and ironies, that we err if we think that we can distinguish poetry from truth, *Dichtung* from *Wahrheit*; we get close to truth by discounting its sure objective claim and by confessing, as it were, the inevitability of bias and subjectivity. The obligation to truth, to mirroring, veers in the direction of becoming an obligation to sincerity or to authenticity. If we cannot be true to an original, to a fact, to a score, and if imaginativeness and distortion will surely intrude, then how much ought we to feel a responsibility to truth, to the facts, to the score?

The sense of the inevitability of imaginativeness has pervaded our thinking and is relevant to considerations of interpretation, criticism, and performance. The notion of an object or work or score out there, to which interpretation and criticism can be true, has been replaced by the notion of a series of creative commentaries or criticisms, with no beginning or first term to the series. There are only interpretations of interpretations and performances of performances. In some ways, because of a kind of indifference to texts and scores, we seem to be reverting to, or recapitulating, the beginning conditions that obtained before there were texts and scores.

Art is often a commentary on art and a performance is one instance of such commentary. One encounters such commentary in essays, of course, but also in paintings about paintings and in music about music. A mustache on a copy of the *Mona Lisa* is a rudimentary form of this, but whole art shows have consisted of paintings done about paintings, with the original frequently alluded to in some disguised or barely recognized form.

So when art comments upon art—in performance and criticism—substantial departure, a thoroughgoing recreation, can be regarded as entirely appropriate because entirely inevitable. There can be said to be as much or more obligation to the new art as to the old, to the work being created by the performer as to the work of the composer (score or performance) that was the nominal focus of attention. It has been said of some critics, say the writers in *The New York Review*, that they are more interested in the pieces they write than in the works they write about. Critical writing is not exactly a performing art and I do not wish to conflate all distinctions. Yet the impulse to use another's work, or body of works, merely as an occasion for one's own artistic creativity, or intellectual virtuosity, is rampant in our times. Even performing artists attempt radical novelty and, as we have seen in some detail, the parameters of score and notation are less binding than they seem.

While some performers try conscientiously to obliterate themselves for the greater glory of Beethoven, the usurping tendency is currently more pronounced than the self-effacing one. The self-centeredness of a performance, highly stylized, doesn't present itself as correct but as interesting and as true to the performer. Such stylizations require much venturesomeness with respect to tone, nuance, rhythm, expression, tempo, and so on, sometimes appearing as wrong or perverse. Harold C. Schonberg complained about this tendency: "We have the mistaken idea that Romanticism in performance means excess liberty. . . . My contention is that the Romantic style, far from being anarchistic or egocentric, is aristocratic, highly controlled and, if anything, classic. . . . The amusing thing is that young artists today take unmentionable, idiotic liberties in rubato and tempo, with the crazy idea that this is 'Romantic' style."[28] Whether connected with Romanticism or not, there is no doubt that many performers are generating self-conscious art works that are personal, idiosyncratic, and remote from any original.

A Beethoven sonata exists as a physical score and as a series of performances. But it also exists as an abstract or ideal notion of its correct rendition. We cannot talk about an obligation to accuracy without generating the idea of prior existence and correctness. But our sense of obligation supersedes the past as it aims for a perfection as yet unknown. The sense of obligation generates its object as much as the object generates the obligation; the object generated has an indefinite future, a future linked with an unfolding self.

We might imagine Beethoven playing a faultless *Hammerklavier Sonata* on an appropriate *Hammerklavier*, with no wrong notes and at the right tempo. (The probability of playing this awesomely difficult work without any wrong notes is close to zero. Goodman will never hear a live performance!) And then there are all the subsequent performances by others, with degrees of approximation and accuracy. Yet what Beethoven himself might at best have done must be seen as an interpretation. The true *Sonata*, the Platonic form, prior and subsequent to his efforts, was likely something that poor, deaf Beethoven was loath to think he could approach. Seen this way, performance is a continuation of a search, not the presentation of a settled discovery. A performance is not so much a member of a class as a longing for an impossible way of being.

The object toward which a performer feels an obligation has a twofold, paradoxical nature. It is at once a prior existence and independent standard, and it is also the vision of excellence that the performer here and now generates and approximates with the skills available to him. The obligation, as with ethical obligation in general, is to something both internal and external, to artificer and to artifact, to antecedent being and to self not yet unfolded. Each is remote and elusive. The obligations of performers are not uniquely aesthetic; they are complicated ethical tasks in a particular interpersonal setting.

The conspicuous double loyalty, to self and to other, to inner demand as well as to outer command, is at the core of ethical existence in its most difficult and hence most meaningful moments. The performer has to make his choices, and nobody can guarantee that he makes them well; not the composer-performer ready to give infallible personal guidance, and especially not the aesthetician, who portrays problems of performance as a series of silent modulations among his own cultivated indecisions.

FIVE

A MOZARTIAN RECOGNITION SCENE

1976

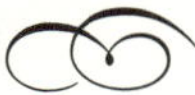

Accounting for the aesthetic pleasure found in a musical passage is a challenge because of the difficulty of describing sounds with words and because of the risk of confusing expressions of sentiment with explanation. An attempt to do so may also choose to face the dangers of drawing an analogy with literary art. In the present case, the last scene of Mozart's Le Nozze di Figaro *is considered in light of Aristotle's account in the* Poetics *of recognition and reversal, while remaining wary of the claim that different arts do the same thing with different materials. The chosen operatic scene presents an opportunity to determine whether and how one might articulate a moment "of transformed moral resolve" in music. The aim is to describe how music might convey character and so to examine in yet a different context an aspect of the tension between art and morality.*

Most music-lovers know special passages in classical compositions—moments that rise out of their musical contexts as haunting melodies or even as peak experiences. To enjoy them should suffice, but there is an impulse to want to know why we enjoy and why something affects us especially. We might even tend to suspect that such knowledge will enhance, or at least intertwine with, the accompanying pleasure. There might even be an extra-musical appropriateness, a rightness that goes beyond music. I dwell here on one such musical passage and attempt to see resemblances with other moments of transformed moral resolve in art.

There are at least three obstacles to the task of writing about music. First, there is the sheer difficulty of describing sounds with words. Second, there is the futility of waxing eloquent and allowing the outpourings of irrelevant sentiment to assume the guise of explanation. Third, and most to the point, I here venture a difficult analogy to literary art, specifically to Aristotle's account of recognition and reversal in the *Poetics*. Such analogies are precarious. Lessing's *Laocoon* still stands as a constant rejoinder to the dubious claim that the various arts do the "same" thing in different media.

The passage I focus on is in the last scene of Mozart's *Le Nozze di Figaro*. It begins Allegro Assai, in G major. Eighty-six measures later there is an Andante, following a fermata over a rest. The Count says (i.e., sings):

Contessa, perdono! Perdono, perdono!

These four measures were preceded by a fermata, the last two notes have fermatas over them, and then the rest afterward has a further fermata! We are thus reminded of the special quality of this line, at a new tempo, practically italicized or bracketed by Mozart. It is as though he confirms the importance of the previous passage, in which the plot halted, and of which these measures are the special outcome.

It is the earlier passage that is the recognition scene, the nineteen measures, 68–86. It is full of chord changes, excitement, violins rushing up and down in staccato frenzy. Its duration is as brief as its intensity is enormous. While the external action, the plot, of the opera has temporarily halted, the Count undergoes an internal transformation. He has to come to terms with what has happened and begins to understand what he must do. Like Macduff (as I have several times said), before he can act or "dispute," he must first "feel." Along with the facts the Count has newly acquired, there is in him an obbligato of transforming, almost

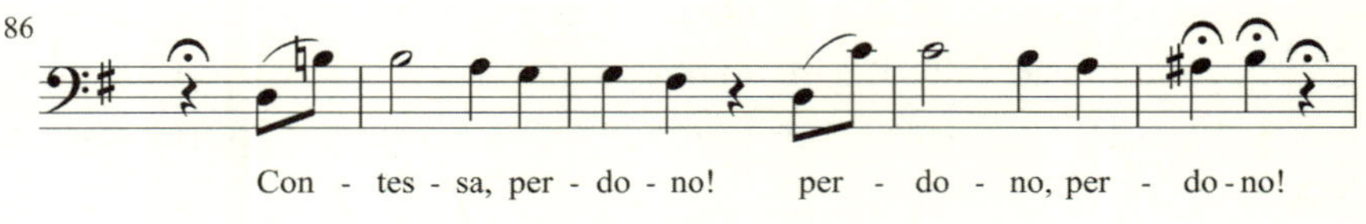

Figure 5-1

unmanageable, emotion. He must undergo it and come to a stop in order to undergo it. We have a musical recognition and reversal.

Count Almaviva, let us recall, in an age of *droit du seigneur*, has been pursuing Susanna. While he philanders, or attempts to, the neglected Countess pines away, her love for the Count unrequited. A complicated trap has been devised by the ladies that will publicly expose the Count's intentions. Susanna and the Countess exchange costumes. The Count attempts to seduce the Countess, thinking she is Susanna. (It is an intimation, in his state of ignorance, of where his heart and the rest of him truly belong.) Along the way he catches the "Countess," really Susanna, compromised (as he thinks) with Figaro. Susanna, in the guise of the Countess, asks the Count for forgiveness. No, he says. Figaro and the others also plead with him, "Perdono." The Count (measure 61) is adamant,

"No, No, No, No, No."

He seems to mean it, to know his mind, and the notes of the dominant seventh seem to presage a return to G major.

It is at this point that the Countess sets aside her disguise, identifies herself, and the reversal begins. Given the aforementioned plot complications, it takes the Count a few moments to grasp what has happened. It remains for him to transform a new objective knowledge of the facts into a new subjective awareness of his feelings. Before he can act he must know contrition, experience a change of heart and renounce his former self (rather like the Pasha Selim in a parallel moment in Mozart's *Die Entführung aus dem Serail* and even like Macduff, who must feel before he can act).

Measures 68–86 confirm the recognition and accomplish the reversal on the emotional, internal side. There is no further action and no further

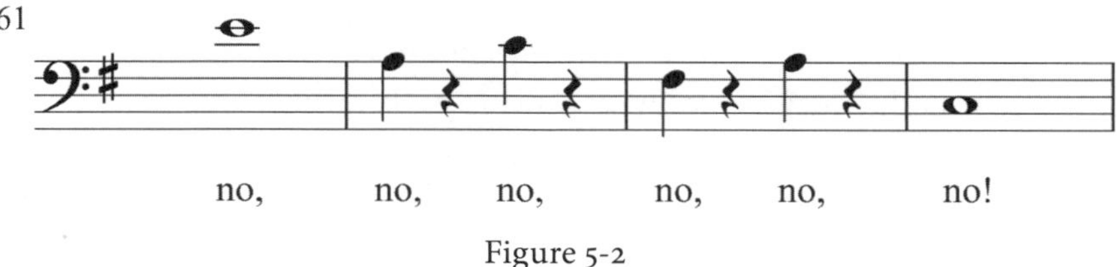

Figure 5-2

dialogue. Perhaps the best way to appreciate the force of this passage is to test the effect of omitting it. One could imagine the Count responding to the Countess without delay. She gives up her disguise and expresses her hope for forgiveness ("Almeno io per loro perdono otterroi") ending on G of measure 68. After the fermata of measure 86 (indeed, the fermata would no longer be needed), the Count could pick up his "Contessa Perdono" without hesitation in ongoing G major, and without modulation. It "works" this way. It carries on the conversational exchange without interruption, more or less as occurs in Beaumarchais's *Le Mariage de Figaro*.

But what would have been lost by such omission, by this simpler musical procedure, is the emotion of recognition and reversal, the internal churning that must occur before the Count can accomplish his metanoia. He is a different person at measure 68 than he was before measure 68. In this instance the music rather than the words has made us feel the change. The Countess's G, measure 68, is not part of an ongoing G major but is suddenly and unexpectedly accompanied by a G minor chord. There are hurried chord changes, suggestive of a musical review of earlier scenes: G minor, D minor, E♭ major, C minor, B♭ major, and finally a D major chord, which prepares for the return to G major from which the passage departed. Measures 68–86 provide an enormous flurry of musical movement within their brief extent, but they return us to the harmonic point from which measure 68 diverged. During this passage the plot does not advance at all. The count does not receive any new information nor does he say anything. Yet an important transformation has taken place. The information he previously received has been turned into personal and emotional truth for him. The words previously spoken by the Countess, when she reveals her identity, have given him a reason for change. But as with Macduff, though it is time to act, he must first fully feel his changed self.

The classical tragic recognition scene often precedes the hero's death, destruction, or exile. His discovered wickedness, like Oedipus's or like Othello's, is not forgivable by others or by himself. And he acts accordingly. But there is an element of affirmation, of triumph, even in the tragic hero. He has moved from ignorance to knowledge, which for the Greeks, if not for some gloomier moderns like Brecht, is always a positive accomplishment.

But *Figaro* is a comedy, the recognition (we can presume) is happy, and we are made to expect good feelings and lasting contentment. Though my concern here has been the transformation, there is no need to be dogmatic about the scope of it. Given my tendency to look for art/morality opposites, we might imagine Figaro still hankering after Susanna despite the responsibilities of marital love, and we might imagine a still unhappy Countess suspecting that the Count's glowing words are not as enduring as his philandering disposition. If suffering is usually the consequence of the reversal, as Aristotle suggests, there might be some suffering whatever the overall direction of the reversal.

Whatever the qualifications about the move from ignorance to knowledge, the passage in question is an example of how music can mirror an Aristotelian recognition. Aristotle emphasized plot in the "change from ignorance to knowledge." Recognition is sometimes a discovery of whether "a person has done a thing or not,"[1] and in Figaro the recognition is one of clear intention rather than of act. Will he feel prepared to do something, recalling Macduff? Asking for pardon is at least a beginning.

We cannot know what specific music might have accompanied Greek drama. There are fragments in Greek texts of undecipherable markings that might have referred to actual sounds. The music, undoubtedly wonderful, is not available to us as the Mozart operas are. But Aristotle does tell us that tragic language was embellished by rhythm, harmony, and song. So, we can very well imagine that the music which accompanied or embellished Greek drama might have provided the kind of recognition we have here exemplified as uniquely musical. That Aristotle links recognition only with plot might be connected with the difficulties of writing about music. Describing how music conveys character—which I have here attempted—is surely a more difficult and dubious task than describing how plot conveys character. And even my example is grounded in plot, with the musical recognition enhancing and enriching what the plot basically provides.

SIX

A NOTE ON ECONOMY AND ART

1974

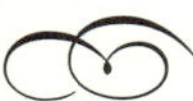

The strenuous effort to provide food, shelter, and security may result in relief from immediate threats and satisfaction at a difficult task accomplished. This pleasure, though, is not fully understood in simple terms of instrumental means and satisfying ends. The means themselves have immediate pleasures, and with this realization one is "in the realm of art, or at least involved in activity that has some resemblance to art." The relationship of economy and art is further understood by approaching it from the perspective of the fine arts. Art is often praised for the economy in a poet's words, the painter's brush strokes, the architect's materials, the dancer's movements. Why should the un-urgent, free activity of art make a virtue of economizing? Economy in art can be understood as "a kind of parable of the economic situation of scarcity in life," and the aesthetic pleasure comes from "the deep echoes of urgency that are apparently awakened." The artist, then, is compelled to "feign life urgencies for the sake of their aesthetic value" and this turns out to be a "creative deception . . . at the heart of the artistic process."

Ultimate origins are lost to us, which is the reason that ultimate ambiguities remain with us. We humans are heirs to a fantastically long biological tradition of accumulating and managing and expending our worldly goods. Even in the lives of the lowliest animals, there is a time for gathering and saving, and a time for using and consuming. The whole of a creature's existence can be seen as a series of diurnal and seasonal cycles in which these things are done. Though man brings skill and sophistication to these activities, he still must do essentially what the prudent ants and squirrels do in order to survive and thrive. If ants and squirrels ate only in the summer and did not store for the winter, they would die. Human economy operates on the same principle, as when a farmer plants and harvests, as when a homeowner stores food and fuel in a cellar, as when a housewife stocks up a larder or a freezer.

But human economy involves a calculation and a subtlety that go far beyond what even the fabled ants are capable of. Though men are partly propelled like squirrels, and caged in the bargain, man brings to his activities an understanding and purpose that give those activities a richer complexion and significance than they have in subhuman life. We know more clearly what we are about; we operate in terms of ends that are foreseen; we do not merely respond to biological urges and instinctive drives, even though we are not free of them. And the direction and awareness that accompany our economic activities give them a meaning and a reward that extends beyond their primal or biological purpose.

When an estate or a household is well managed, when things are done efficiently with the resources that are available, when activity and rest, work and leisure, are brought into some kind of appropriate balance, a sense of satisfaction accompanies the effort and the planning. There is an ordering and control of materials, a budgeting of time and energy, an extended series of interrelated and modifiable choices. These choices, continuously reviewed in retrospect and prospect, and bearing the stamp and the sanction of ulterior purpose, give us a cumulating and ongoing pleasure. It remains true that as you sow, so shall you reap, and reaping leads to eating and surviving. But the simple structure of means and ends, or whatever simplicity we may hastily have ascribed to it, loses its simplicity upon elementary reflection. Sowing and reaping are themselves satisfying and rewarding, before and independently of eating and surviving. We are in the realm of immediate pleasure and intrinsic satisfaction as these accompany manipulative activity. We are in the realm of art, or at least involved in activity that has some resemblance to art.

The above sketch is designed to show a process of transition. Economic activity was first seen as directed toward some end, such as food and the alleviation of hunger in the winter. That activity would not have been engaged in, it would have no rationale, if the end of it were not what we can characterize as a "life" urgency. The discomfort of effort, the proverbial sweat of the brow, are more than counterbalanced by the satisfaction of eventual food and survival. And it is only the counterbalancing (according to this initial strict interpretation of economic activity) that justifies the discomfort and the sweat in the first place. The activity of harvesting and storing food seems to be purely economic when taken at first glance, a means of feeding ourselves out of season, a way of avoiding winters of discontent. But it has all been going on too long, in our lives, in our species, in the eons of animal evolution. In gathering and hunting food we inevitably satisfy ourselves directly, avoiding the displeasures of anxiety, restlessness, and boredom, and enjoying the pleasures of lively attention and movement, awareness and planning, skillfulness and art. The analysis that interprets hunting (let us say) as exclusively economic, directed to the end, and only to the end, that food shall be available, does profound violence to the facts of the matter, important facts having to do with the nature of man and the fulfillments available to him. Men will hunt and fish when they do not eat what they kill or catch; and even when they do eat it, the activities of hunting and fishing might well be more satisfying than the activity of eating.

We do not have to go any further to see how the aims and ends of economic man become transformed and complicated. Energies originally directed toward a clear end, and clearly subservient to it, acquire momentum and become playful, voluntary, and artistic. What began as a compelling, goal-oriented, and urgent activity turns into a partly compelling, partly free activity directed toward multiple ends, among which (and often superseding the originals) are the enjoyments of organized and organizing purpose.

The "artistry" we have been attributing to economic activity is of course not quite the same as the artistry of the fine arts. To explore further the relationship between the two, we jump now to a consideration of the fine arts, particularly to the "economic" quality that is so frequently attributed to particular works of art.

The role of economy in art is so notorious that economy is often taken to be an aesthetic virtue, even the fundamental aesthetic virtue. Criticism alludes to it endlessly. The critic will say of an artist how well he did with a few strokes of the brush, with a modest string orchestra, with the scant material at hand, and so forth. It has been said of Frans Hals that, unable to afford the more expensive oil paints, he made do with, and gave remarkable scope to, the narrower range of colors he *could* afford. And it was said of the architect Pier Luigi Nervi that he had almost as much pride in the economy of his designs as in their elegance and beauty. He himself said that "beauty does not come from decorative effects, but from structural coherence," and "in the absence of good taste, economy is the best incentive for art."[1] He maintained that "with economy, clients will accept daring and even beauty. Low costs have a high esthetic value."[2] Ezra Pound was enthusiastic about economy in poetry, the basic economy of fewness of words. The examples could be multiplied endlessly. Over and over again in artistic criticism, considerations of economy apply. The beauty of the finished art work always expresses and reflects the budgeting and the restraint, the planning and the thrift, that went into the making of it.

This is puzzling. Earlier we related economy and art to the transition from urgent to freely joyful activity. But now art itself, *un*-urgent, free activity, is esteemed for its economies, for urgencies it is reluctant to relinquish. Can there be, *need* there be, life urgencies in art activities?

Before pursuing this question we need to make a further distinction between our aforementioned examples of economy in art. If one must engage in artistic activity (the need to create may have an urgency of its own), one needs the wherewithal for it. This would include paints for painters, paper for poets, stones for sculptors, drafting tables for architects, and even maybe muses for musicians. For the sake of art these things are urgent, provided anything can be urgent apart from what has to do with life and survival. These examples suggest an economy imposed upon the artist from without, an absolute restraint on his absolute freedom, having to do with materials, costs, and the like.

But what about *words* for poets and *sounds* (as over against performing instrumentalists) for musicians? Why be sparing of what is freely available? Is there any need to be mincing of resources that are as abundant and easy to come by as the act of will that summons them up? Is economy with respect to such abundant resources anything else than a pretense, an imitation, and mere echo of life urgency and real economy?

A composer with his own eighty-man orchestra might compose a work for an orchestra that size. If only forty instruments were available, he might do without clarinets, trombones, and large string sections, while adapting to those limited forces. A critic praising the work for small orchestra might make some familiar and time-tested remarks about "economy of means." The composer has made a virtue of his limitations.

But have the limitations made virtue for (i.e., contributed excellence to) the composer? Does the eighty-man orchestra provide undesirable abundance? Is there always some value in the curtailment of resources that are at hand? And is it always clear when the curtailment is voluntary and when it is imposed?

It is just possible that a composer with a thousand-man orchestra at his disposal might choose to write a string quartet. Or there might be an artist (unlike poor Frans Hals) with tubes of costly chrome and violet among his effects who yet might choose to do a charcoal sketch. Has the virtue of economy been lost to the resultant art because the restraints were not absolute? Why is there any aesthetic virtue or merit in material restraint if materials are freely and abundantly available? Is the habit of economy, of the preservation of materials and energies, such an absolute and pervasive human virtue that any semblance of it, anywhere, will give aesthetic satisfaction?

The answer to this last question seems to be an astonishing "yes." *Every instance of economy in art is a kind of parable of the economic situation of scarcity in life*, and is aesthetically pleasing because of the deep echoes of urgency that are apparently awakened. The situation of original life urgency is never entirely irrelevant to an aesthetic effect. When real deprivations are absent they will be self-imposed or imitated. The artist simply cannot afford to be overindulged, or to overindulge himself. If he is or if he does, the results of his efforts will be regarded as aesthetic failures. The Rayburn House Office Building in Washington, DC, is vulgarly lavish, or lavishly vulgar, no matter how great the resources of the United States government, or how much money the architect had at his disposal.

The artist, then, is in an ambiguous predicament. Without being pressed to it, he feigns life urgencies for the sake of their aesthetic value, attesting (if it can be so put) to the urgency with which he is disposed to value real urgency. Or put another way, since urgency feigned is never as urgent as urgency thrust upon one, the latter is invented under the guise of being sought after, in that creative deception which is at the heart of the artistic process.

To summarize, life urgencies impose real ends upon us, and these we must pursue for the sake of life itself. But sometimes the real urgencies of life are gone, or mostly gone, or misunderstood, and the only lingering real urgency is what to do about this lack of urgency, and how to fill the ever-persisting moments of life with the kind of contour, enjoyment, and purpose that once afforded us our satisfactions. And so we have to feign and invent, stipulate our goals, create our obstacles and, in a word, engage in play and art. But the hold upon us of the need for real urgency is fantastically strong, produced in the millennia when we were puppets of forces beyond our control, and always vanquishing us more surely than we ever vanquished them. It is not, then, easy to be free, and even the freedom of art must sustain itself by the fancied consolations of economic restraint and by the nostalgic remembrances of ancient purpose.[3]

SEVEN

AN AESTHETIC GLANCE
AT THE CONSTITUTION

Style, Intention, Performance

1975, 1989

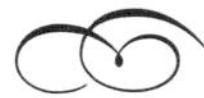

The United States Constitution is considered primarily a legal or moral document, but it is not without an essential aesthetic character, attention to which can lead to unexpected insights. The artistic nature of the Constitution may be approached through the topics of style, intention, and performance. Gouverneur Morris was arguably the most influential stylist of the Constitution, and his capacity for vagueness grounded in precision and for graceful and economic language resolved conflicts and invited vital engagement with the document. The intentions of the framers of the Constitution are as difficult to divine as those of any artist, and the well-known intentional fallacy is as applicable to the Constitution as to any literary work. Dogmatic assertion of original intentions is an interpretation that attempts to block all further interpretations. Further interpretation is necessary for upholding the Constitution, which may be compared to playing a musical score. In both cases the government official and the performer have dual obligations of fidelity and creativity. The latter obligation entails attention "to the array of options between what is prescribed, and what is left unprescribed," and attending to these options is required for successfully navigating unknown future crises.

That language has different functions is one of philosophy's recurrent claims—if not one of its actual insights. These functions have been explained with the help of different typologies—sometimes using simple terms like "informative," "directive," and "expressive"; sometimes with subtler (though comparable) terms like "assertive," "active," and "exhibitive." Several functions of language can obtain simultaneously, for example, the aesthetic (expressive, exhibitive) and the moral (directive, active)—though one is usually thought to prevail. "Thou shalt not kill" has its touch of eloquence, as does the Golden Rule. But such statements are essentially moral precepts, laws, rules, or commandments. What artistry they have is secondary. To dwell on the artistry when something else is more important might seem a misguided, if not a perverse, aestheticism. Surely the Constitution is primarily a legal or moral document, not an aesthetic one.[1] In terms of the aforementioned distinctions, it is informative and directive, not exhibitive.

However, the Constitution is not without art. Looking at it aesthetically—creatively misreading it, taking the text for something other than it obviously is—can be a way of gaining unexpected insights.[2] Even deliberate distortion, as in caricature, underlines as it undermines the truth of what was distorted. Hermeneutics at its best surely involves an openness to the mysteries and obscurities of texts, their multiplicities of function, and the possibility of various critical approaches. Here I make some remarks about the Constitution from an aesthetic perspective. While I use three headings—style, intention, and performance—they are actually interrelated and inseparable. And I single out Gouverneur Morris for his important but neglected role in creating the Constitution.

Style

The Founding Fathers were themselves not without an interest in literary artistry. They were habitual and practiced readers and writers. Their concern about style as such is a tribute to their awareness of the connections between linguistic form and substance. Proposals and drafts at the Constitutional Convention were referred, in the final days, to the Committee on Style. Three members of the committee were from Harvard, Yale, and Princeton, with two from Columbia.

Fashioning a good text is rarely a joint enterprise, and ungainly camels, we know, are created by committees. Elegance and shapeliness require an individual hand. Gouverneur Morris, though not the chair of the Committee on Style, was the decisive fashioner of the document and it was he who gave the Constitution its literary cast. Overall, he was second only to James Madison in his textual and other contributions and he spoke up during the Convention even more than Madison did. Taking style and substance together, looking at the Constitution in its broadest scope, Morris can be said to have been its author.

Gouverneur Morris was an outstanding writer, eventually about matters as varied as fiscal policy and the French Revolution. An elitist and aristocrat, cultivated and witty, he had read widely in Shakespeare, Sterne, and Swift. Morris had his own constitutional agenda—a powerful president elected for life, a Senate appointed by the President, suffrage to property holders, and so on. But these preferences were essentially aesthetic and detached and not connected with political and financial ambitions—of which (compared with so many of the other Founders) he was relatively free. As the dramatic orchestrator of the Constitution, as someone always ready to relinquish his personal preference for a gained harmony, Morris's human and intellectual traits were precisely the ones that were needed for the task. Those mincing critics of Morris, who praised his brilliance but mistrusted him and despoiled his character, simply did not understand the source and scope of his contribution.

The Constitution was hammered together out of enormously competing interests. Gouverneur Morris, and his Committee on Style, did more than superficially modify the texts that were handed over. As aestheticians remind us, poetry is not spread on prose the way butter is spread on bread, and style is not a gloss on substance. Style in a measure is substance. The force of the Constitution is not only in its precise and prosaic details ("The president shall serve. . . .") but in its occasional moral eloquence, its well chosen and provocative phrases, and, not least of all, its cultivated ambiguities. The artistry and the eloquence of the document have influenced how it has been honored and hence have been factors in its practical effectiveness as an enduring instrument. The ambiguities have invited, indeed necessitated, interpretation. To be sure, creating language that was occasionally cryptic and vague (Morris was particularly good at this) had the immediate practical function of making acceptable to the Convention what otherwise would not have been accepted. But it also left leeway for future interpretations that specificity would have constrained. Whatever the reasons for the vaguenesses, and the "intentions" behind them, the possibility of varied interpretation is inherent in the document and is one of its most important stylistic properties.

The gift of vagueness, stylistically understood, is not an aberration of the power of precision, nor is it even distinct from it. Morris's capacity for vagueness went hand in hand with his skill at streamlining language and giving it strength, grace and economy. When necessary, he could and did eliminate downright sloppiness of construction. Morris was the Convention's English professor as well as its literary artist and shifted easily between his creative and remedial roles.

Consider Article I, Section 8, Clause 10. At one point the Committee on Style had this before it: "To define and punish piracies and felonies committed on the high seas, and punish offences against the law of nations." Morris removed the second "punish" so that "define and punish" would carry over from the previous clause, an apparent instance where precision and streamlining went together.[3]

But even here there was a subtler relationship between precision and vagueness than meets the eye. To the objection (from James Wilson) that it would be arrogant of one nation to pretend to define the law of nations, Morris objected that the latter was often too vague and deficient to be enforceable without statutory definition! Morris could create or undo vagueness with equal skill. To summarize the point, when vagueness is not mere confusion it is grounded in precision and, as in Romantic art, is a calculated departure from it.

The transformation of substance by style is best seen in the preamble. The original draft went as follows:

> We the people of the States of New Hampshire, Massachusetts, Rhode-Island and Providence Plantations, Connecticut, New-York, New-Jersey, Pennsylvania, Delaware, Maryland, Virginia, North-Carolina, South-Carolina, and Georgia do ordain, declare, and establish the following constitution for the Government of Ourselves and our Posterity.[4]

Omitting the states in the actual preamble made the document more open textured, inviting the states that would actually sign to a performative action that determined the initial scope of the union. The preamble also veered the emphasis from the states to the people, and added the vagueness of the phrases "establish justice," "insure domestic tranquility," "promote the general welfare," and "blessings of liberty." Some have argued that the Preamble is not itself a substantive part of the Constitution, that it states purposes but assigns no powers. But they have simply neglected the actual power of artistic eloquence and stylistic embellishment, its important invitation to interpretation, and its practical consequences.

Intention

Intention and intentionality are variously explored and puzzled over in life, law, psychology, ethics, and aesthetics. Ever since the Beardsley-Wimsatt essay, aestheticians have had a go at intention with a vengeance.[5] My guiding assumption here is that aestheticians have seen sooner than others, and more clearly, the pitfalls associated with attributions of intention. Specifically, the lesson of the "intentional fallacy" is that the artist's intentions are perhaps interesting but do not have much bearing upon (let alone do they exhaust the meaning and value of) an artwork. Artists are not privileged with respect to knowing their intentions, and even their precisely stated intentions do not reflect what they have accomplished. The wider value, then, of looking at the "intentional fallacy," with its undermining of naiveties and assurances about artworks, has been to raise comparable questions about any intentions—not only the artist's. Just as it is risky to attribute a clear and univocal intention to an artist, it is equally precarious to do so with a law giver or a legal document. Such attribution is a political or moral act of interpretation, itself in need of further interpretation. The dogma of univocal intention is an interpretation that tries to close off further study and interpretation. The "intentional fallacy" then, though originated in discussions of art, is remarkably relevant to all kinds of persons and documents, not least of all to the Constitution. I offer one example of the absurdity of laying too great store by "the intention of the Founding Fathers" and of how we can commit the "intentional fallacy" with respect to the Constitution. I quote from *Mr. Madison's Constitution* by Frank Donovan:

> The Committee of Detail had reported that new states should "be admitted on the same terms with the original states." This displeased most of the delegates, particularly Gouverneur Morris, who claimed that he "did not mean to discourage the growth of the western country. . . . He did not wish, however, to throw the power into their hands." The Convention readily agreed to his substitution: "New states may be admitted by the legislature into the Union." This clause was so ambiguous that it could be interpreted in any of a variety of ways. Sixteen years later, in reply to an inquiry about the Louisiana Purchase, Morris himself interpreted it by writing: "Your inquiry . . . is substantially whether the Constitution can admit, as a new state, territory which did not belong to the United States when the Constitution was made. In my opinion, they cannot. I have always thought that, when we should acquire Canada and Louisiana, it would be proper to govern them as provinces, and allow them no voice in our councils." Had Morris had his way, Florida, Texas, California, Alaska, Hawaii, and several other states would now be the "provinces."[6]

So much for the intention of one Founding Father with respect to his own Constitutional text! The wonder is that Gouverneur Morris was a Founding Father and not a Loyalist. Sticking with George III would have been natural to his temperament, consistent with some of his in-laws, and much in accord with what I would call—with obvious glibness and irony—his deepest "intention."

Performance

Interpretation is closely connected with both style and performance. Symphonies and plays are performed, and aestheticians have wondered about the moral and aesthetic mysteries attendant upon acting in a drama or playing a piano sonata. There is an obligation to an original, a text or score, but also an obligation, in performing it, to interpret creatively, to do something that in the nature of the case cannot be rule-governed and precise.[7] Aestheticians have been aware of, and have carefully spelled out, the ambiguity of these separate obligations. They exist together; they tug against each other; each needs to be honored, and there is no finality in any one performance decision with respect to how they are separately honored.

As with a literary text or musical score, so with the Constitution. "Playing it" needs to be seen in its double aspects, as an occasion for and indeed as requiring both freedom and constraint. Performance demands not only fidelity to the text or score (as legalists would like it) but meta-attention, so to speak, to the array of options between what is prescribed and what is left unprescribed.

The Constitution is a text, a score, that has much in it, admittedly, that is clearly and narrowly prescriptive. Its details have at times been ignored, or performed not badly but wrongly, even by those who have dutifully sworn to uphold it. It is possible to show how, where, and when this has happened. But as a text it is open to interpretation and invites interpretation. Respect for it, like respect for a work of art, is not realized by attending only to its precisions and its demands and by refusing to interpret; it is manifested by attending to its possibilities and daring to interpret. Interpretation and performance go hand in hand. Interpretation might be said to be the words that explain the original text. Performance might be said to be the executive, legislative, and judicial decisions, depending upon interpretation, that have accumulated in the making of the tradition.

Because the Constitution prescribes a great deal in unequivocal detail, it is sometimes mistakenly (unaesthetically!) seen as imperfect for failing to prescribe everything; or it is mistakenly seen as capable of prescribing everything—if one could discover the original intentions of its authors. Composers sometimes specify *a piacere*, in a precisely articulated invitation to freedom. Any critical study of the Constitution, and of its history, shows that it implies such invitations.

We are keenly aware of the freedoms we enjoy, or think we enjoy, because concretely specified in so many words in the Bill of Rights. We are perhaps not as readily aware of the importance of the open texture and built-in drama of the Constitution. Judge Antonin Scalia made this point effectively in the hearings before the Senate Judiciary Committee.

I think most of the questions today will probably be about that portion of the Constitution that is called the Bill of Rights, which is a very important part of it, of course. But if you had to put your finger on what has made our Constitution so enduring, I think it is the original document before the amendments were added.

Because the amendments, by themselves, do not do anything. The Russian constitution probably has better, or at least as good guarantees of personal freedom as our document does. What makes it work, what assures that those words are not just hollow promises, is the structure of government that the original Constitution established, the checks and balances among the three branches, in particular, so that no one of them is able to "run roughshod" over the liberties of the people as those liberties are described in the Bill of Rights.[8]

No one of the branches is able to ride roughshod over the others because the three are part of a dramatic (i.e., artistic) structure and not a logical one. The relation between the branches, since it is not precisely and logically given, needs to be constantly determined and invented by active interpretation and performance.

In those instances in the Constitution where there is some attempt to specify checks and balances, we have possible inconsistency or paradox, and some loss of needed open texture. For example, Article III, Section 2: "In all the other cases before mentioned the Supreme Court shall have appellate jurisdiction, both as to law and fact, with such exception, and under such regulations as the Congress shall make." Such "exceptions" and "regulations" could run head-on against the Supreme Court's power of judicial review, intimated by Article VI, Section 2, and Article III, Section 1.

Contradictions in a legal text tend to be looked upon as mistakes while contradictions in a literary text (e.g., Plato) are (or can be) seen as part of a dramatic structure. Here we do well to see that even a legal text, or what is essentially a legal text, can be buttressed by non-logical components. Going even further, and keeping the Russian Constitution in mind, we might say that a legal text can be too tightly structured.[9] In a word, the resilient richness of the artistry of the Constitution is neither a gloss nor legally irrelevant; the Constitution is its artistry as well as its structure; both influence how the Constitution has worked. The ultimate artistry of the document lies beyond all overt specificity and all covert intention, certainly beyond any one interpretation or performance.

At the birth of the Constitution, and for some time thereafter, there were grave doubts about its merits. Hamilton called it "worthless." John McHenry gave as a reason for having signed the Constitution that he distrusted his own judgment! Gouverneur Morris himself was thoroughly disillusioned with it a quarter of a century after fashioning it. In 1815, he was ready to have New York and New England secede from the union!

Though we regularly honor the Constitution, particularly on its anniversaries, there are lots of differing opinions about both its weaknesses and its merits. However, even some of those who see the Constitution as flawed recognize its "mythic" might, its positive power (which must be essentially inspirational and aesthetic) to offset the deficiencies of its details. The ongoing reevaluations of the Constitution are reminiscent (to pursue my analogy) of the way works of art require time and testing and performance to manifest their richnesses, and of the way in which historical judgments keep changing. The matter is never finally settled.

George Washington sent the new Constitution to Congress with a cover letter drafted (characteristically!) by Gouverneur Morris. It said, "It is not easy to be wise for all times, not even for the present, much less for the future. . . ." I, for one, hope that the Constitution will continue to be performed in a hundred years at its tricentennary celebration.[10] If we think to know now how it will then be interpreted, we are artless in our vision of history.

EIGHT

HUMAN RIGHTS AND ARTISTIC APPRECIATIONS

1979

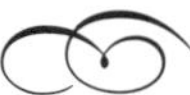

A difficulty with specifying human rights lies in the relational nature of a right. One person's right is another's obligation, so that one's right needs to be recognized by another. But the priority in this relation is not clear. A claim and a recognition of a right implicate and further each other. The specification of a human right is similar to the process of art criticism. Criticism transforms the perceived object (work of art) into the felt object (art object), but there is no priority among perceptions and feelings. Describing an object can lead to an articulation of feelings; and expression of feelings can lead to a more sensitive description. Just as priority is unimportant in art criticism, it can be forgotten with respect to human rights as well; and in both cases the relation is key. "The work of art (human being) is a physical construct that the artist (nature) has fashioned. But the art object (human right) has to be critically perceived and appreciated by others, and acquires its rich and flexible nature by such attention." Human rights, then, are "emergent . . . of critical caring" rather than external attributes.

Human rights are often proclaimed during or after wars. Such rights in the making occurred notably at the time of the American Revolution, when the colonists had grievances and felt that they were dealt with unjustly. They pleaded for redress of those grievances and conflict developed. Some colonists wanted independence, some did not; but most lived in ambiguity and uncertainty, forced to momentous choice. They sensed what their rights were before they could exactly define them. Finally, in the midst of this energized situation, in a climate of debate and battle, Jefferson wrote the Declaration of Independence, with its solemn assertion of human rights.

The eloquence of the words persists: "All men are created equal . . . endowed by their Creator with certain inalienable rights . . . among these rights. . . ." The Declaration is anything but a political or objective study of the nature of man. It is a work of moral art or of impassioned criticism. Looked at coolly, it is a rhetorical mix of description functioning as exhortation and exhortation finding justification in the actual sentiments and concerns of men in a predicament. The statements in isolation, as verbally precise descriptions, are thoroughly inadequate. Men are not created equal, the hypothesis of a Creator is moot, the further listing of rights is arbitrary. But what cannot stand alone and out of context does stand well as a fitting articulation of that caring phase of history. The Declaration is a verbal culmination of an historical process, and the culmination and the process are linked.

The problem of specifying human rights, indeed of their "existence," usually involves the following difficulties. The rights that are said to exist cannot be seen in any generalized inspection of human nature, and those rights that have been proclaimed have in fact varied greatly in the course of history. But there is another related sense in which rights are not readily discoverable. A right is ontologically peculiar; it is relational; it has to do with an implicit or explicit moral demand made upon others, perhaps upon a king. *My* right is *your* obligation; what presumably exists in *me* is something that *you* should recognize and respect. Nor is there any clear priority. You might accord me a right I haven't yet claimed; I might claim a right you haven't yet recognized. Each implicates and furthers the other.

The denial that human rights exist, since they do not seem to exist anywhere clearly, is one way out of the difficulties. The concept of human rights can simply be seen as one that is confusing and ambiguous. Philosophical comment will then consist of detailing the ambiguities and confusions and nothing more. However, this approach does not seem to come to grips with the fact that human rights—utterances of them and caring about them—are important. Perhaps there is a suitable intellectual flexibility that can get to the concerns and ambiguities about human rights without such hasty dismissal.

I propose here to deal with human rights with the help of an analogy with works of art, and how such works function as objects of literary and artistic criticism. Problems having to do with the ambiguous locus and status of works of art have already been given much philosophical attention. If there is any parallel between works of art and human rights, the long consideration given to the former might shed some light on the latter. Analogical argument is itself precarious and is as much an artistic as a theoretical device. It involves, equivocally, the making and the discovering of a connection, as with any good metaphor. It is a procedure that is not inappropriate to my theme.

A peculiarity of artistic criticism, intellectually disturbing to some, is that it helps to generate the very object of its attentions, an object that in some proximate way has "existed" prior to the attentions given it. The function of criticism is to produce the transformation, to turn the "work of art," as the attributed starting point of the process is sometimes called, into an "art object," the presumed terminus of our critical attention. There is a beguiling and paradoxical aspect to this process. We explain and generate interchangeably, at one and the same time.

This can be seen in the basic language of critical judgment, which has often been separated into two components: expressions of feeling (A, "I like this painting") and descriptions of objects (B, "This painting is beautiful"). In actual situations of appreciative response, A and B are easily interchangeable utterances, and it is even possible to regard A as a description (of an emotional state) and B as an expression (of a feeling). Because of these ambiguities, any attempt to view the critical process as following a clear temporal path is dubious. It is tempting to say that feelings come first ("I like this painting") and that the judgment ("This painting is beautiful") is emergent or subsequent—a kind of clarification or consequence or objectification of the feeling. But it is an intellectual prejudice to claim that vague feelings precede clear ideas or descriptions. In criticism and in art the pathways are multitudinous, and feelings and descriptions generate each other. Furthermore, feelings are not necessarily vague and subjective, and concepts or descriptions are not necessarily clear and objective.

Another way, then, of looking at the critical or appreciative process is to set aside all claims to precedence—with the question, "Is it beautiful because I like it, or do I like it because it is beautiful?" left deliberately unresolved. Or rather, we reject the notion that the alternatives are mutually exclusive. We find beauty as we articulate our likes; we express feelings as we respond to a claim or judgment that something is beautiful. It is the relation that is important, the process of expressing and finding, not the claimed locus as subjective *or* objective, internal *or* external.

Some philosophers have incorporated these difficulties into their attempts at definition. Thus, Santayana defined beauty as pleasure regarded as the quality of an object.[1] Santayana's definition might have said quite the same thing, for his purposes as well as for mine, if he had called beauty the quality of an object when experienced as pleasure. Both definitions are ambiguous with respect to both the locus and timing of the pleasure and the beauty. The notion of regarding emotion as the quality of an object suggests that the object is created, or re-created, by the process of attending to it. But that art objects stir emotions in us attests to the other direction in which the process simultaneously occurs.

Arnold Isenberg, a more recent aesthetician than Santayana, made a somewhat similar claim when he suggested that we come to see in the process of criticism certain qualities of the art object that are not directly transmitted by the designative or denotative aspects of the critic's language.[2] Such "descriptions-without-describing" must occur, must come into the picture, so to speak, because of what we have been calling the expressive or feeling components of the critical process. The evidence is overwhelming that the language of criticism, quite apart from its clear designations and denotations, helps us to experience and indeed to get to "know" the art object. Critical language, like art itself and as an accompaniment to it, produces feeling transformations that modify our perceptions. Appreciation of the work of art in terms of description alone never suffices (a point developed at length in Chapter 3, "Music, Modulation, and Metaphor").

Aesthetic value does not simply inhere in a work of art. The critic or appreciator who says that it does is neglecting, at least momentarily, his own performance, the fact that he writes or attends to the art with whatever sensitivity and intelligence he can muster. And, according to my analogy, critical response (with its mix of feelings and judgments) functions similarly in the area of human rights. A human right, then, is some actual desire or care reflected upon and made articulate[3] so that it is worthy of the consideration, attention, and respect of others. Eliminating the aforementioned considerations of priority, we can also say that a human right is a recognition upon the part of others of our desires and cares. So we preserve the relationship, the double locus. The right inheres in the individual; it is something that has to do with one as a human being with feelings and desires. But *qua* right it has to be accorded by others, by "society," sometimes by a critical or legal document. To reanimate my analogy, the work of art (human being) is a physical construct that the artist (nature) has fashioned. But the art object (human right) has to be critically perceived and appreciated by others and acquires its rich and flexible nature by such attention.

Human rights, like objects of the art-critical process, are not entities of an ordinary sort. They are not like arms and legs, rationality and animality, and other fixed properties of a human being. Rather they are the emergents, though tentatively envisioned and proclaimed in advance, of processes of critical caring. Human rights involve humans making claims with effort, feeling, and argument. But human rights also involve others according us dignity, freedom, and legal options.[4]

The original prospectus of the journal *The Public Interest* states: "The public interest is not some kind of pre-existing platonic idea. Rather, it emerges out of differences of opinion, reasonably propounded."[5] I would argue, as in the case of human rights, that the nature of the public interest is bidirectional. The platonic idea, constantly modified, pre- and post-exists its search.

This account of human rights might be clarified by considering examples of what happens when rights are externally attributed, or attributed at a distance. There is then the danger of abstraction and remoteness, of emotion that becomes blind to its true sources. I refer to the putative rights of the dead, the unborn, and future generations. I claim that such seemingly generous attributions of rights to past and potential persons constitute an illicit and improperly explored articulation of one's own rights. In such cases we borrow from the honored dead, and unborn, an air of legitimacy and authority to do what we wish to do on quite other grounds. When the living argue with the living about the rights of the dead and the unborn, the rights actually being contested and formulated are those of some of the living against others of the living. Under the guise of a disinterested righteousness there is an assertion of an interested claim. It would be better to focus on the immediacy and the interest in the forging of a right for ourselves. The unborn, when they are born, will soon enough proclaim themselves; the dead will have to rest in peace.

Here is an example of how deception can enter the picture when rights are attributed to the non-living. Suppose two sons contest their father's will. What is contested is obviously not the right of the father to feel, think, or decide anything—that he can no longer do. He had a right to make a will, and he vivified that right when he did. The sons, in their litigation and their differences, might be disposed to argue about the dead man's rights. What is honestly at stake, however, is the right of each son to interpret the will and to try to derive legal support for his viewpoint. The sons have the actual right to use a document and to evoke whatever memories and devotions they might manage to share. The father's rights are so much pretense; he has done what he would, and willed, and can do or benefit no more.

The issue of abortion is similar. Opponents of abortion sometimes argue abstractly about the rights of the unborn human baby. It is said that fetuses have God-given rights, or that they have reached a point in development where souls have joined their bodies. As a consequence, certain things ought not to be done to them, even by their mothers. (The mother's motives, characteristically, are seen as wilful, selfish, personal— incapable of blossoming into a full-fledged right.) Since fetuses cannot articulate their claims and desires, their defenders do it for them. The point is that the religious and philosophical arguments do not flow out of the claimant's feelings. Those arguments are not readily persuasive and sharable, and sometimes seem to be animated more by a desire to vivify dying doctrines than to vivify living fetuses. What is sharable as a human rights argument, and what makes a good anti-abortion critique, is the suggestion that the fetus looks like us, feels pain like us, and that to undo him would be a travesty of *our* power of human caring.

Such an approach is the equivalent of what happens in proper artistic criticism. It draws on shared capacities, perceptions, responses, and attempts to gather them together in the formation of a communal appreciation or judgment. There is no guarantee that this will work, but it is at least on a possible track. The intrusion of dubious dogma, "principled" and abstract claims that flow out of hidden feelings, will produce at best a perfunctory or alienated assent.

Such external attribution of human rights is equivalent, in my broad analogy, to the claim that such-and-such is an authenticated artistic Masterpiece, deserving our approval because High Authority declares it to be an honored and even a sacred work. This is not the proper way of criticism in either arena. We may understandably wish, because of our enthusiasms or prejudices, to foist the said Masterpiece (or the said Right) upon others and to support such urgings with borrowed certainties and with the rhetoric of high-mindedness. But such urgings, whether in the domain of art or morality, will not connect human feeling with human insight or judgment. This connection is essential and the plea for it, as well as the description of it, are of course the simultaneous burdens of what I have said. Only in the forges of honest caring and intelligent sharing can something good or beautiful come into being.

PART TWO

ARTISTIC PHILOSOPHERS
AND PHILOSOPHICAL ARTISTS

NINE

INTERPRETING PEIRCE

1985

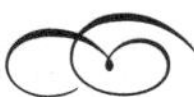

In his famous essay "The Fixation of Belief," Peirce outlines four methods of determining beliefs: (1) tenacity, (2) authority, (3) the a priori *method, and (4) reason (or experience or science). Favoring the fourth, he praises it by comparing it to one's bride, who "should be loved and reverenced." The comparison, remarkable in the context for its literary styling, may be interpreted in four ways: (1) as completely ironic, (2) as partially ironic, (3) as completely sincere, and (4) as all of the above. As completely ironic, the comparison suggests that Peirce has made "an artful and sardonic display of the risks and traps of reason," since the matrimonial devotion to reason would be akin to the rigid emotional attachment found in the other, unreasonable methods. As partially ironic, the comparison suggests "the devotion is qualified but not abandoned." As completely sincere, the comparison presents problems similar to when interpreted as completely ironic yet without the author's self-awareness. Interpreting the comparison as all of the above "recognizes Peirce's refusal to terminate his choice in any one mode, or to decide on final priority or merit," preserves a radical openness, and emphasizes inquiry over either fixation or belief.*

At the end of Peirce's famous essay "The Fixation of Belief,"[1] there is a remarkable simile in an eloquent passage. I quote the final paragraph in full:

> Yes, the other methods do have their merits: a clear logical conscience does cost something—just as any virtue, just as all that we cherish, costs us dear. But we should not desire it to be otherwise.

{ 117 }

The genius of a man's logical method should be loved and reverenced as his bride, whom he has chosen from all the world. He need not contemn the others; on the contrary, he may honor them deeply, and in doing so he only honors her the more. But she is the one that he has chosen, and he knows that he was right in making that choice. And having made it, he will work and fight for her, and will not complain that there are blows to take, hoping that there may be as many and as hard to give, and will strive to be the worthy knight and champion of her from the blaze of whose splendors he draws his inspiration and his courage.[2]

Perhaps I should say that what Peirce gives us is like a simile because a simile usually declares one thing to be like another. Here Peirce is saying that one thing *should be* like another; he gives us an exhortation. It is as though the two things become alike as a result of our efforts. But they are somewhat alike already, and their similarity might actually provoke our efforts. This circularity is part of my theme, so I shall return to it.

Peirce's essay is a discussion of four methods of fixing belief: (1) the method of tenacity, (2) the method of authority, (3) the *a priori* method, and finally, (4) the method of reason (the scientific or experiential or logical method). The first three methods (which I shall call the synoptic methods) are reviewed sympathetically but are discarded as inadequate. Peirce opts for the fourth method, the method of reason, and he carefully justifies his choice.

Is the closing figure of speech Peirce's way of adding a touch of enthusiasm to his preference? Or is there some other point to it? Ordinarily the choice among methods or theories is not looked upon as having the significance of the choice of a bride. It might have greater or lesser significance, but hardly the same kind. At the least the simile is effective, as similes often are, because of the surprisingness of the juxtaposition and the startlingness of the comparison. Elsewhere in the essay, Peirce writes how being in awe of Francis Bacon's grandiloquence can hide an awareness of Bacon's scientific inadequacy. Peirce's closing paragraph is grandiloquent. Does it, too, hide something, and in hiding it artfully does it also reveal it?

What exactly, or even inexactly, is the relationship between the closing paragraph and the rest of Peirce's essay? For a philosopher who can be relentlessly logical, and who has been largely (but not entirely) so un-til his last paragraph, Peirce's literary flourish is something of a stylistic shift. Is it merely that—an epilogical departure from what has preceded it and without relevance to the argument that has gone before? Or is it linked in some thematic way, like a coda, to what has led up to it? Does it perhaps accomplish a closure or finality beyond what the orderly com-pletion of the previous argument was able to provide? Or is it in its own mysterious way an avoidance of finality or closure? In brief, is it con-nected or disconnected with the body of the essay in ways that may not be immediately apparent?

I propose in a somewhat literary critical way to show that there are connections and disconnections, and that they are both complicated and revelatory. Approaching Peirce in anything but a severely logical way might appear wrong from the start. But the simile, the literary figure I dwell on, is Peirce's, not mine. Why not see what happens if we take it seriously, or ironically, or both, or neither? In the history of philosophical criticism there has often been a lack of correspondence between the method employed by the critic and the method examined. There are analytic philosophers who write on Nietzsche and there are literary philosophers, even poets, who write on Kant. The methods used to still doubts and fix beliefs about Peirce may be multifarious.

Peirce's essay is an attempt to resolve doubts about the best way of resolving doubts, that is, the best way of fixing belief. "To satisfy our doubts, therefore, it is necessary that a method should be found by which our beliefs may be caused by nothing human, but by some external per-manency—by something upon which our thinking has no effect."[3] The best method needs to be found, but the best method had better be used or it will not be found! Putting it another way, Peirce's essay is his method or way of fixing belief *about a method*, and the methods reviewed are themselves various ways of fixing beliefs. There is inevitable circularity, but is the circle vicious? Does Peirce trip up on his dilemma or is it bril-liantly displayed?

The bride image focuses the issue of circularity. It is necessary to come to believe in a method by which our beliefs "may be caused by nothing human." The bride is surely human, or is she? Is "bride," for Peirce, a mere concept containing the idea of commitment and permanency? Or is "bride" a lady, a human person, someone we respond to with timely passion and thought? Is she both?

Peirce was a divorced man, a fact, I take it, that was of no small consequence to his professional as well as his personal life. His bride, his wife, was an early feminist. Do we dare to let these facts have any bearing on our study of the bride image? Perhaps we shouldn't dare, but the hovering ironies are hard to overlook. When a chosen bride, or wife, is divorced do we have a contradiction in terms ("divorced wife") or simply a woman who has acquired a new status? Is the method of reason something to which we have, or should have, an ongoing attachment so long as our commitment to it persists, or is the method of reason something that has an independent reality as a Real and excellent thing (to borrow Peirce's words) forever? In the cases of both the bride and the method of reason there are parallel equivocations, which is why Peirce's simile is so apt.

A bride is both permanent and transient. In one sense, a bride is a woman chosen to be one's wife always (as religions like to remind us) apart from circumstances of choice and apart from present and subsequent feelings. In another sense, a bride is "a woman at her marriage; a woman just about to be married or very recently married." This is from the *OED*, which says that the term is "frequently used from the proclamation of the banns, or other public announcement of the coming marriage." Note the institutional intrusion here, the fixation of status by the method of authority. The *OED* reports a parliamentary debate on Prince Leopold's allowance in which Gladstone spoke of Princess Helen as a bride. "Mr. Gladstone, being criticized . . . said he believed that colloquially a lady when engaged was often called a 'bride.' This was met with 'Hear! hear!' from some, and 'No!, no!' from others. Probably 'bride elect' would have satisfied critics."[4] I can only add that "bride elect" would have satisfied some critics but not others.

It has been asked whether a lady is lovable because she is loved or loved because she is lovable. The same question in its very early philosophical garb was posed as follows: Is the pious that which is dear to the gods, or is that which is dear to the gods pious? The presumption behind the question is that it is one or the other, an either/or. The other possibility, both/and, pervades Peirce's essay. The further and subtler possibility is to reveal the either/or and the both/and in both either/or and both/

and fashion. This is what Peirce did, or ought to have done, or both. He defies the clear claims of logical priority in his literary and multi-perspectival meditation about the method of reason. Peirce's position of 1878 has been called "a peculiar combination of doctrines."[5] It can be seen as that but it can also be seen as a rich dramatization of perspectives, of which "peculiar combination of doctrines" is merely one.

Turning now to my specific argument, I propose four possible interpretations of the last paragraph of the Peirce essay. I characterize these interpretations as (1) deliberate, total irony, (2) partial irony, (3) no irony at all, or sincerity, and (4) all of the above.

First, I will address the interpretation that the bride simile is totally ironic. The synoptic methods that Peirce repudiates—tenacity, authority, *a priori*—share a common inflexibility based on the bonds of emotion. What makes them unsatisfactory to Peirce is that they involve an attachment and a fixity that resists rational scrutiny and logical emendation. The worth of the method of reason, by contrast, is that it frees us from such fixities and attachments, particularly attachments to possible false-hoods, and it enables us to modify our beliefs and convictions.

The total irony of the last paragraph, and its crucial role in the essay, is then understandable—or can be made to be understandable. The method of reason frees one from emotional inflexibility, and yet that very method is to be one's bride, to be loved with constancy over all other women or methods. Reason, the rational method, which was supposed to be an es-cape from unreason, the synoptic methods, has started out from, gener-ated, become associated with, an unreasonable devotion, albeit to reason itself. So Peirce deliberately undermines the case he has made; ironically, he calls into question the supposedly reasonable method he had used and the conclusion he had reached about its superiority. He is mocking the method of reason and revealing its blandishments and dangers. His earlier encomial conclusions about reason are made to ring hollow, and the whole "reasonableness" of the bulk of the essay—as practiced and proclaimed—is deliberately undercut. The closing paragraph, then, is no confirming epilogue. It is the most important part of the essay, the sting, the reversal that sheds an entirely new light on what went on before.

To sum up this interpretation, we read (or reread, if it was not appar-ent at first) the essay as an artful and sardonic display of the risks and traps of reason. The argument of the essay is not presented in order to arrive at a conclusion that is the outcome of the argument. Rather, the argument is presented in order to show how arguing and reasoning generate, willy-nilly, unavoidable and perhaps even tragic passions that are inimical to argument and reason. The essay is literary, a dramatization with a final recognition scene. The closing paragraph helps to confirm directly what the essay had indirectly sought to reveal. What it conveys, in full irony and by virtue of its structure, is the total unworthiness of the method of reason. (I am tempted to say "near total" because of logical scruples. Total irony, like total sincerity, might be a contradiction in terms and impossible.) So much, in any case, for the interpretation (1) that Peirce was a conscious, extreme ironist artfully structuring his essay from its outset in order finally to reverse his judgment about the nature and role of reason.

Interpretation (2), partial irony, is in greater accord with the actual ways of irony. It is also more acceptable if the claim of total irony is seen as dubious and self-contradictory. Certainly there can be partial irony, degrees of irony, and we can look upon Peirce as both the victim and the master of his method. On this view, Peirce becomes ironic in spite of himself, in the course of the essay, without being ironic totally and all the time. The last paragraph, then, is a reluctant irony, something that happened to Peirce rather than something that he clearly caused to happen. The closing bride figure is an *arrière-pensée*, an afterthought, whimsically mocking and unsettling. But it is not intended to undo, quite so thoroughly as was proposed in interpretation (1), the propriety of a devotion to reason. The devotion is qualified but not abandoned.

Partial irony, then, is possible, and equivocation about devotion to a bride (or to reason) in lifelong fidelity is a frequent human condition. It is a matter with respect to which a man can oscillate between various degrees of seriousness and irony, earnestness and playfulness, passion and distance. The oscillation can be rapid and unstable and can run to various and uncertain proportions. Peirce, then, has conveyed his devotion to reason in a wavering, irresolute way with the help of the partial irony of the bride figure. I do not regard interpretation (2) as itself vague or wavering. It clearly proposes that Peirce's essay dramatizes various opposed and non-quantifiable views.

By way of an aside, and in order to give some empirical support for interpretation (2) (and also [1]), I turn to the body of the essay to show Peirce's capacity for irony. Indeed, some of the earlier ironies might be seen as preparations for the sharper irony of his ending.

Peirce is genuinely sympathetic to the synoptic methods of fixing belief even as he develops his misgivings:

> But most of all I admire the method of tenacity for its strength, simplicity, and directness. Men who pursue it are distinguished for their decision of character, which becomes very easy with such a mental rule. They do not waste time trying to make up their minds what they want, but, fastening like lightning upon whatever alternative comes first, they hold it to the end, whatever happens, without an instant's irresolution. This is one of the splendid qualities which generally accompany brilliant, unlasting success. It is impossible not to envy the man who can dismiss reason, although we know how it must turn out at last.[6]

This is a real tribute to a method of non-reason. Perhaps it begins to reverse its course, to become ironic, with the simile "fastening like lightning"—which suggests a firm, irrevocable, Zeus-like choice of a bride. The closing lines are not too forceful, not too heartfelt. Is Peirce really complaining about the "brilliant, unlasting success of the synoptic methods"? Can success with reason last? Isn't some eventual consensus arrived at by some uncertain, future community of scientists as unconsoling as the assurances about Heaven that Peirce elsewhere disparages? It is indeed impossible not to envy the man who can dismiss reason— and Peirce is our very man!

Peirce comes up with other sarcasms and ironies, including ironies directed at himself. For example, with respect to the tenacious man:

> It would be an egotistical impertinence to object that his procedure is irrational, for that only amounts to saying that his method of settling belief is not ours. He does not propose to himself to be rational, and, indeed, will often talk with scorn of man's weak and illusive reason.[7]

Surely Peirce could not mean this unironically, since it is in palpable contradiction with what he elsewhere says about reason. And Peirce himself, as a man among men, also talks with scorn about man's weak and illusive reason. Writing about the method of authority, he remarks that, "For the mass of mankind, then, there is perhaps no better method than this. If it is their highest impulse to be intellectual slaves, then slaves they ought to remain."[8] There is irony and some bitterness, and like Swift's irony not merely directed at other men. So the end of the essay can be seen as part of a process of sustained, if intermittent, irony, not as an irony coming out of nowhere.

I now turn to (3), a reading of Peirce as unironic or sincere. On this interpretation, the enthusiasm that Peirce expresses both for the method of reason and for what he compares it with, a lifelong devotion to a bride, is proper, fitting, and consistent. There is nothing problematic or embarrassing about the comparison or the enthusiasm. I find (3) the most difficult interpretation to defend, even though it is perhaps the usual one and has much authority behind it. But with respect to the presence or absence of irony in *any* text, it is good hermeneutics to examine the view opposite the view one is first inclined to take for granted. If one ends up with two or more views, so be it.

In support of (3), sincerity, it might be argued that the unreasonableness of the methods of tenacity, authority, and *a priori* are pointed up by reason, without reason sharing in or becoming corrupted by these synoptic tendencies. The reasonableness of reason was discovered, arrived at in due course by a truly reasoning process that was unknown to itself. This is the way the bride was chosen, after some deliberation and effort, and after some comparison with other women. The bride wasn't there from all eternity but had to be found; and comparably, the worth of reason is an emergent discovery, a choice in time. (That the *merits* of the true bride and true reason were always there to be discovered is something the sincere man cannot allow.) For the sincere man, fidelity either to reason or the bride is not a matter of prior commitment or hidden passion. Passion accompanies but does not precede its validation. Fidelity, on this interpretation, is the ongoing validation of the choice, of the reasoning or loving process; it consists of a passion constantly justified by its joyful exercise and by a continuous confirmation of its own excellence. There is no lapse of time, there is no unconscious in the sincere man, nothing *is* prior to its discovery.

The structure of pure sincerity is perhaps as complicated, as unstable, as impossible, as the structure of pure irony. In the matter at hand, the sincere man must avoid seeing or acknowledging that the discovery of the method of reason as worthy might be connected with the use of the method in making the discovery. (As we saw, if any passionate commitment to reason preceded the use of reason, then the synoptic methods have intruded themselves, and the value of reason is not a reasonable discovery but in part an unreasonable, an emotional, starting point.)

Peirce, taken as sincere, must not allow any prior passion about reason to be part of what he discovers. If such prior passion were present, the unironic man would be marred in his efforts by a lack of self-knowledge. We might say that the sincere man thinks he has no hidden passions, and the ironic man thinks he reveals his hidden passions by conveying them ironically. Both are wrong, but both are needed postures and help us in our final way of interpreting Peirce.

Interpretation (4), "all of the above," brings together (1), (2), and (3). It might seem that (4) is frivolous and that (2), partial irony (with its continuum of possibilities between the impossibilities of total irony and total seriousness), is all that is needed to understand Peirce. As we saw, (2) ranges fully between (1) and (3) and might have been our definitive interpretation. It certainly was very tempting and would have been less wearying than adding (1), (3), and (4).

It is possible to be ironic about seriousness, serious about irony, both, and neither. Interpretation (4) recognizes Peirce's refusal to terminate his choice in any one mode, or to decide on final priority or merit. Interpretation (4) is not exclusionary, as the method of reason is not exclusionary of the synoptic methods, as a bride is not exclusionary of other women. So interpretation (4), combining (1), (2), and (3), is the one to which we must adhere. We should give it all our devotion and recognize it as the best and only way to interpret Peirce.

Yes, interpretations (1), (2), and (3) have their individual blandishments and merits, and the refusal to choose from one among them costs us dear. The genius of a man's life is to be open to radical diversity, even to simultaneous and contradictory choices, to honor what he can, where he can, and as long as he is able. A worthy knight, playful or earnest, whether of cheerful or doleful countenance, should be able to ride off at once in many directions.

It is time to return to the themes of circularity and closure, to what the text has taught and can teach. Peirce dismantles and reassembles himself, using what he has written not as a repository of the discovered but as an occasion for a quest. The text turns out to be, and always was, more expansive and rife with possibilities than we realized, and yet realize. It provokes us to be more open in our critical methods than we ordinarily are. There is an ending to the essay, but also an opening to unknown vistas. The text before us, yellowing, paginated, and finite, can be and should be seen as warmly off the press, garbed in white, ready for further opportunities to dazzle us and to be known. Peirce is committed not to a fixation of belief in any easy sense of either fixation or belief but to inquiry, to the method of reason writ large. Inquiry was Peirce's master passion, his religion, his philosophy, his life. He clung to it because of the social authority behind it, with *a priori* arbitrariness, and with incredible tenacity. He generated it and it generated him. It was his tremulous lady and his immortal bride, neither and both. It was his way of being, giving bearable unity to a vision of brilliant and unbearable variety.[9]

TEN

ON RUF'S *THE CREATION OF CHAOS: WILLIAM JAMES AND THE STYLISTIC MAKING OF A DISORDERLY WORLD*

1992

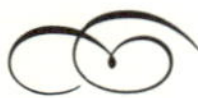

The Creation of Chaos: William James and the Stylistic Making of a Disorderly World, a book by professor of theology Fredrick J. Ruf, reminds one "of how much of mainstream philosophy has become a clear but isolated flow along the fringes, and how much 'real philosophy' . . . is now being done by people who work outside of departments of philosophy." Though examining James as a religious thinker, Ruf usually "lets 'philosophy,' 'religion,' and 'literature' freely roll against each other and interpenetrate." The approach suits an examination of "the stylistic varieties in James." Ruf finds in James various chaotic worlds, in which some kinds of chaos are liberating while others are disruptive. Ruf observes of James that "there is a chaotic destructiveness from without that overwhelms and that cannot be managed. But within, there is an openness and fluidity that embraces and may even affirm the chaotic—but that is victorious over it for accepting it." Ruf goes on to find in James a sort of feminism and a religion of ordinariness, both exemplifying James's responses to and uses of different kinds of chaos.

If the style is the man, then to understand a philosopher is to understand more than his arguments. It is necessary to consider his style. Frederick J. Ruf writes, "it is easy to emerge from [James's *Varieties*] primarily moved not by a theory but by a man."[1] He also says he is looking at the "man, philosophy, and manner of writing."[2] Stylistic studies of philosophers have now become widespread. There is growing conviction that style and substance, if distinguishable, are hardly separable. Ruf says that James's "style does not efface itself" and refuses "to be a mere vehicle."[3] Style, of course, is in the revealing as well as the revealed, in the hiding as well as in the hidden, and if it appears to function as an "effacing vehicle," that too, if we probe it, becomes a stylistic quality! James himself said "Style is not my forte,"[4] but that is about as revelatory as, "Humility is not my strong point." Others have commented on James's style and Ruf uses as a section heading Ralph Barton Perry's characterization of that style as "meanderings, zigzags, and circles."[5]

Did I allude above to philosophers? Ruf is in a theology department, the book is in a "Series in Rhetoric and Theology," and Ruf says, at one point, that he is examining James as a religious thinker. But he is not at home with such limitations. In the spirit of chaotic fluidity that Ruf much recommends, it might be a good idea to efface categories like "philosophy," "religion," and "literature." Ruf is versed in a wide variety of writers that includes Freud, Bakhtin, Barthes, Borges, Coleridge, Nelson Goodman, Pascal, Schleiermacher, and Charlene Haddock Seigfried, plus some ordinary names quite unknown to me. His book is a salutary reminder of how much of mainstream philosophy has become a clear but isolated flow along the fringes and how much "real philosophy" (an admittedly fluid expression) is now being done by people who work outside departments of philosophy.

In his last chapter, and against his prevailing ways, Ruf briefly tries to put everything under the aegis of religion. More usually he lets "philosophy," "religion," and "literature" freely roll against each other and interpenetrate. We know by now that they always had lustful linkages (even when one of them was only supposed to be a handmaiden) and naturally vague boundaries. Only the Puritan keepers of "academic disciplines" want them forcefully kept apart. Ruf is not so inclined. At one point he says his book has employed "a literary, not a sociological or anthropological, analysis."[6] Literary, psychological, religious, philosophical— Ruf has many voices of his own to reckon with the stylistic varieties in James.

Ruf quotes Peirce as criticizing James's *Principles* for its "idiosyncrasies of diction and tricks of language."[7] Ruf indicates that the genre of textbook is supposed to be "discursive" and not "narrative or dramatic." Yet isn't "textbook of philosophy" an oxymoron? American philosophy has never been textbookish, and American philosophers (except, as J. H. Randall used to say, when they went whoring after foreign logicians) have not been merely mincing arguers. They have been literary persons, theologians, moralists—and academic mavericks.

Chaos is a paradoxical concept, since every chaos is a cosmos and things are chaotic in different ways. The "different ways" are what Ruf elaborates. These involve various degrees of order and disorder. Sometimes the order is oppressive, sometimes the disorder is liberating for providing an intellectual "fluidity of mind." Chaos often involves a needed "rupture of the expected."[8] Henry Adams is quoted: "chaos often breeds life, when order breeds habit."[9] For Ruf, James's *Principles* and *Varieties* epitomize the kinds of chaotic worlds.

Principles exemplifies a domesticated "good" or "soft" chaos; it is coherent, inclusive, and the different voices in it add up. *Varieties* exemplifies a more dangerous, damaging, disruptive, "bad," or hard chaos; it is incoherent, unstable, discordant, and the voices war with each other. So Ruf divides his study into two parts. By design, or chaotic happenstance, these parts echo, and are emblematic of, the "healthy soul" and the "sick soul," the source of the moral conflict that is James's ongoing agon.

The tensions of chaos, and even its kinds, defy boundaries and are not readily fixed. Whether chaos is domesticated or disruptive is a matter of perspective or voice. The domesticated is disruptive from a particular point of view, the disruptive is domesticated from another. These meta-viewpoints exist in a degree of tension, and whether *that* tension is disruptive or domesticated would be another viewpoint. Ruf can't quite fix his kinds of chaos, perhaps deliberately, and there is something chaotic (whether disruptive or domesticated!) in his attempts to do the fixing.

Ruf makes clear, but no more clear than is appropriate or possible, the astonishing range and play of voices in James. We are given a detailed and psychologically credible account of James's immersion in, and extrication from, his suicidal moments. There is a chaotic destructiveness from without that overwhelms and that cannot be managed. But within, there is an openness and fluidity that embraces and may even affirm the chaotic—but that is victorious over it for accepting it. The resulting gain of "orientation" is more momentous than any gain that streamlined arguments could give. Why line the stream? To avoid turbulence, to create an unbroken flow, and to manage things mechanically? In a word, why halt thought?

Ruf suggests the linking of James and "feminism" and others have elaborated the connection. If Camille Paglia had extended her study of sexual personae from Henry to William James (she alludes once to the connection between them), she would have had a comparable field day with William's masks and his androgyny. The "feminine" in James—the chthonic, the liquid, the vague, the inconstant, the chaotic—almost destroy him as he is about to bring a gun to his irresolute self. Suicide for James seemed a "manly" form of daring.[10] The "embrace" of the feminine—the acceptance of the vague, the inchoate, the irresolute, the liquid, the emotive—saves him. Will (in the Nietzschean sense, not Hank's brother) provides not only a masculine defiance of chaos in favor of order, habit, hard-edged words, and weapons. William also accomplishes a feminine embrace of chaos in favor of nature, abundance, inventiveness, fecundity, and superfluidity.

Feminine embraces, and embracing the feminine, are notoriously fluid processes and lose all "inner-outer" clarity and reference points. Just where, or in what direction, is the *hinan* toward which Goethe says the eternal feminine draws us? Ruf works hard on the internal-external distinction but never quite nails it down. But should he? Nailing things down, of course, whether they be distinctions or anything else, may not be the best way of relating to them. Even metaphors, if we would have them serve us well, sometimes have to be coaxed out of their metallic brazenness.

"Religion" was promised at the beginning of the book, and Ruf returns to it at the end. It is defined as that which "orients" us;[11] is it perhaps that which gives us "ultimate orientation"? As though to reverse his tendency to give religion great centrality and elevation, the religion that Ruf finally turns to is of an unusual, even an unconsecrated, sort—indeed it is called a religion of "ordinariness." I hear a waggish voice in some of this, but once we start hearing and inventing voices—as Ruf has fully illustrated—it is hard to know when to stop! Ruf quotes T.S. Eliot on "our *lived* religion" as including (among other but no better things)

"Derby Day . . . the dart board . . . boiled cabbage cut into sections . . . and the music of Elgar"—of which Ruf says he appreciates the cabbage most.[12] Religion is at once mundane and yet, quoting one Clifford Geertz, it can "tune human actions to an envisaged cosmic order."[13] So religion is sanctified and yet can include quite anything sensed, thought, or experienced. Chaos is no longer "a vehicle for a divinity."[14] From the "chaosmos," as Joyce called it,[15] we get back to the cosmos and finally the comic. What could be more comfortably trivial than cut cabbage, *Pomp and Circumstance*, and the *Enigma Variations*? Ruf concludes, "I would urge that we not concentrate solely on the arduous, extraordinary, and rare but examine, too, the very ordinary."[16] How apt the choices of Eliot and Elgar for this purpose! But could one imagine living long in Eliot's world, or in a world of Eliots? Wouldn't some fluid impulse incline us away from cabbages to kings?

Ruf hasn't departed from James. He quotes James as saying that the purpose of religion is "not God but life, more life, a larger, richer more satisfying life."[17] Ruf has given us, with much daring and scope on his part, some remarkable and original glimpses of the largeness of William James.

ELEVEN

HOW SARTRE MUST BE READ

An Examination of a Philosophic Method

1968

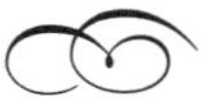

Jean-Paul Sartre's method of ordered distinctions simultaneously distin-guishes and fuses "in the interests of both the divisiveness of truth and the wholeness of being." In "What is Writing?" he distinguishes, first, signi-ficant words and immediate colors or sounds; second, meanings and imme-diacies of colors or sounds; and, third, poetic and prosaic words. Presenting the distinctions as "an ordered series of finer focusings" suggests a contin-uum or gamut and keeps any individual distinction from rising to an on-tological division: "each distinction unbinds the previous one and removes from it its false force and divisiveness." Furthermore, even as Sartre's method reveals a continuum, it also shows that "we are never either on it or out of it but rather in 'double reciprocal relation,'" because any attempt to distinguish two worlds would block the further serial distinguishing that relates and unifies things in process. "Our intellects, our prosaic selves, our tendencies and capacities to use words significantly, keep sundering what is essentially unsunderable. Our poetic sensibilities, our tenden-cies to express the significant, attempt to undo the damage that cutting intellect wreaks, and they do this by relating and combining and reconnecting."

Philosophers, like other people who would like to understand and to know, have to make distinctions. But unlike other people (and here we must make a distinction) philosophers are perhaps more sensitive to the risks and the commitments, the difficulties and the traps, with which the making of distinctions is fraught. Particularly, there is the danger of dichotomizing in thought what is in fact not separate in nature, and of dualizing a world that is in fact one. Avowals of the hypothetical or explanatory functions of distinctions, before or after he makes them, do not leave the philosopher immune from the charge of hypostatization. To say that a distinction is merely explanatory and not divisive does not keep it from being divisive in effect. How, then, can the philosopher keep the mind's categories from impersonating and parading as nature's definitive structure? How can he keep from turning what he knows he thinks into what he thinks he knows?

This task of both making and undermining distinctions is one that some philosophers have set themselves, and Sartre attempts it in his essay "What Is Writing?"[1] What is involved is the making of distinctions in such a way that they are exhibited as an order of related distinctions; so that what is significant is not the bindingness or pertinence of any one distinction but rather the revelation of a gamut, the theoretical awareness, or vision, of the nature of an ongoing process. It is a sundering and a connecting at one and the same time, in the interests of both the divisiveness of truth and the wholeness of being.

Sartre begins his study of literature by commenting upon the various arts. Like Gotthold Ephraim Lessing, he reminds us that they are indeed different and that their functions cannot be assimilated one to another. It follows that the demands made upon the writer ought not to be the same as those made upon the musician or the painter. There is no parallel, Sartre says.

> It is one thing to work with color and sound, and another to express oneself by means of words. Notes, colors, and forms are not signs. They refer to nothing exterior to themselves.[2]

And so we have our first, basic distinction. There are words that point to things beyond themselves (signs that signify) and there are colors and sounds, sensations that simply are. "There is green, there is red, and that is all. They are things, they exist by themselves."[3]

But almost immediately Sartre begins to lead us beyond the crudity of this first proposal. He qualifies his distinction practically in the same breath that he makes it:

> To be sure, it is quite impossible to reduce [tones and colors] strictly
> to themselves, and the idea of a pure sound, for example, is an ab-
> straction. As Merleau-Ponty has pointed out in *The Phenomenology
> of Perception*, there is no quality of sensation so bare that it is not
> penetrated with signification. But the dim little meaning which dwells
> within it, a light joy, a timid sadness, remains immanent or trembles
> about it like a heat mist; it *is* color or sound. Who can distinguish the
> green apple from its tart gaiety? And aren't we already saying too
> much in naming "the tart gaiety of the green apple?" There is green,
> there is red, and that is all. They are things, they exist by themselves.[4]

So Sartre subtly undermines his own distinction by taking with one
hand what he has given with the other. There is green, a thing, but also
green-gaiety, another thing. There is never complete absence of signification; there are "dim little meanings" that attach to sensations; these
meanings both are and are not one with the sensations they are linked
to. Who, Sartre asks, can distinguish the green apple from its tart gaiety?
I, you, Sartre can; anybody can who is able to discriminate meanings.
But to do so is to lose the sense in which these things are, and perhaps
ought to be, experienced undiscriminated. It is to lose the sense in which
they can be brought together and fused in the unity of metaphor.

Sartre gives other examples where meanings abound, or are fused
with, sensations:

> Tintoretto did not choose that yellow rift in the sky above Golgotha
> to *signify* anguish or to *provoke* it. It is anguish and yellow sky at the
> same time. Not sky of anguish or anguished sky; it is an anguish
> become thing, an anguish which has turned into yellow rift of sky,
> and which thereby is submerged and impasted by the proper quali-
> ties of things, by their impermeability, their extension, their blind
> permanence, their externality, and that infinity of relations which
> they maintain with other things.[5]

And we are reminded that the same applies to music:

> Similarly, the signification of a melody—if one can still speak of
> signification—is nothing outside of the melody itself, unlike ideas,
> which can be adequately rendered in several ways.[6]

After providing a number of instances of emotions (or ideas) that are
conjoined with, or incorporated into, colors, shapes and sounds, Sartre

falls back, by way of initial summary, on his primary distinction. Setting aside some of the qualifications he has already introduced, he says that painters and musicians create things and that it is the writer, the man of words, who "deals with significations."

But then, as part of what can be interpreted as his artful architectonic, Sartre proceeds to offer what we shall call his secondary distinction. "The empire of signs is prose; poetry is on the side of painting, sculpture, and music."[7] After having begun with a primary distinction— words on the one hand and colors, shapes, and sounds on the other—he finds in words a need for a further distinction. Words divide themselves into prose and poetry, and poetry is rather like the colors and sounds of the first, or primary, distinction.

In what follows, Sartre continues to operate within the framework of this secondary or sub-distinction. "The poet . . . considers words as things and not as signs"[8] pretty much as painters and musicians consider colors and tones.

> The man who talks is beyond words and near the object, whereas the poet is on this side of them. For the former, they are domesticated; for the latter they are in the wild state. For the former, they are useful conventions, tools which gradually wear out and which one throws away when they are no longer serviceable; for the latter, they are natural things which sprout naturally upon the earth like grass and trees.[9]

And so we see that although this sub-distinction is seemingly a new one, it bears a striking resemblance to the primary distinction.

But Sartre's analysis, his progression of distinctions, does not terminate here. He introduces another, which we can call a tertiary or sub-subdistinction. The words, even the words of poetry, are not so indivisible as was first suggested, and they too have their aspects or their divisibilities. For if the poet

> dwells upon words, as does the painter with colors and the musician with sounds, that does not mean that they have lost all signification in his eyes. Indeed, it is signification alone which can give words their verbal unity. Without it they are frittered away into sounds and strokes of the pen.[10]

In other words, even for the poet words are not quite like colors and sounds (insofar as these are regarded as atomic). Words, too, admit of and invite a further breakdown. They, too, have an element of signification as well as an element of sonority, a meaningful aspect as well as a physical aspect, a pointing quality as well as a thing quality.

> For the poet, language is a structure of the external world. The speaker is *in a situation* in language; he is invested with words. They are prolongations of his meanings, his pincers, his antennae, his eyeglasses. He maneuvers them from within; he feels them as if they were his body; he is surrounded by a verbal body which he is hardly aware of and which extends his action upon the world. The poet is outside of language.[11]

> Not knowing how to use them as a *sign* of an aspect of the world, he sees in the word the *image* of one of these aspects. And the verbal image he chooses for its resemblance to the willow tree or the ash tree is not necessarily the word which we use to designate these objects. As he is already on the outside, he considers words as a trap to catch a fleeing reality rather than as indicators which throw him out of himself into the midst of things. In short, all language is for him the mirror of the world. As a result, important changes take place in the internal economy of the word. Its sonority, its length, its masculine or feminine endings, its visual aspect, compose for him a face of flesh which *represents* rather than expresses signification. Inversely, as the signification is *realized*, the physical aspect of the word is reflected within it, and it, in its turn, functions as an image of the verbal body. Like its sign, too, for it has lost its pre-eminence; since words, like things, are increate, the poet does not decide whether the former exist for the latter or vice-versa.[12]

This is difficult, perhaps unnecessarily obscure, but close to Sartre's heart or to his fundamental project. In his autobiography, *The Words*, Sartre sees his whole life's work as an effort to use words as a trap to catch a fleeing reality. In any case, the gist of what is here described with respect to poetry seems to parallel what was described and distinguished earlier. That is, a distinction can be made *within* poetry as surely as it was made *between* the words of poetry and the words of prose, and as originally it was made between words in general on the one hand, and tones and colors on the other hand.

Sartre's analysis down to his tertiary distinction has now been outlined and skeletonized, perhaps unduly pared of its poetry and verbosity. There was the first distinction between "significant" words and "immediate" colors and sounds, the second distinction between the meanings and the immediacies of colors and sounds, and the last distinction which finds within words themselves poetic immediacies alongside their usual meanings. What is the upshot of Sartre's procedure?

Three terms can define a series, and three distinctions can suggest or generate a sequence of distinctions. What is argued here is that an ordered set of distinctions accomplishes what any one of these distinctions could not of itself do. Each distinction by itself has a certain naiveté; it dichotomizes arbitrarily and creates (or might be taken to create) an ontological division that cannot stand up under severe scrutiny. But the presentation of these distinctions in an ordered series of finer focusings takes the sting out of each one of them. Because these distinctions constitute an array, with the latter distinctions more refined than the earlier, the hypostatization or ontological division seemingly proposed by each one yields to a suggestion of a continuum or a gamut. In a sense, each distinction unbinds the previous one and removes from it its false force and divisiveness. The display of sequence and connectedness gives to the relationship of these distinctions a kind of significance different from what each tends to claim for itself. It is like the tapping of a series of different-sized wooden sticks; each by itself is a mere noise, but taken together one hears a tonal array and hence the tonal element in each. This structure of distinctions has to be put together carefully and artfully; otherwise the relationship between them, the relevance of their connectedness, will go unseen. Sartre's distinctions have such a relationship and invite, indeed necessitate, being taken together.

What is the further upshot of this method? First, there is the suggestion of a continuum between poetry and prose, but second, there is the simultaneous suggestion that we are never precisely *anywhere* on this continuum. There is not, then, a world of poetry and a world of prose, or a world of words and a world of colors and sounds. Poetry and prose are not even different kinds of words, but aspects or functions that are discernible in all words, or for that matter in all sounds and shapes and colors. They are the polarities that suggest a spectrum or gamut, and not categories or baskets in which things and words, paintings and symphonies, can be boxed. Any thing or experience we turn to or undergo yields the kind of distinction of which the three previously reviewed are so many instances. But only by exhibiting the instances can the kind be fully suggested and the continuum be stretched out and defined.

Sartre's method creates a continuum on the one hand, but on the other hand also reminds us that we are never either on it or out of it but rather in "double reciprocal relation." We objectify it, or detach ourselves from it, at our peril—though it is a peril we cannot escape. There is not a world out there, or anywhere, to be signified by our prosaic words; nor is there a world within, or any other where, that is closed, expressive, and poetic. This continuum, if we would understand and see it truly, is the perpetually "continuumable," our existing predicament, the abidingly elusive world in which we live. Our every attempt to distinguish two worlds, or two anything, does violence to or cuts off the further distinguishing, the further activity, that shall bring things together in their relatedness and wholeness.

Our intellects, our prosaic selves, our tendencies and capacities to use words significantly, keep sundering what is essentially unsunderable. Our poetic sensibilities, our tendencies to express the significant, attempt to undo the damage that cutting intellect wreaks, and they do this by relating and combining and reconnecting.[13]

We have seen that Sartre's procedure does two things: it suggests an actual, objective gamut between poetry and prose, but it also denies that gamut by making it internal to any thinking or experiencing. When Sartre turns away from his method of ordered distinctions, he gets into difficulties that his method had succeeded in surmounting. This seems to be the case in several of his qualifying footnotes and asides, some of which we now examine. In one of them Sartre writes:

> It goes without saying that in all poetry a certain form of prose . . . is present; and vice-versa, the driest prose always contains a bit of poetry . . . no prose-writer is *quite* capable of expressing what he wants to say; he says too much or not enough; each phrase is a wager, a risk assumed; the more cautious one is, the more attention the word attracts; as Valery has shown, no one can understand a word to its very bottom. Thus, each word is used simultaneously for its clear

and social meaning and for certain obscure resonances—let me say, almost for its physiognomy. The reader, too, is sensitive to this. At once we are no longer on the level of concerted communication, but on that of grace and chance; the silences of prose are poetic because they mark its limits, and it is for the purpose of greater clarity that I have been considering the extreme cases of pure prose and pure poetry. However, it need not be concluded that we can pass from poetry to prose by a continuous series of intermediate forms. If a prose-writer is too eager to fondle his words, the *eidos* of "prose" is shattered and we fall into highfalutin nonsense. If the poet relates, explains, or teaches, the poetry becomes *prosaic*; he has lost the game. It is a matter of complex structures, impure, but well-defined.[14]

At the outset of this note we have a denial of an actual gamut with clear-cut termini. That is to say, there isn't a continuum with pure poetry at one end and pure prose at the other. It is only for clarity that Sartre has considered, that is, invented for explanatory purposes, the extreme cases. (Odd—it always seems—that clarity results from discriminating the nonexistent.) The reason, then, for pointing out the pure extremes is to indicate or define a process of discrimination, and the pure extremes, the "ideal limits," must be understood as heuristic aids.

But though there is a rejection of the possibility of pure poetry and pure prose, there is a suggestion, or establishment, of two actual, well-defined categories: of one seeming set of words that is prose and of another that is poetry. It is not a question of purity now, but of clear and desirable dominance. There is the prose that avoids the nonsensical and the incorporation of too much poetry; there is the poetry that avoids the prosaic and the addiction to too much didacticism. These are not now pure or ideal extremes but the traditional and acceptable ways of writing.

However, if there is no passage from pure poetry to pure prose, since these are not places on a scale but ideal limits, how about a passage between conventional poetry and conventional prose? Is there not a real passage, a real gamut, here? Sartre seems reluctant to allow it. Apparently to admit of gradation between poetry and prose, to admit an actual continuum, would be to allow, for example, a midpoint where poetry and prose were in some half-and-half condition. But no: "It is a matter of complex structures, impure, but well-defined." Just how the traditional structures of poetry and prose can be complex and impure on the one hand but well-defined on the other is dialectically elusive. The very fact of impurity would seem to guarantee a real gamut. The evidence of many actual and successful instances of writing shows them to fall all over the continuum.

Paradoxically, much of Sartre's own writing is of the sort that involves a rich and evenly impure mixture of poetry and prose and does *not* fall into any traditional or conventional or easy category. One might go further and say that his own literary brilliance derives in part from the way in which he runs the gamut of fusions of poetic and prose techniques. It is this varied fusion, defying tradition, that enables him to generate both the feel of ideas and the significance of sounds, the prose that reverberates and the poetry that teaches.

Here is another passage, another qualifying distinction taken in isolation: "A cry of grief is a sign of the grief which provokes it, but a song of grief is both grief itself and something other than grief."[15] This is perfectly legitimate, comparable to R. G. Collingwood's distinction between the *betrayal* of emotion and the *expression* of it. But here, too, we can use Sartre's own analysis to undermine this distinction. That is to say, we can interpret the cry much as we interpret the song, that is, as a fusion of grief itself and something other than grief. A cry, then, is an incipient song, somewhere along a gamut that chooses to hold it as different in degree but not in kind.

There are other comparable quibbles that might be raised. We have already seen how Sartre unites the "tart gaiety" and the "green apple" and how he can regard them as indistinguishable. But in the same portion of his essay he goes on to consider conventional meanings that attach to certain things. His example is the association of fidelity with white roses:

> But if . . . white roses signify "fidelity" to me, the fact is that I have stopped seeing them as roses. My attention cuts through them to aim beyond them at this abstract virtue. I forget them. I no longer pay attention to their mossy abundance, to their sweet stagnant odor. I have not even perceived them. That means that I have not behaved like an artist.[16]

Now this tendency or direction is certainly possible. The white roses can become rich in signification and minimal in importance with respect to color, shape, odor, and so on. In Sartre's own terms the flowers can become prosaic, functioning, as it were, like a non-mellifluous word or pointer. However, as Sartre's many other arguments show, the flowers as color-shape-odor and the flowers as conventional sign can unite and fuse in the unity of a new thing. The thingness of the flowers, then, will not be merely their color-shape-odor but these *along* with the idea of fidelity. (It would be like Tintoretto's yellow sky and the anguish it is at the same time.) The fact that the signification is conventional, or historical, or personal (and rather unlike the way in which clouds signify rain) subtracts not one iota from the *possibility* of the complete fusion of thing and signification. Sartre readily acknowledges this when he discusses the word "Florence" and what he calls "the insidious effects of biography." The word unites for him the city, the flower (the Florentine lily), and a particular actress of that name whom Sartre once liked. Here a private association, much more idiosyncratic than even a conventional one, submits to thoroughgoing fusion.

But again our intention is not to point out a contradiction in Sartre. It is rather to suggest the inevitability of contradiction if one takes his distinctions in isolation. Such contradiction is not a manifestation of blindness or intellectual error. It follows from Sartre's synthetic procedure (when it is his procedure), in which a controlled display of contradictions is his constructive method. The dialectical dilemmas Sartre gets into are more than surmounted by his own larger awareness of these dilemmas and by the way in which he exhibits and overcomes them in the subtle deliberateness of his juxtapositions.

Our caveats and objections, then, are largely beside the point, just as Sartre's notes and interpolations are sometimes beside the point of his original, methodical presentation. The sequence of distinctions accomplishes something that the mere collection of distinctions could not, and the collection inevitably has a dialectical vulnerability that the sequence does not. Sartre might have let his original sequence stand by itself, without belated qualifications and props and *ad hoc* arguments, which perhaps turn us from that initial and crucial sense of sequence. These asides and qualifications are like the filigree in baroque music. They can become excessive and can divert us from the basic melodic line. But they are quite acceptable and even desirable if we can manage to hear them as enriching counterpoint to their underlying theme.

In one of his notes Sartre writes:

> Human enterprise has two aspects: it is both success and failure. [This can be read "both prose and poetry."] The dialectical scheme is inadequate for reflecting upon it. We must make our vocabulary and the frames of our reason more supple. Some day I am going to try to describe that strange reality, History, which is neither objective, nor ever quite subjective, in which the dialectic is contested, penetrated, and corroded by a kind of antidialectic, but which still is a dialectic. But that is the philosopher's affair. One does not ordinarily consider the two faces of Janus; the man of action [i.e., the prose writer] sees one and the poet sees the other.[17]

There is a rhetorical flourish in "Some day I'm going to try . . ." and a pretense, hardly more than playful, that Sartre is not already deeply involved in the "philosopher's affair." One does not ordinarily see the two faces of Janus, but this is precisely what the philosopher tries to see in what has been called a binocular vision.[18] Sartre, in this essay as elsewhere, attempts such vision. He is, *par excellence*, the poetic man of action, the prose stylist, the philosopher.

TWELVE

ON BEARDSLEY'S "AN AESTHETIC DEFINITION OF ART"

1983

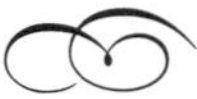

In spite of the stark distinction that Monroe Beardsley maintains between the task of philosophy and the artworks that philosophy considers, there remains an aesthetic dimension to Beardsley's philosophizing. The most interesting issue this raises is not with his particular definition of art but rather with his method and the issue of "whether writing about art . . . should be limited and restricted by a philosophical method which presses for the exclusionary tendencies of definition and analysis." Philosophy can do more than identify and eliminate false claims in search of final definitions; it can also appreciate the drama of arguments and counter-arguments. A reading of Beardsley that takes this broader view finds that his "definition and its supporting arguments cannot quite do what they purport to do. But the interplay between the definition, and the larger sympathies in which it is embedded but which it cannot comprehend, constitutes a lively philosophical dialogue. . . . Beardsley repeatedly qualifies his own precisions as his broader sensibilities and insights lead to a detection of the inadequacy of those precisions. But the interaction of these distinct but not separate components of his essay constitutes a discoverable aesthetic intention."

By bringing within itself what it had traditionally been regarded as logically apart from, art transforms itself into philosophy, in effect. The distinction between philosophy of art and art itself is no longer tenable, and by a curious, astounding magic we have been made over into contributors to a field we had always believed it our task merely to analyze from without.[1]

For, the Intentional (contrary to the doctrine of Romantic hermeneutics, for instance) cannot be transhistorically fixed once and, for
all, and both invites and requires (for its very life) the "response" or
"reception" of historically, variably placed interpreters.[2]

Aesthetics, particularly in some of its contemporary manifestations,
is the most ironic of disciplines. It is possible to philosophize without
having much interest in, or acquaintance with, art. It is even possible to
be a philosopher of art without having large sympathies and awarenesses of art. (Kant was in this case.) But, by and large, philosophers
have turned to art not merely to extend their systems but because of
genuine, and sometimes even prior, enthusiasms for the creation and
experience of art. The irony is that aestheticians have sharply distinguished, and sought to separate, the tasks of philosophy and art when
the connections and togethernesses might have been so obvious to them.

Aestheticians, after all, understand the non-cognitive, mirroring, self-
referential aspects of artworks. Their cast of mind is not so theoretical,
so merely analytical, that non-cognitive structures which are not *about*
anything elude them as a possibility. They have experienced and are fully
aware of the charms and non-rational seductions of music, dance, and
even philosophical dialogue. Nonetheless they tend to be horrified by
any manifestations of art in the enterprise of philosophy. They want to
put a paper curtain between the philosophical tasks to which they
address themselves and the non-cognitive or less-than-cognitive artworks that they write about. They do not want aesthetic qualities and
intentions to enter into and mar the fabric of philosophy—*their* philosophy. The art, then, that does not elude these aestheticians as experience
and as subject matter is resisted methodically (but not always successfully) in their deliberate philosophical intentions and choices.

Some inroads into both a breakdown and revelation of the irony can
be seen in the writings of Arthur Danto and Joseph Margolis. The former
has suggested, perhaps with some surprise and reluctance, that the philosophy of art is itself becoming art. But the irony persists and philosophers
of art, in some cases even artist-philosophers, have vigorously resisted
the notion that philosophy is in part an artistic enterprise.

Monroe Beardsley is one such philosopher, and his sense of a "philosophical task" carefully delimits what he thinks he should be about.

Nonetheless, the openness of his mind, even the artistry of his efforts, run counter to the precisions he proclaims. Might he, too, come to entertain the notion that the philosophy of art is becoming art? My task here is to deal with the irony of a philosopher of art who distances but does not quite separate himself from doing philosophy in the aesthetic mode. I frequently follow or paraphrase Beardsley's own language and try to uncover the "aesthetic intention" behind Beardsley's professed philosophical task. Philosophy, I aver, is not "becoming" art but has always had within it an aesthetic dimension or intention. Some philosophers are belatedly discovering this intention; it was there, and could have been inferred, from the outset.

My strategy is to direct various arguments at Beardsley's proposed definition of art. But my point (and more later about making points) is not to undo his definition, since Beardsley himself has directed the essential challenges to it. My concern is more with philosophical method than it is with the virtues or weaknesses of particular arguments.

Beardsley himself perhaps undermines his otherwise sure sense of what philosophy is about by proclaiming his "assumptions and biasses."[3] For if philosophy is philosophy, all that clearly and indubitably, then Beardsley need not have been concerned about bias. Beardsley immediately turns away from "further defense or apology,"[4] as though his personal caveats were non-philosophical and even unnecessary. For me, this opening, hesitant note about what is properly philosophical is itself properly philosophical. It is an uncertain note that is happily sounded again and again, particularly in Beardsley's critical discussions of possible artworks.

Could it be that a combination of biases, none of them eliminable, constitutes the enterprise of philosophy? Following Beardsley, let me state my countering biases. There are no clear philosophical tasks. Philosophy is constantly attempting to define philosophy, and a recognition of this as a feature of philosophy (perhaps its most permanent and endearing one but not its only one) is more essential to philosophy than any agreed upon definition of it that might be available or forthcoming. A corollary of such an assumption is that any approach that might give us some general insights into the nature of art (or anything else) cannot be ruled out in advance by virtue of conforming or not conforming to a perceived philosophical task. This exactly parallels the view that any approach to a purported art work, whoever does the purporting, should not be ruled out in advance by virtue of a prior definition of art.

I

I now select for comment portions of the Beardsley text—assuming that the reader has it before him in its fullness and coherence. For Beardsley, the task of the philosopher (I use his words) is not merely lexicographical or psychological; it is not to rediscover the ordinary or to reconfirm the common. The philosopher addresses not only the issue at hand but also what it means to address it philosophically. He makes significant distinctions for the sake of theoretical understanding; he makes decisions and proposals; he distinguishes what he defines from other things. A definition should "mark out a class of things," "fix a meaning," "establish it for some range of contexts."[5] The philosopher "should be curious to know what he is philosophizing about."[6]

Here Beardsley lets the cat, or at least one of several kittens, out of the bag. Philosophy is about something, and its concrete tasks are to find out what it is about by discovering and proposing definitions. What philosophy is about, according to this view, is something other than itself. Whether this is indeed the philosophical enterprise is not seen as a possible question, or as part of a search for a still uncertain definition of philosophy. Only definitions of art are uncertain!

The alternative I offer, pressing to the other extreme, is that philosophy is no more clearly *about* something than is a painting or a sonata or a poem. Perhaps philosophy is at its best and most itself (as art is, too) when it is about itself and about other things.

Beardsley gives some amiable and practical reasons for definition. "Should the dance historian deal with parades and with cavorting bears? Should the architecture historian deal with igloos and Macdonald's [*sic*] eateries?"[7] We seem to have to decide these things—but do we? Suppose someone wrote (and I presume I invent this title) "Igloos: The Frozen Architecture of the North." Would we decide not to read the book because of a prior decision that igloos are not architecture? Wouldn't we rather care to see what wise or foolish, profound or trivial, things the author has to say about the structure and history of igloos? What is the practical advantage of separating igloos from architecture? The case for such a separation might somewhere be ingeniously argued, and it might carry an aura of conviction. But should that close us off to the next arguer— perhaps an Eskimo with a Pei-like flair and Mumford-like sympathies? No, the case for practicality is unconvincing, impractical, and hardly even philosophical.

I almost see aesthetic intention (in the form of irony) in Beardsley's professed practical concern about "which important objects to exempt from duties."[8] After all, Beardsley asks, how can customs collectors know which objects are art and which are not? But would anyone seriously argue that that kind of decision will be based on the ingenuity of the definitions of aestheticians? To bolster the irony, imagine a customs collector, after having his hound dog sniff for marijuana, pull out a card with Beardsley's terse but subtle definition and proceed with its help to separate art from non-art!

Beardsley appreciates the difficulties and challenges of borderline cases. He repeatedly bounces them against his definition and confesses the dilemmas. From igloos and dancing bears he turns to the "art" of "medicine, of salesmanship, of motorcycle maintenance, of cooking, of war."[9] While we might want to rule out the above as proper examples of art, what will we do with the speculating, the analogizing, the aesthetic theorizing that explores the difficult connections, say, between cooking and the established arts? Has it not been fascinating, at least since Aristotle, to dwell on the differences between the tasting tongue, the feeling finger, and the seeing eye? Will aesthetic journals forbid such speculations and lucubrations even if they are good (and they can be good)? Will defining cooking and war out of art help editors make their practical and exclusionary decisions? Ironically, in banishing certain activities from the domain of art, Beardsley himself displays a genuinely art-critical interest in them.

Beardsley connects another practical need for definition with "which allegedly artistic projects should be funded by the National Endowment for the Arts."[10] The ways of funding in these matters are sometimes as strange and as unaccountable as the ways of customs collectors. I think, particularly, of how the National Endowment for the Humanities has funded "philosophical" projects that (to me? de facto?) are quite without humanist orientation. I wish that there could be a properly fierce, constraining, and dentilated definition. But decisions in these areas are not likely to be based on the subtle and ongoing refinements of proposed definitions. Such decisions are rooted in different kinds of persuasions and power ploys, in the arena where the art of politics (rather than the art of philosophy) is practiced.

Later in his essay, when he is concretely testing his definition, Beardsley takes to task two artworks or "artworks," and I pursue his discussion here. One work is by Cone, the other by Duchamp.

> I would incline toward generosity and a welcoming attitude toward novelty—but I would look for evidence of some aesthetic intention, and I see no reason to twist my definition to make room for something like, say Edward T. Cone's one hundred metronomes running down with nobody silly enough to wait around for them—even if this "musical composition" is titled "Poème symphonique."[11]

When do we twist by definition, and when do we make room by definition? I am pleased that Beardsley does not allow Cone's work to take its place even among second rate *poème symphoniques*. Away with the metronomes! But my questions are these: Is it Beardsley's definition that rules out Cone's "musical composition"; is it Beardsley's interpretation of his definition, which might be interpreted differently by someone else; or is it Beardsley's rather direct negative response to those flailing, failing, and futile metronomes? Can we say of those running-down metronomes that one cannot infer (that they are incapable of allowing one to infer) the property of aesthetic intention, as well as an appropriate desire and belief on Cone's part?

I am convinced that Beardsley does not like Cone's work. But might it not be more accurate, sincere, and artful to say so directly? Appropriate would be a clever critical piece, perhaps in the form of an extended and derisive sneer, in which the work is satirically chastised. Beardsley's dissatisfaction with Cone, as I read or misread his text, is in fact less an application of his definition than it is a gentle taunt. Personal unkindness is so remote from Beardsley's nature that he seems to want quickly to transform any such tendency on his part into an objective judgment, supported by definition. Finding such an objective correlative for one's feelings is of course an artful process, even if cast in a theoretical mold. But it is difficult to do in the case at hand. I am reminded of the memorable Dr. Fell who in the brief poem about him is directly disliked, but for reasons that cannot possibly he made manifest.

Putting the matter another way, to remove Cone's work from the domain of art on the basis of a definition is to demand of a definition more than it can possibly do. It leads to the exercise of power under the guise of objectivity, a more dangerous habit than the exercise of power on the basis of frank preference or antipathy.

We can directly share or not share, be persuaded or not persuaded by, a properly articulated expression of contempt. Such an expression, coming from a person and not from a definition (or an institutional use of a definition, if the National Endowment for the Arts had one) conveys the intention of being aesthetic and eschews pseudo-philosophical objectivity.

Duchamp's *Fountain* gets Beardsley's same short shrift. Beardsley claims that Duchamp did not think of it as art or as having aesthetic capacity, and that may be the case with respect to Duchamp's avowed intentions and the actual perceptions of the (first) jury. But that does not quite settle the matter. Beardsley writes:

> If there was a point, it was surely to prove to the jury that even their tolerance had limits, and that they would *not* accept anything—at least gracefully.[12]

Beardsley assumes that this point is external to the *Fountain* and without aesthetic relevance, but the point he mentions can come to be seen (and, I think, has come to be seen) as a (conceptual) property of the *Fountain*—in a word, an aesthetic feature. Furthermore, and following Beardsley, one can infer an aesthetic intention, and if that first jury did not make the inference, it is because the work had a capacity (again following Beardsley) that at the time they failed to detect. This ties in with a later observation:

> It follows from my definition that once an artwork, always an artwork. Anyone who holds that something can become an artwork

and cease to be an artwork will object to my definition, and be inclined to adopt an institutional definition.[13]

Beardsley presumably circumvents the problem of "acquiring" aesthetic intention. The intention is there or not. If *there*, the work has the capacity to satisfy the aesthetic interest whether anyone (Duchamp, the jury) at any particular time can make the inference or not. Nonetheless, including the word "capacity" in the definition, and thus giving to "real" art a timeless potential that might have temporal vicissitudes, still leaves us with the obscure task of inferring aesthetic intentions. What good is it to proclaim the eternal and essential nature of the artwork when this process of inferring aesthetic intention is apt to be so variable and problematic, when, in Margolis's words, the intention "cannot be trans-historically fixed once and for all."[14] Beardsley attempts to preserve the integrity of his definition by a characteristically rational maneuver. But the precision is gained at the price of the uncertainties in the formidable process of inferring aesthetic intention. The inferential judgment that a work has aesthetic intention opens all of the sluices and partakes of the general difficulties and subjectivities of criticism. Make the judgments and open the sluices, but let us be aware that we are doing so, and that we forever need to be timely and circumspect in the interpretation of the timeless and secure definition of artwork.

Beardsley's devotion to the changeless animates his strong opposition to institutional definitions of art.

> If some versions of the institutional theory are right, and there is an implicit or explicit performative act by which nonart can be given art-status, then it seems the process should be irreversible by a converse act, as marriages can be annulled, names changed, contracts declared void, cabinet appointments rescinded, votes overturned, priests defrocked, and so forth. But the notion of taking away an object's property of being art is prima facie puzzling, and the puzzlingness is accounted for on the aesthetic definition.[15]

Beardsley's litany of changeable things, some of which are deplorably if unavoidably changeable, provides (by way of telling dramatic contrast) a sense of his loyal attachment to his devoted object of unchangeability—the sought-after definition of art. We can only enrich this Platonic devotion in the ironic attempt to gainsay it. The counter devotion—to art as an undefinable and changing enterprise—is itself a Heraclitean attachment to a different kind of changelessness and fixity.

It is also clear that Beardsley wants a stable definition for the purpose of protecting the best art, in Platonic fashion, from the inroads of philistinism, debasement, and barbarism.

> It is this narrower concept that we must aim to capture in our definition—or at least *some* concept that will make a significant distinction and in so doing show us how to gather up into a single class a great many paintings, poems, and musical compositions and performances.[16]

Who would not be in favor of such a defining enterprise if it could accomplish the necessary gathering? But just as the cerebral ramparts of the ideal Republic have been ineffective against the spreading of latter-day banana republics, so definitions of art have little to do with what is coming to be foisted upon us in its name. The barbarians (creators of trash, kitsch, graffiti) have taken over and are offering semblances of art in the name of the real thing. So let us, with Beardsley, fight the quixotic battle of definitions, knowing that we are distinguishing the better from the worse only in the citadel of the mind's free fancy, and engaged in an enterprise that is both lesser and greater than any practical purpose. Beardsley is caught, like definers and artists since Plato, in a struggle between contrary aims: a moral one (to save the world) and an aesthetic one (to leave it for something better, or at least different). That, of course, is my own ongoing theme. Beardsley compounds the irony of his pleas for practicality (morality) and his concerns for excellence (art) when he says that he wants his definition to be value-neutral, not to exclude bad art from its provenance, and to embrace even "tawdry and negligible objects."[17] One recalls Socrates's misgivings about including hair and dirt among the Forms.[18]

Beardsley is at times constraining with his definition and at other times generous. He is so well intentioned and tentative with it, so aware of its "softness" and inadequacy for borderline cases, that it is perhaps graceless to belabor one's criticisms of it. But the larger issue is neither the merit of the definition (and it surely has merits) nor the merit of any undermining arguments, some of which Beardsley himself makes. The issue is whether writing about art, or the nature of art, should be limited and restricted by a philosophical method that presses for the exclusionary tendencies of definition and analysis. Such method thinks to withhold art from its own inevitable, and occasionally less than methodological, processes.

Seeing either a definition or a repudiation of a definition as "falsifiable" is to look at the matter narrowly. The larger and more generous philosophical task is not to eliminate or separate out the false. Rather, we can see proposals and refutations as part of a structure in which arguments are juxtaposed to preserve their visible contrariness. Such a dramatic way of dealing with arguments is a traditional aspect of philosophy and is directly connected with aesthetic intent. I conjoin it repeatedly with the dialectical way, which presses for elimination and the arrival of definition.

What, may I venture to ask (like the film comedian who looks at the camera, breaks the spell and comments on his own performance), is the status of the gathering of essays in which this essay originally appeared?[19] That some arguments in that book might permanently dislodge other arguments from any proper place in a coherent system does not get at the only or central or primary intention. The essays were gathered, side by side, for the momentary yet permanent display of their rivaling interdependence. As with the personae in more standard drama, there may be some wholesale slayings in the process—yet Hamlet and Ophelia live!

This applies to all arguing, which is why it is so hard to know what point we make, or what we clearly *intend*, by arguing. We can see any argument that repudiates another as a way of getting rid of or falsifying the second argument. But we can always infer that one of the intentions of argumentative repudiation—and I borrow Beardsley's words—is to lift our experience

> in a certain way that is hard to describe and especially to summarize:
> it takes on a sense of freedom from concern about matters outside
> the thing received, an intense affect that is nevertheless detached
> from practical ends, the exhilarating sense of exercising powers of
> discovery, integration of the self and its experience.[20]

In a word, we are not privy to our purposes, and aesthetic intention lurks at the heart of what the philosopher sometimes thinks of as his defining task.

II

Beardsley develops his definition of art in part by arguing (as we saw) against making "noninstitutional artistic activities impossible by definition . . . such as rural whittling and bluegrass music-making. . . ."[21] He writes:

> At least, we should want our definitions to leave open the possibility of new forms of artistic activity appearing before they become encompassed by institutions.[22]

This is laudable, but it is reminiscent of those who object to *any* definitions of art on the grounds (to rephrase Beardsley) "of leaving open the possibility of new forms of artistic activity appearing before they become encompassed by *definitions*." The definitions, for Beardsley, have prescriptive force, and there is indeed a linkage between the coercions of (private) definitions and (public) institutions. In proposing his definition it would seem that Beardsley is looking for institutional support for it in the form of a community of scholars who might share it—even if it never quite gets to customs collectors and the National Endowment for the Arts. Put another way, the furtherance or discovery of agreement in any group is minimal institutionalization. In any case, with respect to the possibilities of their exerting unfortunate constraints there is little difference between institutional and other definitions of art.

The matter of priority is less clear than Beardsley makes it out to be. He writes: "I see no good reason to withhold the label 'artwork' from art-production undertaken before or independently of a tradition."[23] But is any art, or any person, *sui generis*? Again:

> To define any form of activity in terms of the concept of institution, rather than the other way about, seems to be to invert logical order: how can we conceive of religious, political, artistic, and other institutions except in terms of the forms of activity that they sponsor and regularize?[24]

There is no logical priority, and a given analysis depends upon the issues at stake. A spatial sense of whole and part is inappropriate. Institutions can be explained in terms of persons, and persons in terms of institutions.

Beardsley continues his critique by ruling out the claim "that anything is art if anyone says it is."[25] What to me seems germane is *how* something is said to be art. Is the saying an external observation, a prior or subsequent comment that such-and-such is art? Or is the saying a live response to the living work, searched out with critical flair and uncertainty, and terminating in a discovery of aesthetic intention that Beardsley says we have to infer? So one kind of saying, properly by proclamation so to speak, Beardsley properly rules out. But another kind of saying, a critical inference that the appreciator can make, Beardsley finds acceptable. On this theme, Beardsley says that calling something art is performative

> so the sentence "That is art" can never be *false*, no matter what it is said of or who says it. Sentences that become true merely by uttering them can be interesting if there are rules to follow in uttering them, and hence some restrictions on when and by whom they can take effect. But sentences governed by no such rules have no point; on this proposal, the word "artwork" simply loses all content and becomes empty.[26]

Such lack of content and emptiness follows from Beardsley's sense of what a sentence, a philosophical sentence, is about, and particularly from the connection between meaning (or content, or fullness) and falsifiability.

But consider the following paraphrase of the above quoted Beardsley sentences: "Art works that become art merely by making them can be interesting if there are some rules to follow in creating them; but professed art-works governed by no such rules have no point; such artworks lose content and are empty." The point of my paraphrase, obviously, is to create a sentence that is manifestly false. Artworks might be undefinable, there might be no rules or definitions that govern them and their making, and still they might be interesting and rich in content.

What is the point of a *point*? Is it only to reveal univocally and to be falsifiable? Might not the point of a philosophical utterance be to satisfy an aesthetic interest? Beardsley would not aver such an intention. He gets to the crux of the matter by referring to attempts "in our age, to get us to cease to make any distinction between artistic and non-artistic activities, and between artworks and other things."[27] He deplores this:

> This effort, I think, partly reflects a confused notion that if we allow a distinction we will encourage a separation; and it is partly a confused way of pleading for a far wider range of artistic activity than has ever before been recognized.[28]

This may be the case, and there is such pleading. But it is not necessarily confused, and distinctions, in fact, sometimes encourage separations. Beardsley distinguishes, and encourages a separation, between philosophy and art in this current essay and elsewhere. I think he sees art for its lack of precision and rigor as something that can contaminate philosophy.

Whether distinctions separate or bring together, or perhaps do both, is a complicated matter. Beardsley points out that a single activity, "carving or dancing in a ring," can be both religious and artistic.[29] In making the distinction, Beardsley is right in noting that we do not prevent the "same act" from being religious and artistic, and we might add that we only discern that the one activity can have these two aspects or dimensions *by virtue of making the distinction*. But Beardsley distinguishes philosophy and art to ensure that the "same act" can *not* be both philosophical and artistic. Santayana distinguishes between poet and philosopher (in *Three Philosophical Poets*) in order to bring them together in a single great enterprise. One can distinguish the moral from the aesthetic, life from art, in order to keep them apart or to bring them together. The aesthetes have done the former, the moralists the latter. Santayana most characteristically does both. Making distinctions eludes any easy discovery of the intention behind them. It is an aesthetic as well as cognitive process and requires interpretation. The western world became convinced that Plato separated body and soul, and the practical implications of such an interpretation were enormous. Some Plato scholars assure us that he merely distinguished body and soul.

An ultimate and ironic distinction that always faces us is whether (1) to make distinctions or (2) to not make distinctions. We can make this distinction between (1) and (2), as I just have, either for the sake of deciding between them, that is, exercising a moral preference for (1) or (2), or else for the sake of displaying (1) and (2) as dramatic alternatives. This is the way of philosophizing for the sake of art, or vision, or Wittgensteinian silence.

III

I now move more closely to Beardsley's "terse" definition:

> An artwork is something produced with the intention of giving it the capacity to satisfy the aesthetic interest.[30]

Beardsley's appeal to intention might take us aback. He has claimed in his essay "The Philosophy of Literature"[31] that "The Intentional Fallacy" was not meant to distinguish between art and non-art. Therefore, if such a fallacy intruded improperly in evaluating particular works of art, the appeal to intention is not ruled out for Beardsley's task at hand—a definition of art.

I have already suggested in my discussion of Cone and Duchamp that Beardsley sometimes conflates the distinction between distinguishing art and non-art (on the one hand) and evaluating particular works of art (on the other hand). Therefore it seems to me that the problems of the intentional fallacy are perpetuated in Beardsley's task of defining art.

Here is what Beardsley says further about intention:

> Once we discover that people in a given society have the *idea* of satisfying an aesthetic interest, and once we know at least some of their ways of satisfying this interest, we can reasonably infer the aesthetic intention (that is, the intention to produce something capable of satisfying the aesthetic interest) from properties of the product.[32]

First of all, by referring to society and a general aesthetic interest Beardsley may be bringing in institutional considerations that he previously wanted to avoid. But more to the point, this is an unusual way of referring to intention. Ordinarily a person has an intention and this intention belongs to him before or while he does his thing. The properties of the product must either be subsequent to, or at least in a different locus from, the place of intention. This straddling, this move from emotion (intention for Beardsley involves desire and belief) to the property of the artwork is reminiscent (to me) of Santayana's definition of beauty: pleasure regarded as the quality of an object.[33] In both cases, emotion has an ambiguous status and the definitions seek to capture an elusive kind of transfer. The feel, the awareness, the sense of beauty cannot be broken down into the separate, "defining" parts, pleasure (subject) and art work (object), in Santayana. Intention (subject) and property of the artwork (object) is parallel in Beardsley.

In both cases the definition reveals a mystery by partaking of it. It is as though one were to explain a metaphor by calling it a magic power that teases unrelated things into forced togetherness, or an incredibly speedy rocket that allows us to be in two places at once. Our metaphors explain, but only metaphorically.

Beardsley metaphorizes "inference," which has perhaps always needed such enlarging. The word "inference," of course, is drawn from logic and involves seeing necessary connections. The other meaning of inference has to do with finding connections that seem necessary and convincing, that we think others should see as we do, but that cannot be confirmed by reason. In Beardsley's discussion, inferring requires orders and techniques of persuasion that go beyond logic and into art. Hence the need for metaphor, the combination of two perceptions or meanings. It is a good metaphor because it explores a primal mystery, an "astounding magic" (as Danto calls it in the epigraph to this essay), in which certain inexorable processes of art partake of and resemble the assurances of the steps in an argument.[34]

In a proper overview of Beardsley's essay, and by way of recapitulation, we need to see that the severity and narrowness of his avowed philosophical method is in constant struggle with his wider sympathies and appreciations. Whether it is an intention he intends, or merely an intention we find, his essay reveals the drama between his "philosophical task" on the one hand, and, on the other hand, a generosity and openness to art's richness and variety. The definition and its supporting arguments cannot quite do what they purport to do. But the interplay between the definition and the larger sympathies in which it is embedded but that it cannot comprehend constitutes a lively philosophical dialogue. As we saw, Beardsley repeatedly qualifies his own precisions as his broader sensibilities and insights lead to a detection of the inadequacy of those precisions. But the interaction of these distinct but not separate components of his essay constitutes a discoverable aesthetic intention.

The sharpness of Beardsley's philosophical method and the recalcitrance of the materials to which he would apply it illustrate a prevailing but gradually changing approach in contemporary analytical aesthetics. One might think it analogous to the sculpturing process. Ordinarily the sculptor is adept with his tools, handles them well, and even has affection for them. But they are his instruments, to be set aside for the glory of his finished work. Sometimes that work will show touches of roughness, and the visible effects will deliberately make manifest the cutting and gouging tools that lie behind them. The work might even be finished with reluctance.

Beardsley's essay presents the sculpturing almost as pure process. The sharp and merciless tools, chipping away at the resistant rock, are never set aside. No definition is ever secure and no clear shape is ever established. But the shaping activity, full of virtuoso touches, intellectual anarchy, and sparks of light, remains before us to be admired.

And why not—for there, too, are muses.

THIRTEEN

LESSING AS PHILOSOPHICAL DRAMATIST
On Nathan the Wise

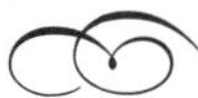

Gotthold Ephraim Lessing (1729–1781) is best understood as a poet-philosopher whose method went beyond reason, consistency, and system, and included poetry and drama in order to encompass a wider range of human values. He employs his method against religious bigotry in his play Nathan the Wise. *By dramatizing in the play the conflict between traditional religion and reason, Lessing aimed "to display, to reveal and to mirror the contradictions of the human condition rather than to disentangle and eliminate them." But he was not content merely to observe his subject, and he tried "to understand charitably, to render dramatically, and to improve morally." He thought the opportunity for moral improvement appeared in dramatic mirroring, which could reveal the identity in emotions and conceits among opposed partisans. An audience might then see particular arguments and resentments become less important in light of "the newly visible common structure of such adversarial claims and arguments." Awareness of shared tendencies leads to insight: "we move from ignorance to knowledge." The larger point is that dramatizing conflict is as philosophically relevant as analyzing arguments. Metaphor and drama are as vital to the conveyance of profound ideas as systematic thinking.*

I

Gotthold Ephraim Lessing was a philosopher who was a literary person—a poet-philosopher. For some critics this is practically a contradiction in terms or an impossibility. Such critics are committed to one kind of philosophy that stresses reason, consistency, and system. However, another kind of philosophy sees in poetic and dramatic art an alternative vision and avenue to truth, one that does not eschew reason but that encompasses other human values, purposes, and ways of being. This sort of philosophizing was Lessing's. It was his way of existing as a person and as a writer. But these alternate ways of doing or defining philosophy are strangely connected to the specific issues with which Lessing grappled.

Lessing's major moral stance was his attack on the religious bigotry of his age. His play *Nathan the Wise*[1] is both an attack on such bigotry and an insight into the reasons for its persistence. In broad but undoubtedly crude terms, Lessing's writings consist in large part of a rational rejection of traditional religion. He was in favor of deism, of a religion of reason, if not outright irreligion and atheism. However, his writings are also a rejection of attempts to see in traditional religion, in Christianity, only that which is rational. He defends Christianity against attacks from both right and left, taking his stance in response to the antagonist of the moment. In his polemics and plays Lessing constantly shifts his ground, working back and forth among various perspectives. Though he devotedly studied the rationalist philosophers Leibniz and Spinoza, his own dramatic accomplishment is to sustain contrasting viewpoints rather than bring them together into a single system. And in doing this he spontaneously introduces feelings, commitments, and moral purposes into his vision. The sometime mistake of a narrow rationality is to minimize the role of non-rationality in life, the mystery of it in art and religion, and the wonder of it in philosophy.

II

Lessing's *Nathan the Wise*, on which I focus, dramatizes the contrast between traditional religion and a religion of reason. There are arguments for each in the voices of the different characters, but these arguments go beyond logic, reflecting various kinds of passions. Drama often needs to be *ad hominem* and is as much a revelatory as it is a rational enterprise. In *Nathan the Wise*, the multiple mix of reason and emotion is rendered in minute and subtle ways, and the philosophical message *of* the drama (if it can be said to have one) takes us well beyond any statement or statements *in* the drama.

Lessing, then, is not *only* a supporter of a religion of reason, let alone a full-fledged rationalist philosopher. In the ironic and dramatic complications of his arguments with others, with the natural theologians, and always with himself, he defends traditional religion. (Christianity, of course, but obliquely even Judaism and Islam.) The Christianity he defends is no longer the incubus, the external dogma, of the Middle Ages. It is a feelingful subjectivity that men can create and develop for themselves. It is a harbinger of the kind of faith and truth that Kierkegaard was to further in still another major move into modernity. Like other artists and writers of the eighteenth century, Lessing was attuned to the century to come, to the value of Romantic and subjective impulses.

Kierkegaard, in fact, acknowledged Lessing as a great influence and the source of the idea of truth as subjectivity. And Lessing's reluctance to gain an easy, rational victory over Christianity can be seen as the existential, or proto-existential, element in his thought. Lessing certainly rejects old-fashioned Christian revelation, but he is wise enough to realize that the reasons for rejecting it could by no means undo the faith and sometimes the fury that often accompany it. And so for Lessing there is a truth of faith, of feeling, of traditional attachments, of subjectivity; in other words, there is an existential truth that cannot be conflated with the truths of reason. In a strange way Lessing, the rationalist, was discontent with ongoing attempts to reconcile reason and faith, to bring them together into one clear vision or "position."

One can easily extract from *Nathan the Wise* a statement of a religion of reason as it comes from Nathan. But that statement is conjoined not only with the Patriarch's distastefully dogmatic and cruel notion of faith but with other statements, even from Nathan, that qualify pure reasonableness. Nathan is something of an anomaly. While truly reasonable and wise, he still identifies positively with his ancestral tradition, with its elements of the historical, the arbitrary, and the non-rational. Lessing does not resolve these contradictions, he deploys them. Nathan (the editor suggests) is a freethinking Jew, a seemingly contradictory yet not impossible state of being. Lessing's aim is to display, to reveal, and to mirror the contradictions of the human condition rather than to disentangle and eliminate them.

To be a dramatist does not preclude being a moralist, and that fact complicated Lessing's art. He had a passion to improve the world and the people in it, not simply to see it, and them, as they were and to leave them unbothered. For one thing, they would not leave him alone. Since he wanted some viewpoints and behaviors to prevail over others, he took practical stands. The result is that elevated ambivalence that sometimes signals an exalted life. It involves the effort to understand charitably, to render dramatically, and to improve morally, though these impulses pull in different directions.

III

Partly to understand how Lessing accomplishes his complicated dramatic and moral purposes, I elaborate on the aforementioned idea of "mirroring" the human condition. The notion that the stage mirrors us and provides truth is an old one. The most famous reference is surely by Shakespeare's Hamlet, who talks of holding "as 'twere the mirror up to nature."[2]

The "as 'twere" is not gratuitous since the process of mirroring is not always simple and very often precarious. To see ourselves reflected in stage characters is often indirect. It occurs against resistance and through time. The mirroring, in fact, cannot be instantaneous. If we saw ourselves suddenly on stage, with our flaws and faults, with the precision and verisimilitude of a George Segal sculpture, we would simply deny what we saw and the mirroring process would never start. We would see a person other than ourselves, unrecognizable, and the drama would fail. The stage mirroring can significantly occur only if we see and learn about the person or persons onstage slowly and thoughtfully, with much feeling, affect, and cognition.

The resistance to seeing ourselves as we are, of knowing ourselves, is enormous and proverbial—a major concern of depth psychology. We are willing to observe stage characters and even to observe stage characters observing stage characters because we have initial assurances and all kinds of superficial evidence that they are *not* us. We are helped by their interactions among themselves and their slow revelations to each other. We only gradually come to see ourselves reflected in them. The mirroring develops in time, not instantaneously like a Polaroid print. We look at the developing character, fascinated by the image that is coming into being, without at first realizing, as Pogo's friend the porcupine might say, that the enemy is us. So we gain insights about those fabricated stage persons before there is any psychological need or impulse to build resistance. By the time the resemblances and significant mirrorings occur, we have succumbed to too many details to block out the difficult, the damaging, and the painful. By then we are made to stand in our own judgment and to discover that we, too, are part of the agon and that we, too, are on trial.

Dramatic mirroring works because we can look at others without the initial foreboding that we are heading for a fall, that is, a painful look at ourselves. When we finally do look inward, it is too late to look away. By then we are transfixed and, like the flawed character or failed hero, can no longer deny what we had once been reluctant to acknowledge.

IV

"Being-in-the-theater" is a special mirroring that sometimes occurs. It has been said of Euripides that his "patent subject was the workings of the theater itself"[3] and that he always suggested such mirroring. When we are in a theater we presumably know that we are in a theater, at least in a peripheral way, even when our emotions are absorbed by actions on stage. We are not like the country bumpkin who steps up on stage to pick up the heroine's fallen handkerchief! But the dramatist might want to bring special attention to our viewing predicament and make us part of the scene, perhaps for special moral reasons. By making the play work for some internal righteous purpose, as in *Hamlet* and also *Nathan the Wise*, our own playgoing status is inevitably italicized.

Hamlet expects that as the visiting players mirror Claudius's murderous activity, the "real" king, watching the proceedings, will presumably reveal his guilt. But what mirroring do we, as second level viewers, experience? Who is watching us and are we learning anything, or benefiting at all, by being in the theater? Consider the possibility that Claudius, wicked indeed but dense, might merely enjoy the play the players put on and learn or remember nothing about himself! Isn't that our usual condition at entertainments? To be mirrored requires effort and involvement, along with some suspension of belief or disbelief. Can we, watching Claudius, escape asking ourselves what we are doing in the theater, and why? Has Shakespeare set us up? Are we benefiting?

Both Shakespeare and Lessing, in commenting on the theater ambience, are perhaps similarly ironic about its usefulness and similarly probing in their quest to make us think about it. In *Nathan*, there are specific reservations about theater-going that allow Lessing to look at himself ironically—and that invite us to look at our own meta-level of theater-going.

In theater, in general, the mirrorings and moral lessons that are learned onstage, by the characters from each other, are compressed. They transform each other far more easily and quickly than they transform viewers and readers. This surely happens in *Nathan*.

Resistance in us remains considerable because of resemblances that cannot be easily stomached. The mirroring that Dürrenmatt attempted in *The Visit of the Old Lady* was resented by characters within the play. Also, there was a hue and outcry at the time of the publication of Shirley Jackson's *The Lottery*; readers could not tolerate the story's intimations that they and the characters shared the same tendencies toward cruelty. Ironically, the resistance against a literary work might mark the extent, if not the success, of its mirroring. Failed mirroring might be the measure both of a drama's moral urgency and its artistic imperfection. It could be argued that the mirrorings in *Nathan* are very effective for the characters *in* the drama, but do not leap out as mirrorings and moral lessons for viewers. The characters change rapidly and everything ends happily. What of the viewers of the drama? Looked at historically, Hitler was Pastor Goeze's revenge upon *Nathan the Wise*. Ultimately, Lessing failed miserably as a public moralist, presuming that his moralism was a large or intended part of his art.

Lessing himself is thoroughly aware of the difference between mirrorings onstage, what characters learn from each other, and what might happen to, that is, be mirrored by, the audience. He did not, in fact, have illusions about the didactic power of the theater. In *Nathan*, in his theater piece, Lessing mirrors some self-referential reflections about the theater and about his own precarious hopes. His characters advance morally more than he expects that the readers will. This must frequently be the case. (Tolstoy surely thought the same thing with respect to his *Death of Ivan Ilyich*. See Chapter 15, "Art and Death.")

V

Let us recall, before looking still further at *Nathan*, that the mirroring process, absent its layered complications, is what generally happens in drama. Thus, Oedipus presses his search for truth before he realizes that he is finding out about himself—and when he finds out, it is too late to stop. Meanwhile we come to see ourselves, or a bit of ourselves, in Oedipus. Oedipus (possibly) mirrors us. However, there was no one on stage who particularly mirrored Oedipus. In more complicated mirroring, the dramatist promotes the process in us by having several of his characters see, reflect upon, and learn from each other—as in *Nathan*. This mirroring on stage precedes, and sometimes expedites, the mirroring between those characters and ourselves. The mirroring has several phases, and they do not necessarily achieve equal success.

In *Nathan*, Lessing gradually uncovers the evil of religious bigotry by showing its prevalence, its near universality. He illustrates the attitudes of Moslems toward Christians, Christians toward Moslems, and both toward Jews. We get multiple mirrorings of malice, in which characters come to see their traits in others. The drama spurs the characters to probe themselves and each other, and finally it invites readers to reflect upon themselves. Do they also share the faulty human nature that they are inclined to attribute solely to the "other"?

The mirroring reveals that what is parochially right and obvious to one character, the vaunting of his own religion or beliefs, is exactly what other persons do with remarkably similar emotions and conceits. The mirrored repetitions lead us too to see that the claims, arguments, and resentments among people dwindle in importance, or at least in conspicuousness, as compared to the newly visible common structure of such adversarial claims and arguments. Our attention has been made to veer from our personal passions and assurances to an awareness of our shared tendencies, and hence we gain insight: we move from ignorance to knowledge.

The mirroring I choose to focus on here goes beyond mere bigotry. It extends to antagonism of a subtler sort—the more modern bigotry of patronage, of elitism, of "tolerance," of unconscious feelings of superiority. It takes especially keen mirroring to achieve this. The passage that appeals to me and that involves such mirroring is an encounter between Friar Bonafides and Nathan in Act IV, Scene 7. The two men have cooperated, collaborated, and developed a genuine appreciation for each other's virtues. They easily understand and share ordinary goodness, love, kindness, and right feelings. But Nathan is the wiser of the two, and since there is a connection between knowledge and virtue, he has a virtue that the Friar does not yet understand or possess. Nathan knows the risk of hasty generalization and of giving exclusive or parochial religious names to one's set of right feelings. He needs to communicate that to the Friar who, overwhelmed by Nathan's goodness, said:

Nathan, Nathan! You're a Christian soul!

By God, a better Christian never lived![4]

Nathan does not allow himself to be quite overwhelmed by the well-intentioned compliment. Indeed, he sees that good intentions and good feelings do not of themselves exhaust virtue. It is necessary to take into account how those feelings and intentions are named and how names can be co-opted and can even become threatening. It is necessary to do some reasoning about words and names.

Nathan had several options for his reply. He could have used a non-mirroring approach and objected that there was no need for the Friar to equate his sense of right feeling and human decency with the word "Christian," particularly when talking to him, to Nathan. But the Friar, though he is very good, is not very clever, and he might not have understood; even clever people have difficulty understanding this point. They will understand in logic that A implies B does not mean that B implies A, but they will not necessarily carry this reasoning over to matters of religious and moral labeling. Sadly, there would be no point in Nathan's telling the Friar what he would not have understood.

As a second option, Nathan could have directly mimicked the Friar's words and turned around the compliment:

> Friar, Friar, You're a Jewish soul!
>
> By God, a better Jew never lived!

Such mirroring might have made its point and the lesson might have been learned. But as educators know, sarcasm directed at the uneducated, even very mild sarcasm, rarely enlightens or teaches them anything. Often sarcasm and irony do not succeed even with the educated, else how could there be so many learned Yahoos after Swift? (I write this last sentence merely to reveal the didactic uselessness of writing it.) The lesson that sarcasm might teach becomes buried under the resentment it engenders and that might have elicited it in the first place. So Nathan justifiably eschews anything that might smack of sarcasm.

The third option, the one Nathan actually chose, is to mirror the Friar's language, *but also to explain the mirroring in the process of doing so.* Might it not be called a mirroring of mirroring? He says:

> And well for us! For what makes for you
>
> A Christian, makes yourself for me a Jew!—[5]

In Nathan's reply, Lessing provides us with both a mirroring and a lesson about mirroring. The immediate mirroring occurs in the two quoted lines. But the mirroring process had to be slowly and gently preceded by accumulations of feeling and sentiment, carefully taking into account the sensibilities of the person being mirrored. Dramatic detail must antecede gained insight; otherwise the mirroring would be futile, like looking into a glass darkly, or at a dark glass. A literal mirror, a non-metaphorical mirror, a piece of glass that is silvered, reflects everything and sees nothing, just as our callous selves sometimes see everything and reflect upon nothing. In successful dramatic mirroring we look, reflect, recognize, learn, and sometimes even change. Recognition, if and when it occurs, in or outside drama, always involves elements of resistance and transformation, a move, as Aristotle put it, from ignorance to knowledge. But not easy knowledge, gained merely by reasoning.

I have already distinguished the mirroring between stage characters and the mirroring of *us* in those characters. These phases sometimes come together, sometimes stay apart, and sometimes remain suspended in complicated relationships. In *Nathan* the characters are mirrored and morally improved, sometimes with more dramatic speed than satisfies credulity. Surely Lessing would have liked to provoke the same effects on his viewers and readers. But his didactic hopes, his poetic artistry, and his philosophical wisdom become conjoined and inseparable. In a scene of complicated theatrics about the theater, Lessing mirrors his characters' views about make-believe and the hypothetical, about his own activity as a dramatist, and possibly about our spectator roles as viewers of mirroring.

It is in Act IV, Scene 2, that Lessing provides us with what can be seen as self-deprecating irony about the moral function and value of theater pieces. He reminds us of the aforementioned "being-in-the-theater." In this scene, the Templar visits the Patriarch in order to discuss, in a hypothetical manner, the situation of Nathan and his adopted daughter Rachel. The Templar has come to care for Rachel, and even for Nathan, and does not want to expose them to danger by identifying them. However, he has real misgivings about Nathan and the possible obstacle Nathan might be to his courtship of Rachel. In his guarded manner, he wants to get information from the Patriarch before he decides what to do. This is the exchange:

> *Templar.* Supposing, reverend Father, that a Jew
>
> Possessed an only child—call it a girl—
>
> Whom with the greatest care in all things good
>
> He had brought up, and loved more than his soul,
>
> And who most piously returned his love.
>
> And now we were informed, the child was not
>
> The Jew's own daughter: he had picked it up
>
> In childhood, bought or stolen—what you will;
>
> The girl was known to be a Christian child,
>
> Baptized; the Jew had merely reared her as a Jewess;
>
> And caused her to remain as Jewess and
>
> His daughter:—tell me, Father, in such case
>
> What should one do?

Patriarch. I shudder!—First, however,

My Lord should state if such a case is fact

Or mere hypothesis. That is to say:

If he has imagined this, or if

It has occurred, and so continues.

Templar. I believed that was all one, if I but wished

Your Worship's judgment.

Patriarch. One? I pray you, mark

How our proud human intellect can err

In churchly things.—By no means! If the case

Presented is but pastime of the mind:

Would it be worth the toil to think it through

In earnest? Then I'd urge my Lord to try

The theatre, where such things *pro et contra*

Could be discussed with general applause.—

But if you do not play some trick on me

With a theatric prank; and if the case

Is fact; and should it even have transpired

Within this diocese Jerusalem,

Our well-beloved city:—then, indeed—[6]

The Patriarch goes on to explain why Nathan should be burned at the stake for the villainous crime of raising his adopted daughter (merely) with loving reasonableness.

The Patriarch is Lessing's villain and this passage, in particular, reveals his bigotry and hatred. (Recall that even the high-minded Thomas More, "The Man for All Seasons," had people burned at the stake.) Lessing modeled him after Chief Pastor Goeze of Hamburg, who among other things attempted to suppress Lessing's writings. Editor B. Q. Morgan writes:

Lessing resolved to employ the stage as pulpit, and to preach the doctrine of religious tolerance in such a way as to confute the bigots and zealots for good and all.[7]

That Lessing did not confute the bigots for good and all is a matter of history. And that Lessing had no easy and optimistic assurances about theater pieces is nicely revealed in the above. True, the criticism of theater and make-believe is in the voice of the Patriarch, the character Lessing dislikes most and whose opinions he shares least. But he sees to it that the Patriarch is seriously reckoned with; over and over again he is portrayed as a shrewd and effective arguer; he knows where power lies and how to manipulate it. The Patriarch's judgment of the moral importance or unimportance of the theater could well be sound and Lessing, in part, gives us a tribute to the Patriarch's shrewdness. In doing this, Lessing makes the most of any chance of a Pastor Goeze, or the likes of him, to see himself mirrored at all.

Lessing would certainly have liked his drama to make a difference. But he had no illusions that it would. By his ironies, and by his manner of mirroring, he frees himself of accusations of naiveté. It is not theatrical arguments, *pro et contra*, that make a difference in the world but rather arguments that are already manifestations of power and feeling. Nothing can be done if the Patriarch and Pastor Goeze (who actually referred to Lessing's "theater logic") refuse to listen, or if they can cause things to happen independently of the merits of arguments. Reason alone does not describe things adequately or cause things to happen. That is Lessing's ulterior wisdom—his theatrical mirroring of his mirrorings.

VI

Finally, to return to my central theme of the philosopher as writer, I criticize a critic who neglects the importance of Lessing's dramatic artistry.

This brings me back to my general observations about Lessing as philosophical dramatist. I now justify my interpretation and defend Lessing's procedures by arguing against a very able philosopher. Henry Allison's *Lessing and the Enlightenment*[8] has been a source of enlightenment for me, but there are some points of disagreement.

Primarily, Allison deals with Lessing as a philosopher in the analytic or dialectic sense, not as a dramatic philosopher. Allison brings a rational concern to Lessing that Lessing sought in himself, as we saw, and that animated much of his thinking. But Allison will not acknowledge that Lessing's status as a thinker and philosopher could have any primary connection with Lessing as a writer and with Lessing's non-rational modes of exploration, some of which we have just examined. A few examples of what I see as a rationalistic misreading of Lessing might clarify, or at least bolster, my earlier comments.

Allison discusses Lessing's speculative interpretation of the Trinity in *The Christianity of Reason* and *The Education of the Human Race*. As Allison explains it, Lessing is dealing with issues of pure philosophy and logic. The Father and the Son of God have to do with the self-contemplation of the conceiver and conceived, and then, "by a metaphysical tour de force, Lessing arrives . . . at the concept of the Holy Spirit, which he equates with the harmony between Father and Son." Allison goes on to say:

> Such a discussion of the Trinity certainly does not reveal any deep concern with Christian doctrine. There is absolutely no connection between Lessing's Son of God, and the Jesus Christ of the Christian Faith. This identical image of God is purely a speculative construction, and not the savior of the human race. Thus . . . we see that Lessing had broken completely away from orthodox Christianity. . . . [9]

This is wrong, or at least without nuance. It reveals the danger of isolating a man in his logic, and from himself, and the fault of not seeing how his philosophy outruns his logic. Lessing, the writer as philosopher, methodically intertwined reason and feeling, and his philosophical deliverance was the rich and changing dramatizations of himself. Lessing never could, or did, break away from Christianity, and in *Nathan the Wise* there are arguments about feeling, tradition, and human identity that indicate why one cannot and ought not to break away from one's past. That past is not something that can be entirely dispelled by any man's reason. It is part of the ongoing burden of a tragic self-awareness. As we saw, Lessing fully understood the power of words and the attachment to words. He was aware of the implicit bigotries that such attachments could produce and cognizant of their capacity to provide solace and comfort.

To see Lessing properly is to recognize that he does not expect words to be reduced to their fighting weights or their definitional clarities; rather, this philosopher-writer cares about words in all of their ramifications.

Philosophers who strive for precision and logic are likely to see only the merit of pure reasonableness in the philosophers they interpret. But, in their unpacking process there is danger of a narrow and insufficient mirroring. Allison at times fails to acknowledge the weight of words for Lessing, which Lessing did not neglect, even when he battled against the obscurities. Philosophers have generally accorded each other the right of stipulative definitions. Such stipulations frequently involve giving old words new meanings. If the meanings are clear, and if the old word has associations that are neutral or not inappropriate, stipulation can be harmless and inevitable. However, when we are dealing with words that have great power for good or ill—when they do service or mischief despite the proclaimed definition—we stipulate at our peril and foolishly isolate ourselves from more comprehensive meanings. "Father," "Son," and "Holy Ghost" are not neutral, indifferent ways of naming logical categories or concepts. Neither are hosts of other religious, political, and moral terms. Defining such terms as we will does not rule out enormous factual consequences that we might not will. We live in a world in which words are not merely counters that we can move about passionlessly. Rather, they explode at us like bombs. Lessing saw this, and, in general, the philosopher as writer sees this more clearly than the philosopher as "philosopher." The poet-philosopher works his way into words by unconcealing their powers gradually and by linking them always with people. He puts reason into a human setting, even protects its humanness, and incidentally its limitations, by his dramatic art.

It is germane that Allison, who knows Lessing so well, can actually defend Pastor Goeze's charge that Lessing engaged in "theater logic." Recall that Lessing also defended Goeze's charge of "theater logic" in the person of the Patriarch. However, Lessing did this ironically, as a mode of mirrored insight, not in a state of self-contradiction or in a mode of ignorance. Here is what Allison says:

> When Lessing became a theologian, or "amateur in theology" he
> never ceased being a dramatist, and this must be kept in mind if one
> is to understand his theological polemic. Self-confessedly not a sys-

tematic thinker, he often plays with ideas . . . simply because they offer interesting dramatic alternatives to the views which he is attacking, and it is largely because of this, as well as the fact that many of his profound ideas are clothed in metaphor, that he has so often been misunderstood.[10]

But who is it that misunderstands? My own essential point, and I make it again, is that the philosopher cannot be disentangled from the writer and that being a dramatist was Lessing's way of philosophizing. Allison assumes that the alternative to systematic thinking (to what *he* understands as philosophy) is play and risky metaphor. Metaphor, to be sure, does not necessarily clothe profound ideas, but neither is it necessarily independent of profound ideas; metaphor and drama are the occasional ways through which certain profound ideas are expressed, albeit not the profound ideas of systematic thinking. If Lessing has so often been misunderstood, it is possibly because of the misguided search for system and consistency in his writings. Allison is in the anomalous predicament of searching and not finding, and yet he sees everything that is there. He uncovers chunks and moments of consistency and is usually careful not to attribute to Lessing more than he finds. But what Allison cannot acknowledge is that a dramatic vision is at the heart of Lessing's profundity and remains his most pervasive philosophical gift.

There is some unwitting drama in Allison's changing approaches to Lessing. On the one hand, he refers to Lessing's playfulness and drama; on the other hand, he can say at one point that Lessing's "apparently contradictory attitudes in regard to the various theological tendencies of his age were all manifestations of a consistent standpoint."[11] There is no such standpoint. Lessing's dramatic playfulness (as a student he was called "moquant") was of a piece with his logical earnestness, struck from the same coin. Allison makes many other attempts to save Lessing from himself.

> Like his other metaphysical forays it is more of an occasional piece than a systematic statement of his philosophical position.[12]

Those attempts are valiant and based on enormous attention to argument and detail. But if we choose to see the writer and philosopher not as two persons but as one, they are incapable of getting to the essential Lessing.

I cannot here resist a specific comparison of Lessing and Santayana, though such a comparison has animated this entire essay. At the end of *Realms of Being*, in his General Review, Santayana connects, analogizes, and metaphorizes his realms into the Christian trinity: the Father (realm of Matter), the Son (realm of Essence), and Holy Ghost (realm of Spirit). Santayana says, "This analogy between Christian theology and my ontology must not be pressed . . ."[13] though he presses it for some pages. He remains a Christian of sorts and an atheist of sorts, as was Lessing. And so what *can* be pressed is the remarkable likeness of Lessing and Santayana. Despite the different ages in which they lived, and their different talents and personalities, they shared a perennial wisdom about art and morality, drama and dialectic, and the nature of the philosophic enterprise.

FOURTEEN

LEWIS CARROLL

Pedophile and/or Platonist?

2005

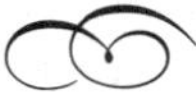

Lewis Carroll has been identified as a pedophile, but any final identification is precarious since identity is "simultaneously created and discovered in the critical process." One problem with identifying the celibate Carroll as a pedophile turns on what counts as evidence. Investigating thoughts would require distinguishing between thoughts of little girls that are intellectual—say, in the mind of an artist—and that are sensuous—say, in the mind of a pedophile. The distinction is dubious and designations based on it arbitrary; hence, Carroll might as easily be seen as a Platonic lover after the example of Dante in love with Beatrice. Ultimately, the real Carroll cannot be identified because "there is only the Lewis Carroll we can both honestly discover and freely create, in an ongoing process. . . . The distinction between [the two] is lost in the process, and blessedly so. . . . The 'real' endlessly precedes, follows, and eludes our best-laid plans and pursuits." Labeling Carroll a pedophile is not objectionable because of the negativity or falseness, but because of the narrowness and irrelevance. To honor Carroll's worthy accomplishments, as a Platonic lover would, furthers the best in his loving idealizations and creates new ideals.

I

Someone suggested that, given my title, I should have two versions of this paper, one for children and one for grownups. The version that follows is perhaps for neither—but for an occasional Mad Hatter or philosopher. This paper is deliberately without illustrations. I gradually discovered that it's about "unpictured" ideas, unheard melodies,

Platonic ideas, and a thoroughly elusive Lewis Carroll. So here it is—only words.

In recent years, perhaps because of the wider availability of Lewis Carroll's photographs, some Lewis Carroll "scholars" have become energetic pervert hunters. Their exaggerated interest in Lewis Carroll's interest in little (Liddell?) girls has become their way of identifying him. This has arisen not merely because Lewis Carroll enjoyed Alice's company and spent a significant amount of time with her—for which there is certainly much evidence. What has really provoked surmises of all sorts, and summary sexual indictments, is that he photographed little girls nude; even fetchingly naked. Could such photos, they ask, merely be the art of a pioneer photographer or was he not a deranged "pedophile"?

Many words and phrases, such as "obsessive," "compulsive," "eccentric," "psychically repressed," "pathological," "psychotic," "perversely erotic," "exploitative," and "sexually dominating" have been used to fix this negative picture of Lewis Carroll, and it is not easy to wash them away. One writer asked if Lewis Carroll's photos "emanate a foul heat of perverse passion."[1] This is an example of identity attribution, or identity creation, with a vengeance.[2]

What is it that makes someone who he is and not someone else? What was Lewis Carroll's relation to Alice? Was there a real Alice and an ideal one, and was either one an object of his passion? Were his passions—can we know them?—either elevatedly abstract or crudely physical? Both or neither?

To offset the above characterizations of Lewis Carroll as a vile pedophile, I propose a counterbalancing Platonic interpretation seeing him as a lover, but high-minded, abstract, remote. I am skeptical and tentative about both interpretations and juxtaposing them might help to underline the precariousness of easy identification. I particularly dwell on claims about someone's presumed thoughts. To study a complicated man is to explore not only what we don't know about him but to begin to measure our own limitations and prejudices.

The attention we give Lewis Carroll depends on who we are and on the sort of appreciation and enthusiasm we have. Our identities are as much at stake in what we say about Lewis Carroll as is his, and both identities, necessarily incomplete, are simultaneously created and discovered in the critical process. I bring no Lewis Carroll scholarship to my task, but raise questions about what I think is the occasional irrelevance of such studies. I focus on the tendency to bring hasty and narrow assurances where summary assessments of persons are not warranted. I look at some of the difficulties of discerning identity and of presuming to pin down a mindset—the contents of a mind.

Understanding Lewis Carroll, I suggest, does not depend on more and more accumulation of biographical and textual detail. Rather, it has to do with the kind of interest, appraisal, and critical scope that we bring to bear on what we already know. Human identity, if there is such a thing, is more voluminous than the discoverable. Approaching it is not a narrowing down to a name but an enlarging to a mystery. In some respects such identity must remain unknowable and is indeed as evanescent as a Platonic ideal.

Much is known about Lewis Carroll. However, much remains unknown, oddly enough, because of the way some questions about Lewis Carroll have been posed. The way we frame our curiosities, particularly our more curious curiosities, can make it fairly certain that we will never know enough to satisfy them. There is simply a limit to what can be uncovered about aspects of an inner life—even our own. Some Lewis Carroll scholars seem convinced that if only we trace a few more facts about Lewis Carroll, find some disappeared journal pages, locate some recollections, we would finally snare the man and discover his essence—his true Platonic essence, I might say, with deliberate irony.

Identity of sorts is sometimes fairly clear, and someone can be a bona fide pedophile—active, arrested, tried, and jailed. (However, not even the vilest criminal behavior fully exhausts a person or can determine what might be his primary or secondary designation—recall Ezra Pound: was he a traitor and/or a poet?) But it is unlikely that Lewis Carroll had sexual relations with anyone, so our concern here is identity in terms of what might be called orientation, something that is vaguer than what a person did, said, wrote, and even thought he knew about himself. One might then call Lewis Carroll a pedophile—as one might call someone a homosexual or a heterosexual or a sadist or a sinner or a Lewis Carroll scholar or a Platonist—even absent any overt activity that might guarantee the designation.

To say that Lewis Carroll was a pedophile by orientation it is not enough that he liked to talk to and photograph young girls, or even that he looked at Alice with "lust in his heart." That well-known phrase, for me, is entirely verbal and produces no imagery. What an orientation might mean, minimally, is something concrete. Suppose after long searches of libraries, purchases of private collections, and so on, we found that somewhere Lewis Carroll actually wrote, "Last evening I had thoughts of sex with Alice, of embracing and penetrating her, of enjoying her supremely. What excitement. My thoughts, my images, affected me physically. It was a white stone day." I would make two observations. First, such writing would be quite out of character. Second, if Lewis Carroll wrote it, or we thought he thought it, it ought not to affect our larger judgment of him. Or even lead us to conclude that he was a pedophile.

Some people are more detailed in their imagination than others. Lewis Carroll at times confessed to unholy thoughts, wicked thoughts, whatever they were. He may have had more wicked thoughts in one afternoon than some of us have in a lifetime. This would not be a measure of his wickedness but of his mental powers. Maybe something like the above quotation I pretended to find, much attenuated and less specific, was among his thoughts. Maybe the thought I attributed to him was more a vague concept of wrongness than an image of an action. As I will soon suggest, we don't always know whether we have concepts or images of actions. We all have countless thoughts, more than we can acknowledge or fathom—imaginable and unimaginable. There is a pervasive elusiveness to what we think is the content of our mental lives, and that elusiveness—which is mostly what I attempt to explore here—is relevant to claims about identity and character. Ergo, even the notion of orientation is problematic. So given Lewis Carroll's celibacy, would such a confession have great moral or biographical consequence, and would such a putatively clarifying text have been worth the Javert-like fury with which it was hunted?

II

I attempted to characterize a sexual orientation by assuming the presence of certain clinching sensual thoughts. However, we tend to assume that we can distinguish between sensuous thoughts and intellectual ones, or know which ones we are attending. I suggest that what seems sensuous—a visual or aural or even sexual reference—may not be that at all. The conceptual and intellectual obtrude upon the sensuous in ordinary experience and even in the arts—in poetry, painting, and music. We are regularly linguistic and conceptual when we might think we are concrete and sensuous. "Orientation" remains elusive.

Arthur Danto, philosopher and critic, wrote about Modigliani's nudes: "We are conscious of them as paintings, and only secondarily as women."[3] Countering Danto, I profess no such divided consciousness. I am conscious of a painting of a woman, or of a woman in a painting, with no primary and no secondary.

I am almost inclined to say that the above remark is nonsense, though I mean it only in the sense of non-sensuous. There is surely a linguistic sense—I mean a linguistic way—in which we all get the drift of the distinction. It is the kind of remark that makes a verbal, not a visual, point and does not get definitively to the contents of our minds, nor to the vagaries of how and when and why we see what we see. Does "secondarily as women" mean erotic consciousness? Would "primarily as paintings" mean aesthetic consciousness? Does "primarily" mean it dominates consciousness to a greater extent, or prevails over a longer period of time?

With respect to time, or duration, at least one defender of Lewis Carroll, concerned with the amount of attention he gave to young girls, pointed out that he was often in church. But where we spend time, what we are outwardly doing, is only a partial index of what goes on in our heads. You can think of sex in church, God in bed, of Alice and Boojums anywhere; you can think or imagine just about anything while listening to music, or attending a tiresome lecture, or reading a diffuse paper.

In Danto's distinction, it is his language, the relationship of the words "paintings" and "women," that determines what thinking we do. Whether we are seeing or thinking, or thinking we are seeing, we cannot separate out a woman from a painting of a woman, or indeed a woman from the idea of a woman. I can make these distinctions like anyone else, but they do not mark out a typology of my mental life. Nor can any presumed tally of someone's wholesome or noble thoughts, as over against his unwholesome or improper fancies, determine quantitatively a mental or a moral orientation.

In one sense thoughts do not matter. The distinction between doing and thinking is crucial for morality and law, and to think about sex or murder is different from doing it. But thinking, especially for some Catholic moralists, can have a moral dimension apart from doing. So further distinctions are needed. First, thinking wicked thoughts is bad because they lead, or might lead, to doing wicked deeds. Even the law sometimes looks askance, perhaps dangerously askance, at thought; nowadays you might be punished for possessing certain pictures, possibly Lewis Carroll pictures. But some mental activity, as Aristotle explained, is superior to other mental activity. Contemplation of mathematics, astronomy, philosophy, politics, is superior, *as an activity*, to contemplating murder, rape, pedophilia; even superior to contemplating licit marital sex, pistachio ice cream, and lots of other things. Lewis Carroll might be faulted for contemplating pedophilia—which he may have. But it led to no action and if he did contemplate it, it surely constituted but a limited part of his comprehensive and wide-ranging imagination.

Regarding the morality of mind content, I was struck by a review in *The New Yorker* by Anthony Lane of Tim Hilton's *John Ruskin: The Later Years*. Hilton wrote, "Ruskin's sexual maladjustment is not an uncommon one. He was a paedophile." Lane wrote, "Which is worse: to be a Humbert Humbert [I may have the last name first, but he of the Lolita connection] who seduces an underage female, with or without her consent, but who at least comprehends what he has done: or to be a John Ruskin, [he would have said the same of Lewis Carroll] who is guilty of no rape or ravishment, but who hardly begins to know his own depravity?"[4] Does Lane know his own depravity in not knowing which is worse?

To get back to Lewis Carroll's orientation, was he conscious of his photos primarily as art objects and only secondarily as naked little girls? Or was it the other way around? I can't clearly make that kind of distinction in my own experience and infer, presumptuously, that you can't make it in yours, and that Modigliani could not make it in his. Minds are mercurial and strange things swim, or are swept, into our kens. I also suggest, speculatively, that Lewis Carroll could not make the distinction in his mind, and so I decide, dogmatically, that calling him a pedophile or, as I shall soon claim, a Platonic lover, on the basis of some presumption about thought primacy or content, is arbitrary at best.

Imagine Picasso, who we all know was an aggressively erotic great master. Would anyone dare speculate on how Picasso was conscious of the various canvases and women he had around him in great abundance? Was anything primary or secondary? Can we divide him up, could he divide himself up, into a curatorial catalogue of his thoughts, specifying when he was the great master primarily conscious of paintings and when he was the leering satyr primarily conscious of women?

After you have the contents of Picasso's mind figured out, what he was thinking about and when, and have tallied the results and determined his orientation, try the same with Rubens or Raphael or Goya.

Some people deny the possibility of a simultaneous mental grasp—say, of the aesthetic and the erotic—without primacy. Some even insist on exclusivity—is it art or is it pornography? Why so? Some things, it has been argued, can only be seen or thought as an either/or and not both together—like the famous duck-rabbit. Why so? (I profess I can clearly see or think a duck-rabbit, not one or the other.) I can now clearly think about, without hearing, contrapuntal scales simultaneously moving in opposite directions in a passage in Mahler's *Das Lied von der Erde*. Neither scale is primary.

Here is a thought experiment, or test of the imagination, that might further illustrate the uncertainties about thought content I am exploring. What do you think of when you encounter the title of Freud's paper called "Dreams on the Death of Beloved Persons"? Or suppose I refer to the Oedipus complex—as, in fact, I just have. Many of you, I trust, will think of that Freudian theory without needing to resort to any concrete mental imagery. I asked a psychologist friend what he thought people thought when they heard the phrase "Oedipus complex." For him it was a concept—but his patients, he thought, would have concrete images!

The capacity to conceptualize is early in us, and it is enormous. The child discriminates the shape of the balloon from the color of it and soon knows what red and round mean. Shapes and colors, when alluded to, are in principle sensuous but they do not occupy the imagination as sensuous. They can become ideas or concepts. When I encounter a poem with colors mentioned in it, particularly remote ones like magenta, fuchsia, ochre, cyan, saffron, and so on, I have a concept of color multiplicity but nothing more specific. I know the names of some flowers I could not adequately describe or even identify.

This capacity to conceptualize occurs in situations where one might think it impossible. Consider chess, Lewis Carroll's favorite game. Proper play and imagining would seem to require shapes, colors, and boards, even if one were playing blindfold, as some players can. But if I go P-K4 and you go P-K4 and I go N-KB3, I know I am threatening your pawn, and Lewis Carroll would know it—without necessarily forming any mental picture whatsoever. Would we be playing chess? Could Lewis Carroll have been bothered by "unpictured" pedophilic mental activities?

In a piece by E. Fuller Torrey, M.D., and Judy Miller,[5] they wrote of skeptical and blasphemous thoughts that kept Lewis Carroll awake. They said that Lewis Carroll refused to let Henry Holiday, whom he had lured to illustrate the poem ("The Hunting of the Snark"), depict the Boojum. Holiday wrote that all of Carroll's "descriptions of the Boojum were quite unimaginable, and he wanted the creature to remain so."[6] This is a kind of reverse Platonism. Just as the Platonic good is unimaginable, can't be pictured, neither can ultimate evil, which is also very real. This notion of evil, to which Lewis Carroll apparently gave some thought, serves my theme of a non-pictured, conceptual object.

III

But now let us move more directly to Platonic love, with its connections to identity, the sensuous, and the intellectual. What is unique to Platonic love is its link to intellectual capacity, literary imaginativeness, and moral passion. And while Platonic love is out of fashion and not now much understood, confessed, or admired, it is not altogether remote from the ordinarily human. "We are often Platonists without knowing it," Santayana says in his *Interpretations of Poetry and Religion.*[7]

When Santayana says, "We are often Platonists without knowing it," I think he means that we can have knowledge beyond the evidences of things present to us, love excellences that are intimated and envisioned. We can conceptualize, move from the specific to the general, grasp ideas and ideals. What we usually don't know—when we are Platonists without knowing it—is this Platonizing impulse as a prevailing rather than as a partial passion, carried far beyond where our own ordinary human experiences and creative talents have so far taken us—and perhaps where it intermittently took Lewis Carroll.

With Santayana's help, here are some examples of Platonic love. Santayana describes how Dante, at a wedding feast in Florence, saw Beatrice, then a child of seven, "who became forthwith, the mistress of his thoughts."[8] Further, "This precocious passion ruled his imagination for life. . . ."[9] Santayana says of Dante that his devotion "was something purely mental and poetical."[10] But it was not an exclusive devotion for Dante who, like Beatrice and Alice, though unlike Lewis Carroll, married. Santayana says that for Dante, "the affection of married life seems to have existed beneath this ideal love, not unrebuked by it, indeed, but certainly not disturbing it."[11] So the different kinds of love can not only coexist, but can do so simultaneously toward different persons. Can we go a step further without contradiction? Can carnal and Platonic love be directed at the same person? Could Lewis Carroll have loved Alice, and thought of her, in both ways?

The tradition of Platonic love puts great emphasis on the physical unavailability, what might even be called the chosen unavailability, of the woman loved ideally. Little Alice would seem to fill that bill. Platonizing poetry was characteristically written to women who couldn't be wives, and who weren't wanted as wives or weren't available as sexual partners. Indeed, the prime sense of the Platonic impulse is to see it as a move from the sensuous to the intellectual, as both an ascent and a departure—not always a complete departure—from the person previously loved physically.

As we saw, Platonic love did not preclude some lovers from having other kinds of loves or even, simultaneously with the Platonic love, a conventional wife. This applied to Dante and his friend Guido Cavalcanti. Petrarch wrote to Laura, not to the mother of his children. Sir Philip Sidney did not write his sonnet sequence to his wife. Shakespeare wrote his Platonizing sonnets not to his wife but to a young man and/or a dark lady, and of course people speculate about Shakespeare's relationship to those persons. So Platonic imaginativeness and idealization can occur independently of whatever else goes on mentally and physically, toward other persons or even the same person.

Stephen Greenblatt, in *Will in the World*, suggests that Shakespeare was drawn to the stage because of his "love of language, his sensitivity to spectacle, and a certain erotic thrill in make-believe."[12] The erotic thrill of the imaginative, especially as it envisions moral excellence, is close to what one might mean by Platonic love. The same kind of erotic thrill appears in Lewis Carroll; it is conceptual, imaginative, intellectual.

Santayana makes these further observations about Dante and his marriage:

> Should we be surprised at this species of infidelity? [Santayana of course means, with much irony, Dante's infidelity to Beatrice.] Should we regard it as a proof of the artificiality and hollowness of that so transcendental passion, and smile, as people have done in the case of Plato himself, at the thin disguise of philosophy that covers the most vulgar frailties of human nature? Or, should we say, with others, that Beatrice is a merely allegorical figure, and the love she is said to inspire nothing but a symbol for attachment to wisdom and virtue? These are old questions, and insoluble by any positive method, since they cannot be answered by the facts but only by our interpretation of them.[13]

Not by the facts but by our interpretation—which is my theme. This insight might bring us back from Beatrice to Alice—and a look at possible similarities. Many writers distinguish the *real* Alice that Lewis Carroll presumably encountered, maybe the one he even wanted to embrace, from the persona, the make-believe or *ideal* girl that he depicted for us and even transformed in his photographs. And then how and whether he loved either or both of them, and whether such loves were mutually exclusive, becomes a puzzle.

"Real" and "ideal" are treacherous words in any discussion of Platonism. Platonic realism means that the ideal, the better, the perfect, the changeless is the most real. Also the object of the highest passion. It actually reverses ordinary discourse about the real and the ideal. It leaves the Alice who rowed on the river and became Mrs. Hargreaves, and the young Beatrice, seen at a distance by Dante, less than fully real. For the Platonist, the real is not the obvious, the first sensed or available. It is the discovered, the final, reached after long effort.

So the Alice that Lewis Carroll first looked at would *ordinarily* be called real. But might we not recognize that an initial image or impression of a person needs more attention to undo our possible blindness and ignorance? Isn't the real always waiting to be found out? The people we come to know well are not mere place-and-time sightings like the initial Alice and Beatrice. No, they are changed, sometimes slightly if we are neglectful or indifferent, sometimes profoundly—if the power of our Platonizing impulses can accomplish it. Or if you want to leave Plato out of all of this—they are changed by our conceptual capacities and moral, emotional, and aesthetic interests.

There are two philosophical, or commonsensical, ways of reckoning with this paradox of changing identities. We can say the people we know haven't changed but we simply get to know more about them, know them better. The other way, acknowledging that Platonic impulses contribute to our ways of knowing, is to see people, recognize them for the qualities that they have, but see them modified by the excellences they *intimate* and that we help bring about by our imaginative attributions. So Dante with Beatrice; Lewis Carroll with Alice. This way of knowing suggests that there is neither a prior unchangeable real person, little Alice just come into view, independent of us—nor is there an eventual person, whom we painstakingly come to know by our efforts and talents, and likewise unchangeable. What is unchangeable is the expression of intimated excellences and imaginative attributions, like the artful creations of Dante and Carroll.

Of course this presumed unchangeable Platonic goal has its philosophical difficulties; it is reachable by being defined as unreachable, like God for the religious. Such problems bother some thinkers, but not inspired ones like Lewis Carroll, who loved paradox more than he loved logic.

Let me compress the philosophical gist of all of this. There is no real and ideal, or metaphysical priority in the ordering of the world or in the way people are—there is ontological parity, a kind of equality in ways of being.[14] The Western search for the *ens realissimum*, the most real of things, is misguided. The person in space and time is real in certain respects. Alice was surely of a certain weight and size, made up of transient atoms, and must have tilted the boat on the Thames with her gravity. But Alice, full of childlike fun, playfulness, and smarts, is real in other respects and might have tilted the boat with her levity. (The swan, or was it a duck, who guided the boat had its own practical worth and identity.)

There is no real Alice and the same can be said, *mutatis mutandis*, for Lewis Carroll. Could we mean by Lewis Carroll the imagined creation of the real Oxford don, or the real creation of our imagined Oxford don? There is only the Lewis Carroll we can both honestly discover and freely create, in an ongoing process. If we think we have found him we have stopped learning.

The word "real," except for particular, limited, pragmatic, or comparative purposes, is not a useful characterization of anything. The so-called real, along with its opposites, unreal, dreamlike, fictional, imaginary, appear frequently in Carrollian scholarship, and to no useful or insightful purpose. If they were removed from such writing, as well as from all of philosophy, we would be less deluded and the world would *really* be a better place!

I have tried, as best as I can, to obscure any assured identity, even as an orientation, that I can give to Lewis Carroll. To float a further philosophical point, I would add that this is what significant imaginative searches are characteristically about. And what literary criticism at its best is about. The distinction between what we find and what we create is lost in the process, and blessedly so. That distinction and its obliteration are with us whenever we are mindfully searching anything. It is not possible to assemble a divine comedy, or a biographical sketch, or a tolerable poem, or even a well constructed sentence without fashioning and forgetting, such simultaneous searching and creating. The "real" endlessly precedes, follows, and eludes our best laid plans and pursuits.

And Lewis Carroll? Pedophile and/or Platonist? Without clear assertion or denial I would say, using opaque modern lingo but also recalling Plato on divine madness, that Lewis Carroll was "mad about Alice." Perhaps that phrase captures the ambiguities and uncertainties that are my theme. It clarifies only as much as can be clarified, and not more, because there is nothing more to be clarified. I think Lewis Carroll was mad about, sad about, glad about, bad about Alice, in a contrapuntal simultaneity that his prolific imagination could easily balance—along with a multitude of other things.

Beware, if you like, the claims that Lewis Carroll was a Platonic lover, but if Lewis Carroll saw Alice as beyond her true worth, his vision is at least inspired, transparent, and deliberate. But beware, even more than the Jabberwock, the person who sees Lewis Carroll as a pedophile. It's not the negativity that is objectionable but the narrowness, not the falseness but the irrelevance.

Selectively faulting accomplished individuals is mean-spirited. Selectively honoring and loving worthy persons, and adding extravagantly to their merits as Platonic lovers do, as Lewis Carroll perhaps did, and as Carrollians often do when they honor Lewis Carroll, may be fanciful but there is generosity to it.

Santayana somewhere said that the same facts in the world make one person a pessimist and another person an optimist.[15] The same facts about Lewis Carroll enable him to be seen both as a pedophile and as a Platonic lover. And as neither. And as I hope I have been suggesting, the pedophile-Platonic pairing is perhaps provocative but largely irrelevant to Lewis Carroll's art and his scope. He remains someone more elusive and larger than such narrow namings.

The same facts in the world will keep us discovering more about ourselves and speculating endlessly about Lewis Carroll.

FIFTEEN

ART AND DEATH

A Sermon in the Form of an Essay

1978

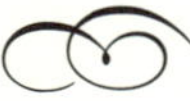

Despite the fact that death is often random and unpredictable while end-ings in art are desired and planned, comparison may be enlightening. Art shows how one may "consider closure and completion while we are im-mersed in a work," such as listening to a symphony and experiencing "rec-ollections and expectations . . . that prepare us . . . for the silence that will be." Such awareness may help in accepting one's inevitable death. "The point is to make one's death part of an acceptable prospect, in the manner in which one awaits the ending of an art work. A sense of artistic process must be applied to living experience; wholeness and direction must be felt as part of an ongoing project." This entails regarding life "not as a triumph of persistence, . . . but as an experience with contour, purpose, and wholeness." Tolstoy's work The Death of Ivan Ilyich provides an example in which the title character accomplished a difficult but not impossible "consummatory judgment that made his life whole and that foreclosed any need to defer death." This "is partly like an artistic recapitulation—a rec-reative survey that is also creative and transforming."

Death is the end of life. It is a bothersome matter, a source of pain and woe and terrible anticipation. It is connected somehow with all deep reflection and brooding. Death is life's end both in the sense of termination and also in the sense of purpose. All ultimate concerns, all attempts to understand, all meditations on life are also meditations on death.

Whatever else death is, or means, it is some kind of closure. It is usually rude and random and unpredictable. When purposeful, as in suicide, it is likely an act of desperation, an act of evasion rather than of fulfillment. Reconciliation to death is difficult; death is usually untimely closure—feared, begrudged, resented.

Why is this so? Why are some closures in life so different from the closure *of* life? Art provides us with experiences where closures in life are timely and satisfying, where endings are proper parts of structures, and where there is fittingness in such endings. After Oedipus has discovered all that there is to know about himself, all that is germane to his search, the drama of Oedipus clearly ends—though in this case his life doesn't, his sorrows continue, and Sophocles has the chorus offer a brief summary lesson. When Bach returns to his theme in his long *Goldberg Variations*, we know that the beginning, literally recapitulated but transfigured in its effects, is also his ending. Termination in art is not a cutting off, a rude interruption. It is a desired and appropriate stop. If death could be seen, could be undergone, in the same way as stoppages in art, it would lose its sting. What we propose here is not quite an attempt to undo death's sting—which might be the whole art of life—but to examine an aspect of the relationship between art and life, that is, the relationship between endings of art and endings of life. The comparison could help us to understand why death both invites and evades analogy to closure in art.

We will consider, first, two ways of examining closure in art. The one way is the retrospective regard, the postmortem analysis, for which there can be no analogy to the experience of dying and which cannot serve our needs here. The other way is artistic anticipation of closure, the ending as aesthetically experienced and undergone. It is this perspective that serves our comparison, for closures anticipated and approached, as experienced in art, can have cultivable life equivalents. Secondly, to illustrate and exemplify our points, we will discuss at some length a particular work of art, Tolstoy's *The Death of Ivan Ilyich*, in which the closures of both art and life are peculiarly related and intertwined so that each serves as a kind of paradigm for the other.

Termination in art, as we have suggested, is not an improper interruption of something that we feel should continue. Such termination is a desirable and appropriate stop. The end of tragedy is such, as Aristotle tells us, that it follows something but nothing has to follow it. Closure in art is not the death of an art work, in any invidious or painful sense, but a requirement. The subsequent silence is not part of a symphony, but it would not be *a* symphony, *a* work of art, if it were not followed by such silence and perhaps then by *an* other symphony. Beethoven somewhere has a fermata over a rest at the *end* of a composition, as though to confirm, indeed to prolong, the contrasting silence that surrounds every musical work. The unity of an art work requires that it not be interminable, that it exist in a context which is other than itself and from which it has been extricated. Art draws from life, selects and omits, includes and excludes, above all, comes to a stop before life comes to a stop. The unity of art, the acceptance of its termination, is apprehended in part in terms of the disordered, the non-unified other—or at least the less-unified surrounding life out of which the art work emerges.

It follows, from this first way of looking at the matter, that the unity and finality of art are qualities that depend, temporally, upon an extra-artistic perspective. It is the silence *after* the symphony and the retrospective judgment that is thereby made possible that confirm the unity and finality. We are no longer, strictly speaking, experiencing the art work when such retrospective judgment is made. This kind of looking and listening, this tendency, is particularly strong in the person with an art-historical cast of mind, for whom long accretions of judgment and scholarship surround a work, and for whom the distant assessment, rather than the living enjoyment, is paramount.

But life has no context for the liver of it, and one cannot conduct one's own postmortem. This suggests another way of reflecting on endings of art, a way that is germane to a possible analogy with the ending of life. This way is to consider closure and completion while we are immersed in a work. As we attend to the latter portions of a symphony or a tragedy there are recollections and expectations, discoveries and directions, that prepare us quite reliably for the silence that will be. They are only directions and intimations while they occur, but they have much intentionality and definitiveness, and eventual terminations, when art is good, cap and confirm clear expectations. So we know and accept an ending by awaiting it well; we experience it in advance of its arrival by the manner in which it has been prepared. It is truly accepted and experienced insofar as correct anticipation is not thwarted.

If dying can have any connection with art it is in this second sense of ending, of immersion in a process whose termination is anticipated and accepted before it literally occurs. The point is to make one's death part of an acceptable prospect, in the manner in which one awaits the ending of an art work. A sense of artistic process must be applied to living experience; wholeness and direction must be felt as part of an ongoing project.

It is not easy to bring to life, particularly to its later phases, the kinds of anticipations and reconciliations we experience vicariously during the last act of a tragedy or the last movement of a symphony. But that life is longer and harder than art does not preclude the possibility of some proximate success. Primarily we have to think about life not as a triumph of persistence, as seriatim joys projected into an indefinite future, but as an experience with contour, purpose, and wholeness. The desire for indefinite persistence is pathetic and understandable; it is an irrational, even an unconscious, thrust after meaningful organization in the face of felt meaninglessness. Where there is a felt absence of structure and direction, then the adding of more detail, mere accumulation of material, becomes a desperate and futile purpose. But every attempt to conceive of excellence, even of joy, in terms of infinite persistence (see Kierkegaard's "aesthetic" stage) collapses under the necessary intellectual scrutiny. This scrutiny is seldom undertaken and meets with enormous resistance. We tend to remain, even late in life, on the nether side of life's suitable organization or assessment, and hence uncomfortable at the prospect of its end. We are like the artist with his first draft, who, when his story doesn't fall into place, thinks to add more material rather than to reorder what is already to hand. But while incipient structures sometimes require more material and detail to flesh them out properly, available material and detail can acquire structure by suitable efforts at seeing and accepting. Right composure and right judgment can accomplish completions of any works and lives in progress.

We turn now to a work of fiction, Tolstoy's *The Death of Ivan Ilyich*, to elaborate certain connections between the ways art and life end. Certain unique qualities of this story make it peculiarly suitable for shedding light on the relationship we have been exploring. For Ivan fully succeeds in what has been called "the art of holy dying," and Tolstoy tells us that "everything that was necessary had been accomplished."[1] Ivan's painful terminal illness precipitates an extraordinary examination of conscience, which in turn produces a conversion and an acceptance of death. Tolstoy does not suggest that Ivan's accomplishment is easy, nor does he suggest (as we shall see) that other characters will do in turn what Ivan did. They will evade Ivan's death and they will continue to evade their own. It is not by seeing other men die, or by reading about the deaths of other men, that the necessary transformations occur. Most men die badly, without ever examining their lives or accomplishing a reconciliation. Ivan's death is the exception that proves the rule. It suggests the possible, not the habitual.

The Death of Ivan Ilyich is so constructed that the death of Ivan coincides with the end of the story. The death of a hero usually comes at a story's end, but not so exactly and precisely as in this one. The last lines are: " 'Death is finished,' he said to himself. 'It is no more!' He drew in a breath, stopped in the midst of a sigh, stretched out, and died."[2] The overlapping, the concurrence, of Ivan's death with the story's end allows for no epilogue, no summaries by other characters, extenuations, or moral lessons. To be sure, Ivan will lie in his casket as a warning to the living; his friends will come to his wake and try hard to ignore what Ivan has learned. This must, of course, happen after Ivan dies, but in terms of the construction of the story it is put at the beginning. To accomplish more powerful artistic closure, Tolstoy begins his story with Ivan's wake, and then resorts to a flashback to lead us to Ivan's death.

Let us dwell on this and on the implications of this artistic procedure. The story, we know, went through several preliminary versions before it received its final form. In one version the narrator is a colleague of Ivan's who responds to Ivan's diary. The diary is given him after Ivan's death by his widow. In this version the narrator writes: "It is impossible, absolutely impossible, to live as I have lived, as I live, and as we all live. I realized that as a result of the death of an acquaintance of mine, Ivan Ilyich, and of the diary he left behind."[3] This is a remarkable statement in view of the final version of the story and of Tolstoy's depiction of Ivan's colleagues in that version. Tolstoy underwent a change of judgment that had to do both with the very meaning of the story and consequently with the distribution of its parts and the ending it finally acquired. In the definitive version, there is no diary, and the response to Ivan's death is put at the beginning. In this beginning, at the wake, Ivan's wife and colleagues evade the meanings and insights that Ivan acquired during the course of his illness. Nobody says anything along the lines of the above quotation, for it is quite clear that they will continue to live as they have lived, badly, like Ivan before his illness, and unheedful of Ivan's painfully acquired insights. And so the natural end of the story is not in any lessons learned by Ivan's colleagues after Ivan's death. Though Tolstoy the moralist would have liked them to learn such lessons, he was too much of a realist and an artist to think that they would. Such a glorious moral ending would have been a lie, or at best an expression of a sermonizing hope. So the reaction to Ivan's death is put at the beginning, and the postmortem review that we are given is calculatedly unemotional, evasive, and outside the decisive experience of dying. What matters, the ending that matters, is the actual dying and the coercive reconciliations produced by the manner of it. The evasiveness of Ivan's colleagues figures in the story as something comparable to Ivan's own evasiveness, something he has to overcome before accepting his death. So though it is out of chronological order, it is appropriate to put the reaction to Ivan's death before Ivan's death. The story's artistic closure is improved by being made to coincide with the description and occurrence of Ivan's death, not with the evasive, inconclusive, and necessarily endless responses of those who remain alive.

Thus Tolstoy strengthened the ending of his story by some rearrangement of parts. Artistic closure was better with an account of Ivan's conversion and death than it would have been if there were subsequent inconsequential responses. Chronology was altered to accomplish this artistic improvement. Ivan himself, a character, a "living" man and not an artist, cannot alter or rearrange the life he has led. He cannot strike out any moments that he has lived or any of the meaninglessness he has experienced. What he could do, what he did do, was accomplish a consummatory judgment that made his life whole and that foreclosed any need to defer death. This judgmental and transforming process, this coming to terms with oneself, is partly like an artistic recapitulation—a recreative survey that is also creative and transforming. This is always possible in life, for Ivan or anyone else, so that we can try to say with him, amid the very tensions of reconstruction and reconciliation, that death is finished.

Ivan's death, we have agreed, is an idealization of what death usually is, a sort of holy dying that rarely occurs in actuality. Such merging of reflection and finality, of insight and choice, tends to elude life as it is lived. Santayana writes:

> There are times, although rare, when men are noble in the very moment of passion: when that passion is not unqualified, but already mastered by reflection and leveled with truth. Then the experience is itself the tragedy, and no poet is needed to make it beautiful in representation, since the sufferer has been an artist himself, and has molded what he has endured. But usually these two stages have to be successive: first we suffer, afterwards we sing. An interval is necessary to make feeling presentable, and subjugate it to that form in which alone it is beautiful.[4]

Good dying is difficult because, as Santayana also says in the same passage:

> There is no noble sorrow except in a noble mind, because what is noble is the reaction upon sorrow, the attitude of the man in its presence, the language in which he clothes it, the associations with which he surrounds it, and the fine affections and impulses which shine through it. Only by suffusing some sinister experience with this moral light, as a poet may do who carries that light within him, can we raise misfortune into tragedy and make it better for us to remember our lives than to forget them.[5]

There is consolation in knowing that the difficult is not impossible, that singing and sorrow can merge in a requiem that is our own. Like Ivan's colleague with the diary, in the ending Tolstoy attempted but could not keep, we may yet come to learn Ivan's lesson without all of Ivan's suffering—that to a life properly reflected upon and examined, death can be an acceptable finish.

I read this paper at a conference at which Charles Hartshorne also participated with a paper, "The Acceptance of Death." I met him subsequently at other conferences and always received warm greetings. I discovered only recently, during a moment of Googling vanity, that he had commented on my paper in one of his books, *The Zero Fallacy and Other Essays in Neoclassical Philosophy.*

> The supreme art is life itself. At the conference at which I first read a paper making this point, another speaker (Morris Grossman) also made the same point in his paper. (I regard this as an illustration of how cultural change tends to bring about situations favorable to a certain idea so that more than one person hits upon it independently.) The special point the two of us stressed was that as in other works of art, in a life there should ideally be a beginning, a middle, and an end. In other words we offered an aesthetic theory of death. In a life that is not prematurely terminated there are the thrills and vague anticipations of childhood, the mature plans of youth, the fulfillment of middle and (with care and good luck) old age. A personality is a theme and like nearly all themes, only a finite number of its variations can avoid triviality, unbearable monotony. This is also the objection to most dreams of heaven. Death together with birth, forms the solution of life as an aesthetic problem: new personality themes.[6]

Hartshorne goes on to discuss religious and ethical values and, reminiscent of Santayana, writes, "religious values are finally aesthetic." If I were argumentative I would suggest that others have surely had the idea of life as art, for example, Nietzsche. But I'm pleased to share Charles Hartshorne's stage with him, alone or with others.

SIXTEEN

BRANCUSI

Some Changing and Changeless Perspectives

1976

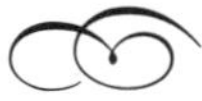

*Among artists, the sculptor is especially concerned with the varying impressions an observer has in considering a work from multiple perspectives. Brancusi in particular has created sculptures addressing the issue of multiple perspectives. "He invites us not merely to look at his works, but to think about what it means to look at them, and to envision in advance, intellectually, various totalities of perspective." The simplicity and purity of form in Brancusi's work allows "an intellectualized preview or survey of change" making actual change of perspective unnecessary. This results in "a kind of Platonic surmounting of motion, a turning of sculpture into static, cerebral art. If morality is a move from the sensuous to the cerebral, this is it." Considering three examples of Brancusi's sculpture—*The Table of Science, The Gate of the Kiss, *and* Endless Column—*reveals "a tension between actual perspectives with their empirical detail and possible content, and the envisioned, ideal, conceptual set of perspectives which require no ordinary experience or motion for their proper grasp." Brancusi's work seems to reach beyond his private experience in search of a "the unspatial and timeless idea beyond all perspective."*

The primary experience on seeing a sculpture by Brancusi is that of knowing it at once. Prolonged attention or the accumulation of a series of views from a series of angles of vision adds nothing or little to the initial knowledge. Time only confirms what the first instant revealed; time continues to reproduce the first sensation.[1]

One aspect of art that might be regarded as central to it is the process of dealing with or looking at the "same" thing from multiple perspectives. I put the word "same" in quotes because the sameness of things in an artistic context—or the sameness of artistic repetition—is always a sameness with a difference. Consider as near an identical repetition as can be attained, for example the visual symmetry of two side-by-side columns, or the aural symmetry of two identical notes sounded in succession. The repetition will introduce elements of relationship and plurality between entities that might otherwise have stood alone. The "same" things are different for being to the right or to the left, before or after, one another— for being seen or heard at different times or from different directions. Justus Buchler, in *The Main of Light*, his study of the concept of poetry, says that, "in the arts the analytical process most significantly takes the form of rotating a complex, delineating it in different perspectives."[2]

Whether anything has an identity apart from the perspectives in which it is seen or conjoined with other things is a metaphysical question I prefer to avoid here. I merely suggest that it makes sense to say that some artistic perspectives involve a great deal of sameness with little difference, while other perspectives involve very little sameness with great difference. A musical theme and variations, for example, will range over obvious and conspicuous degrees of sameness and difference. The twelfth variation of Bach's *Goldberg Variations* is quite different from the opening aria. On the other hand, the *Aria da Capo* at the end of the work is the "same" as the opening aria, or at least much more similar to it than variation twelve. In fact, the symmetry between the aria and the *Aria da Capo* has been stretched out enormously in time and much musical material has intervened, so there is a strong sense of experiential difference between these otherwise "identical" opening and closing sections.

But the sculptor is perhaps the artist most especially involved in problems of perspectival review and the degrees of sameness and difference that such review accomplishes. There is the obvious matter of spatial perspective—the multiple vantage points from which a work of sculpture requires to be seen. One cannot stand still and look at the *Aphrodite of Melos* the way one looks at the *Mona Lisa*. One needs to circle the former to see all of it. While moving to the right and left of the *Mona Lisa* might make some difference with respect to lighting effects, and while moving back and forth in front of it might make still bigger differences with re-spect to perception of detail, it is nothing like the accumulating perspec-tives that result from moment to moment when a statue is encircled.

At each stage of this encircling process, lights and shades, disposition of shapes and masses, change enormously. One can only begin to imag-ine the incredible challenge it must be to the sculptor, who in modifying his work in progress in some desirable way from one angle of vision, might be despoiling it from another angle. What a series of circling at-tentions and compromises the creative process must be for him, and what a temptation he might feel to try to surmount this state of affairs.

The sculptor accomplishes some avoidance of too many perspectives, of 360 degrees of circling, by the design and positioning of his work. Gargoyles on a cathedral, for example, are not likely to be seen up close, or from behind. Often the physical setting of a sculpture in a museum or garden will exclude some vantage points and underline others. High re-lief seems to stand midway between painting and regular sculpture, with its viewability limited to something less than 180 degrees.

But in general it is the condition of sculpture, the very nature of the medium, to have built into it the expectation of spectator circling. It is not surprising, then, that sculptors should give this fact about the nature of their medium some conceptual attention. On one occasion two artists sought to withdraw their works from the Whitney Museum because of dissatisfaction with the way their sculpture was being presented.[3] While much modern art is conceptual in various ways, there is good reason why sculptors should give special thought to the very idea of perspective and how it figures in what they do and how they exhibit.

Brancusi is certainly an artist in this case, and he has given much at-tention to the idea or concept of perspective. Brancusi's work accom-plishes not only the possibility of a series of perspectives of objects, as all sculpture does, but also a conceptual comment on perspective—what might even be called a perspective on perspective. He invites us not merely to look at his works, but to think about what it means to look at them and to envision in advance, intellectually, various totalities of perspective.

This needs elaboration. Brancusi's work, as we know, veered away from representation toward purity of form and simplicity of design. A succession of heads that he made began to look more and more like simple ovoids or spheres with minimal delineation or protrusion of facial features. One characteristic of this kind of art object is that it tends to reveal itself quickly—at a glance. The perspectives that will ensue when the object is circled are acquired and known in advance. The first perspective, if not exactly proxy for all others, gives fairly precise indication of what they will be. Thus, in looking at an ovoid or egg shape, one can anticipate how the shape will vary from different angles. In the limiting case of circular symmetry, as with a column or a sphere, the first perspective, any one, is exact proxy for all others. Circling the circle leaves it with ongoing, unchanging circularity. The advance knowledge of this is conceptual; it is an intellectualized preview or survey of change, making the actual circling experience of change superfluous.

This is surely part of what Brancusi was striving after in his purified, simple forms. Or if we are to avoid the intentional fallacy, we can say that this is what we find—a kind of Platonic surmounting of motion, a turning of sculpture into static, cerebral art. If morality is a move from the sensuous to the cerebral, this is it. Most works of sculpture not only require movement around them, they even seem clearly to propel the direction of circling. In the case of the drastic symmetries of some of Brancusi's work, there is no such indicated direction. Since no angle of vision is different from any other angle, there is no point to choosing to move around the work and to travel to where the mind has already been.

It might help to amplify this problem of stasis and motion by a comparison among the arts. If one were to apply a temporal—timeless, or moving—motionless distinction to the arts, sculpture would ordinarily fall somewhere between painting at one extreme and music at the other. Like a painted canvas, the sculptured object itself does not move. But as with a musical work, there is a temporal dimension to sculpture because the object invites and requires a circling, temporal purview. This purview is not fixed in time, as in music, by the duration of someone else's performance. But while this purview of sculpture can be slow or fast, in principle even endless, it is ordinarily incapable of being fixed or nearly instantaneous—as a glance at a painting might be. Of course glancing at a painting is hardly a way of looking at it. There will be internal dynamics, motions of perception generated despite the picture's and the viewer's fixity. But we are not here dealing with that kind of motion, eyesight motion, rather with the motion that is a consequence of changing physical perspectives.

It is this usual predicament of sculpture—as being within, or involving, an order of changing physical perspectives—that some of Brancusi's work defies. Part of his interest seems to be to overcome not the relevance of multiple perspectives, but the need to engage in motion in order to become aware of how those perspectives would accumulate. Formal precision and simplicity, intermingled with intelligence, suffice to do this. Motion and the pulses of motion are encompassed and prefigured in uncomplicated but carefully conceived structures. Picasso once commented on this simplifying tendency in Brancusi, a tendency he could admire but not quite share. In his private collection of sculpture there was a violin-shaped idol from the Cyclades—a human figure of remarkable simplicity and purity. In a conversation with Malraux, Picasso characterized the head as an egg anchored down by a neck, and said of the ancient work, a bit ironically, that Brancusi should be the only one to love it.[4]

Having made our general point about Brancusi's efforts, it is important to give several concrete illustrations and to look at his achievement from some different angles of our own. The exceptions and qualifications to what has so far been said turn out to be as interesting and relevant as the principles from which they depart.

The three works of Târgu Jiu, Romania, that I identify are good examples for a review of this sort because they are so well known and because they provide so much of the quintessential Brancusi. All three, *The Table of Silence*, *The Gate of the Kiss*, and *Endless Column*, are extremely formal, symmetrical, conceptualized art objects. Their structures are suggested at first glance, and only *The Gate of the Kiss* is elaborated with some surface design, suggesting the kind of motion of the eye that a painting invites. The other two works are undecorated, solid shapes.

We might use the idea of pulsation to refer to the repetitions or rhythms that occur in the process of circling such shapes. Some objects, simple cylinders for example, can be encircled in a single beat, so to speak. Other symmetrical objects, but not rounded, will give rise to recurrent beats or pulsations in the process of circling. *The Gate of the Kiss*, with its front and back, has two pulsations or beats. *Endless Column*, with its

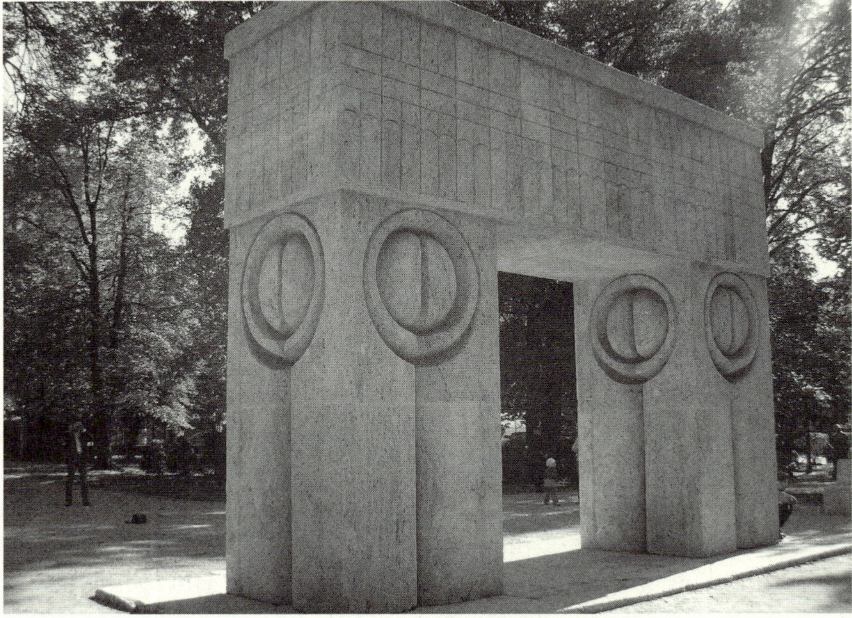

Figure 16-1. *The Gate of the Kiss*. Photo courtesy of Robert and Mihaela Vicol.

rhomboidal modules, has four. But *The Table of Silence* is without pulsations and has but one beat to its circular measure. It is seen, from anywhere, as offering the same, unchanging perspective as from anywhere else.

The low-lying *Table of Silence* can be totally envisioned and circled in the mind more surely than can the other two works. While, conceptually, we can and do anticipate the hidden aspects of both *The Gate of the Kiss* and *Endless Column*, it cannot be with the same degree of certitude as with *The Table of Silence*. This work is awesome in its circularity multiplied upon circularity. With its twelve stools it suggests a clock without hands, or a table without people, and while *The Table of Silence* provides only one pulse in its actual or envisioned circling, the stools can be said to offset this oneness with twelve pulses or beats. However, with a number as large as this it is moot whether they are indeed so experienced—just as the number of modules (fifteen) in *Endless Column* is such as to preclude their being immediately countable. It is interesting that Brancusi may have thought to place the stools in groups of twos and threes—

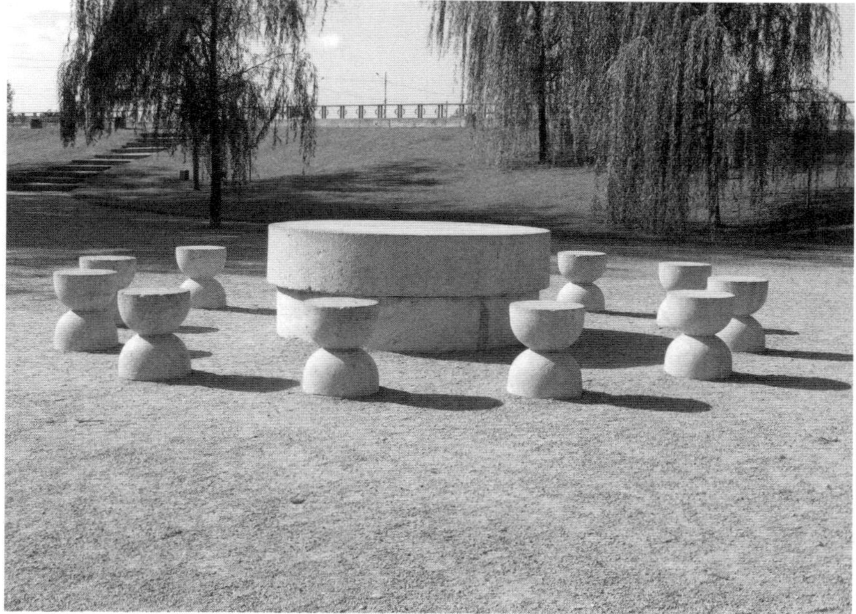

Figure 16-2. *The Table of Silence*. Photo courtesy of Robert and Mihaela Vicol.

which would have vivified the sense of pulsation and variety, but would have taken from the work its general effect of eerie silence and simplicity.

Endless Column with its rhomboidal modules will bring a repetition at every quarter turn around it; or, as I have indicated, it has four pulsations. Sidney Geist says of this: "If Brancusi had wished to make a column the proportions of whose modules remain constant from any point of view he would have made a column of circular section. Such a design would have entailed an increase in labor and a reduction in content—a faulty economy."[5] A brief quibble with this argument. First of all, a circular column might not require an increase in labor. But more to the point, a reduction in content would be consonant with what we see as a repeated tendency in Brancusi's work. This reduction in content is precisely what adds to simplicity and purity and what enhances Brancusi's conceptual purpose. We might want to put the question this way: Does the conceptual interest in the form of a work sustain or balance the dwindling of content or detail? The attractions, mostly intellectual, of ultimate simplicity and purity are

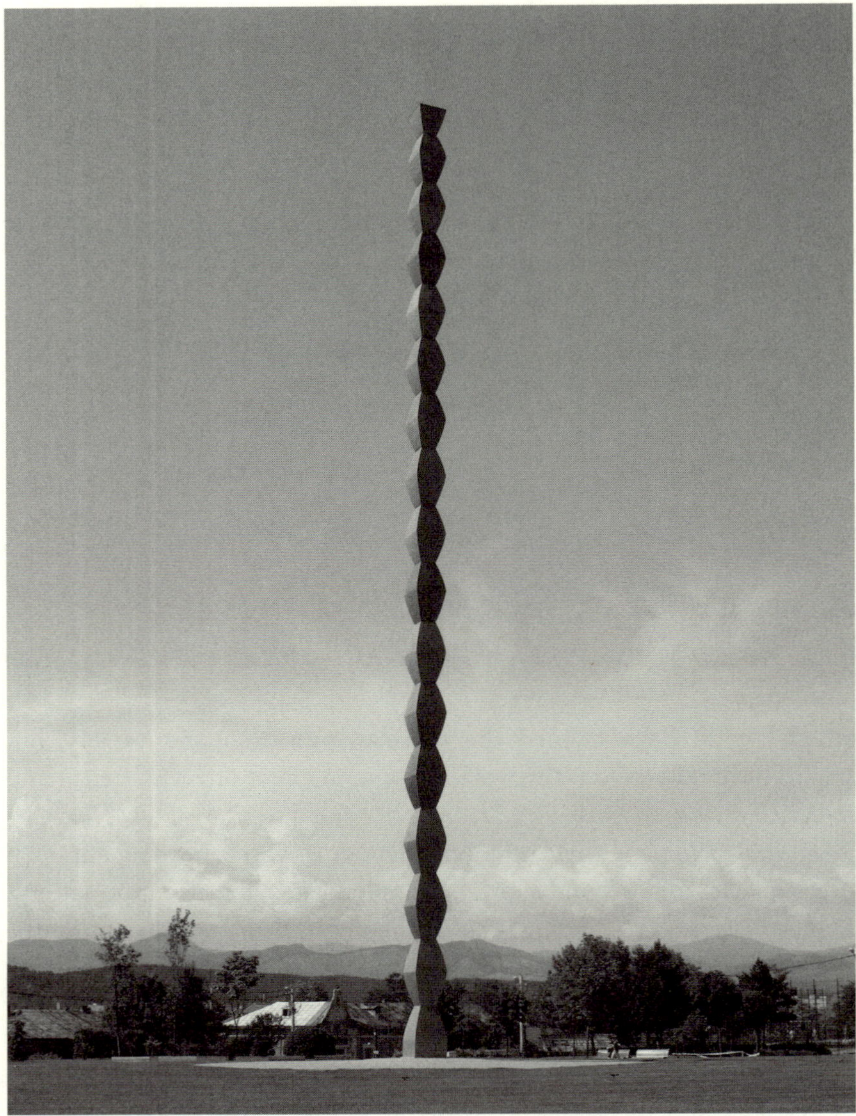

Figure 16-3. *Endless Column.* Photo courtesy of Robert and Mihaela Vicol.

enormous, but equally enormous are the risks in loss of personal perspective and detail. The sphere or globe is the object that has always had this kind of contentless mystical and intellectual fascination, but it is more silent even than Brancusi's celebrated table.

What I have outlined seems to suggest that in the move toward con-ceptual simplicity, the usual contents and traditional values of sculpture are abandoned by Brancusi. This is obviously not so. Brancusi's works at Târgu Jiu are in a natural Romanian park and city, not in some kind of artificial astrodome where circling them would produce no changes of effect. Brancusi thought about backgrounds and settings, and the lights and shades of *Endless Column* produce more variety than the four pulsa-tions I previously suggested; even *The Table of Silence*, since it is not set in the tropics at noon, will partake of the inevitable asymmetries of sun-shine and shadow. And because it is called a table, we experience as an existential negativity the persons who might have been sitting there but are not.

So we have in these works a tension between actual perspectives with their empirical detail and possible content, and the envisioned, ideal, conceptual set of perspectives that require no ordinary experience or motion for their proper grasp. Notwithstanding this tension, the latter preoccupation is very real for Brancusi, and perhaps his deepest one. This may be what Hilton Kramer meant in saying "that Brancusi's late sculpture results from a 'rigorous effort to place the whole of his art beyond the reach of his private experience.'"[6] Part of Brancusi wanted to get beyond the earth-rooted, folk-art, traditional variety of perspectives to the unspatial and timeless idea beyond all perspective.

We know of Brancusi's philosophical interests and of his reading of Plato and Bergson. We are told that in his room there was a globe of the world. Take the world away from the globe, get rid of the slowly moving continents and other trivial details on the face of it, and we have that object that is remarkably the same from all the perspectives of three-dimensional space. We also know that Brancusi stopped sculpting in his later years. Perhaps the globe and the inactivity suggest a halting end to perspectives, even an arrival at that aloneness and silence toward which Platonizing mystics and artists have sometimes veered.

SEVENTEEN

DRAMA AND DIALECTIC

Ways of Philosophizing

1972

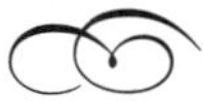

Drama, the "controlled presentation of contrary viewpoints," and dialectic, "the logical elaboration of viewpoints," are integral to philosophy. Drama in philosophy may take the form of irony, the compression and immediate presentation of contrary voices; dialogue, "a natural oscillation between viewpoints"; or soliloquy, a single voice presented in the assumed context of others. Dialectic is a kind of drama aiming to eliminate drama altogether by silencing contrary viewpoints, thereby diminishing the variety of voices. Excessive drama, unable to contain contrary voices, threatens confusion. The key is not choosing one method over the other but applying both wisely. While dialectic "is foolproof, and reason can be nothing but reasonable, the topics upon which it is employed are often arbitrary, accidental, and extraneous to our real interests." Santayana dramatizes the situation, suggesting that no argument is worth eliminating "the multiplicity of alternative sentiments that are always waiting in the wings. To interrupt an argument or to quail before its consequences is admittedly to sacrifice a significant fiber of one's humanity. But to withhold the promptings of those contrary sentiments, and to keep them in abeyance for the sake of that one strand, is to sacrifice the very fabric of one's humanity."

I venture, in the following, to do several things, each one ambitious in intent, but here necessarily tentative and sketchy in performance. First, I characterize what I mean by drama and dialectic and suggest a conception of philosophy that is based on them. Second, I consider drama and dialectic not simply as the major strains of philosophy, but also as foci of a critical and expressive dilemma. I particularly dwell on drama, partly because it is the less obvious category, partly because I feel it needs the stronger plea. In dealing with dramatic devices, and their relation to dialectic, I concentrate on irony. It is for me the paradigm case of drama, and I spend some time analyzing and explaining it.

I want finally—though it is not really finally—to do something other than to argue or explain anything. I want to give expression to the conflict of choice that is my underlying theme—which conflict I genuinely feel and which conflict is relevant to the contemporary philosophical scene. That scene is marked by a breakup of philosophy into separate and warring camps, turning opportunities for creative synthesis into excuses for destructive repudiation. It marks, in my terms, a failure of dramatic containment.

Santayana succeeds in accomplishing such containment and in doing so reveals that deep conflict of choice that makes of the containment a large human and philosophical achievement. I call on him often in the following, as he in turn calls often on Plato. But I call on him on this occasion not primarily for the sake of exegesis, to explain what he means, but to have his help in explaining and displaying what I mean.

I

There is an early essay by Santayana entitled "The Search for the True Plato" in which he discusses some attempts to fix the chronology of the Platonic dialogues. "Was Plato," Santayana asks, "a conscientious scholar, did he subject himself to a scholastic discipline, working over abstruse technical problems, in order to rise afterwards, when his apprenticeship was over, to a poetic treatment of real things? Did he shake himself loose from dialectical scruples in his maturity, and proceed to handle the deepest themes with the freedom and irony of a master?"[1]

Santayana comes to the conclusion that in spite of the varieties of emphasis that one finds in the dialogues, it cannot be claimed that Plato was either a dialectician who gradually turned poet or an enthusiast finally become critical and sober. These strains in Plato of poetry and precision, of enthusiasm and argument, of drama and dialectic, were continuous and concurrent and remarkably intertwined. Santayana puts it this way:

> Without denying the striking variety of Plato's compositions, it may be doubted whether the change in style is due to a permanent change in the man, and not rather to different and reversible poses in the writer. . . . For so imaginative and dramatic a genius as Plato, it is particularly natural to hold various moods and interests in suspense, and to give utterance to them in turn without being obliged to concentrate, for the convenience of future critics, all the poetry in one period of one's life and all the logic in another. . . . There is no difficulty . . . in conceiving that Plato should have tapped his various interests at various times and more or less adapted his expression to each theme he took up.[2]

A little further on, Santayana adds:

> He knew the limitations of art and the often ambiguous complexities of dialectic. What more conceivable, therefore, than that he should have sometimes etched a subject and sometimes filled it in with richest colors, sometimes followed the logic of a problem, and sometimes that of passion? In the *Parmenides*, indeed, we have these extreme phases actually juxtaposed—a singularly picturesque scene, scintillating with brilliant and profound ideas, being followed by a singularly abstruse exercise in dialectic.[3]

When Santayana writes thus he reveals as much about himself as he does about Plato. He is surely characterizing his own ways of philosophizing and indicating what he regards as the critical proprieties. As he reads Plato, so would he also be read and evaluated and understood.

Santayana indeed displays the versatility he attributes to Plato. He employs logic and art, dialogue and analysis, irony and seriousness, with interchangeable abandon. His critics, his close-reasoning Socratic critics, are hard put to deal with him because he defies their charges of contradiction by embracing the multiple attitudes they said he could not hold. Also, in the manner of a dramatist, he often denies that his positions represent chronological and alternative doctrines.

Santayana's occasionally cavalier attitude toward dialectic compounds the critical difficulties. This is in spite of the fact that his powers as a dialectician were considerable. On one occasion he wrote, "I detest disputation and distrust proofs and disproofs."[4] On another occasion, "You might say that although it is impossible for a contradiction to be true, it is possible and easy for me to be guilty of one. . . ."[5] In one of his letters Santayana recalls the Oriental practice of *ketmân*: "It consists in never saying what you think, but if necessary saying anything else. . . . I think that perhaps, without knowing that the thing had a name or was recommended by the wise men of the East, I may have indulged in a little *ketmân* in my earlier days. . . ."[6] In his later days too, one could add, and one wonders whether he might not have been indulging in it at that moment of confession.

Santayana often does two things at once that can't properly or, rather, can't dialectically be done at once. He describes the nature of beauty on the one hand and expresses what he understands by the sense of beauty on the other. He characterizes spirit as a category in an ontological scheme addressed to the nature of things, and he also conveys the sense of a spiritual life, spirit seen and felt inwardly. And he often does these things in close and unexpected juxtaposition.

There is a well-known passage in the preface to the second edition of *The Life of Reason* in which Santayana admits to having confused, or improperly interchanged, nature with his idea of nature and mind with the category of mind. But it is at the core of Santayana's constant procedure to try to reveal what something is by analyzing it and also to convey his idea of it by intimation, by expression, and by dramatic art. And he refuses to surrender what has been called a binocular vision.[7] To perceive what something is, and to perceive how one perceives, can lead to confusion and run into regress. The confusion and regress can be avoided by non-analytical modes of expression that invite participation and insight in lieu of explanation and further analysis.

Certainly Santayana was not always successful in uniting analytical and non-analytical modes of expression. His indifference to, or playfulness about, dialectic can be unexpected and prevents even the most sympathetic reader from always riding his moods. A sudden change of temper is apt to erupt at unexpected moments, perhaps when we are following him most intently and have begun to stake more on the outcome of the argument than Santayana ever intended. Contrariwise, and on other occasions, the reader is inclined to the lightness that Santayana has elsewhere taught him to expect only to find a dialectical ponderousness that refuses to let up. In a word, there is nothing consistent in Santayana's concern about consistency or in his indifference to it.

Santayana confesses his errant tendencies, but at the same time his pervasive irony extends (after the manner of Schlegel's "irony of ironies") to his confessions. Consistency remains for him a relative virtue, in contest with other virtues, and often subordinate to a different kind of success. It is subordinate to the dramatic accomplishment, as in Plato. There is the refusal to relinquish any alternatives that are humanly important, even if they lead to the brink of contradiction and its attendant distress.

Santayana certainly knew and felt such distress and grappled hard with its urgencies. He sometimes made heroic efforts, against insuperable odds, to force the variety of his sentiments through what he called the sieve of reason. Let me report one instance of this agony of decision without here developing it in detail. In spite of his contempt for system, Santayana has an ontology. He deals with the categories of essence, matter, and spirit, and there are for him ways of existing as over against ways of being. One of the things that long preoccupied him, sometimes on a semi-conscious level, was the problem of attributing or denying existence to spirit. (It was a problem perhaps inherited from William James, since what Santayana later called "spirit" he first called "consciousness.") A scrutiny of the texts, and an examination of early drafts, shows an astonishing series of oscillations—statements to the effect that "spirit exists" and "spirit doesn't exist." For those without a special interest in Santayana, this might sound like a verbal tempest in a teapot, a trivial confusion that could perhaps be dismissed with the observation that existence, anyway, is not a predicate. The point, however, is that these alternative and contradictory statements can be traced to powerfully conflicting sentiments and value orientations in Santayana. The further point I would make is that—at times at least—Santayana contradicts himself with a bad conscience and, like us ordinary mortals, squirms to shake loose from, rather than to embrace, dialectical dilemma.

These problems of choice are revealed with particular poignance in Santayana's unpublished scribbles and manuscripts. I think that some of his manuscript drafts were abandoned because Santayana could neither pressure his thoughts into the consistency that would have been required for straightforward exposition, nor could he yet attain the psychic distance and composure that would have been required for proper dramatizing or dialoguing. Or he couldn't decide which of the two to attempt. (*In extremis*, chatter turns into silence.) We see in those scribblings the very sharp tensions that obtained between strivings toward clarity and consistency of outlook on the one hand and diversity of expression on the other. We see those tensions that, elsewhere yielding to choice, more usually resolved themselves in the dialectic that streamlined and eliminated or the drama and irony that sustained and juxtaposed.

These extended remarks of Santayana on Plato, and mine on Santayana, I hope serve to set the stage and to indicate in a preliminary way what I mean by drama and dialectic. They begin to suggest all kinds of problems about philosophical method. How, why, and when, and on what grounds, are dialectic and drama brought into play? What coercions are there on the philosopher to keep him from doing anything he wants at any time? What is it that he wants to do? Is the procedure of shuttling from the warp of argument to the woof of poetry a way giving rise to a patchwork tangle, or a many-splendored thing? Is it accidental literature or occidental wisdom? It is necessary to bring the relationship and the conflict between drama and dialectic into sharper focus and to consider how we get involved in the problems and pressures of choice.

II

By drama I mean a more or less deliberately controlled presentation of contrary viewpoints, or, as in soliloquy, presentation of a single viewpoint with the implied sense that it is one among several. The philosopher stands behind them not as statements that he asserts but as opinions or attitudes or sentiments that he deploys. He is responsible for them, but in a special way. It is the way Shakespeare is responsible for Iago and Othello. He invented them and juxtaposed them and is the author of everything that they say and do. But because he speaks both, he doesn't entirely speak for either.

By dialectic I mean the logical elaboration of viewpoints and a consideration of statements that are entailed with respect to their consistency. Dialectic is what Socrates does in a deliberate ploy. One of his interlocutors has asserted A. Drawn out by Socrates, he asserts B. A and B are presumably unrelated. They have been domiciled in different parts of the brain, have run the rounds of separated neurons, and have never played any circuits together. Socrates turns on the current and puts on the pressure. He shows that one of the consequences of B and C, or B and C and D, is not-A. His interlocutor has in effect asserted both A and not-A simultaneously, in the context of one purview and examination. This temporal focus is important. It is the *confrontation* of A with not-A that is humanly crucial and that brings the dialectical exercise itself to a dramatic denouement. (It is Aristotle's recognition scene in miniature, arising as it does from memory and reasoning, and involving a change from ignorance to knowledge.) Dialectical *skill*, at least this decisive aspect of it, is thus an instance of dramatic art. It was Socrates himself who pulled the strings, who summoned the statements, and who got the colloquy to lead to that moment of recognition. It was Socrates who was aware of the contradiction, who in a sense contained it before he forced the revelation. But the function of this little drama, ironically, is to undo drama and to silence one of the statements that couldn't (presumably) be simultaneously contained. Following the confrontation, the recognition scene, Socrates's friend makes some appropriate exclamation and realizes that he has to renounce either A or not-A, or some of the sub-statements that led up to not-A.

For the dialectical-minded philosopher, or the recipient of such refutation, renunciation seems to be absolutely coercive, necessary, and inevitable. But this is only because his passion for consistency is paramount and he sees himself in an either-or dilemma. Actually such renunciation in the face of dialectical assault is partly optional. It is also possible to embrace the contradiction and to make it advertent, sustain the contrary viewpoints dramatically, and acknowledge the variety and paradox of one's being. In brief, Socrates's interlocutor, instead of yielding to Socrates, could have endeavored to become more *like* Socrates, saying rather less but understanding and encompassing rather more than he did before the exchange got under way.

Santayana had a favorite way of showing how dramatic resolution might overcome dialectical difficulty. On several occasions he called on

Catullus's phrase, *Odi et Amo*, I hate and I love, to suggest that contrary feelings can coexist in a man's mind without impugning his logical integrity. "Who has not said of life *Odi et Amo*? But if you choose to exalt these feelings into maxims, I see no contradiction."[8] Though Santayana here glosses over the point, it is quite apparent that "exalting feelings into maxims" is rife with unexpected consequences. A feeling is without dialectical status. It can be criticized or defended, but it cannot be contradicted. A maxim, however, has the form of a statement and is decidedly uncomfortable in the presence of its contradiction. And so when feelings are exalted into maxims, especially when they are expanded and elaborated, organized and systematized, the dialectical consequences are considerable. By a strange alchemy of utterance, the feelings that initiate comment and speculation, impulsive and half-articulate to begin with, end up as cool statements that are decidedly vulnerable to dialectical repudiation. (Earlier I remarked on how two of Santayana's "sentiments"— his naturalistic preference for being a rational animal and his mystical preference for being a pure spirit—issued in the statements, "spirit exists" and "spirit does not exist.")

The close interplay between drama and dialectic, between statements and voicings, is hard to pin down, and it is understandable that ambiguity of function should frequently pose interpretative and critical challenges. Any statement exhibits at least the minimal preference that has selected that statement from other possible ones. Again, any preference or attitude, if it is not an assertion outright, readily gives rise to subsidiary statements that sound like unequivocal and responsible assertions, meaningful and contradictable.

In order to clarify and trace these transitions more closely, let me introduce a distinction—that between contradictions-in-discourse and contraries-in-sentiment. Contradictions-in-discourse are simply statements of the form "A" and "not-A." Contraries-in-sentiment are expressions of opposite feelings, modal statements of the form, "I affirm A" and "I believe not-A," with the affirmation or belief acquiring some vehemence and taking priority over what it is that is affirmed. It is the extent or degree of voicing, the dramatic stance, that is often an unknown factor. And to the extent that one is unsympathetic to or uninterested in the inflections, it remains an unknowable factor. The voicings are suggested tacitly and by context—my later comments on irony will develop this—as well as by devices like dialogue and soliloquy.

The relationship between contradictions and contraries is exceedingly fluid. The one "converts" to the other sometimes openly, sometimes by sub- or supra-linguistic shifts. This shady kind of shifting, with its glissando-like continuity, constitutes much of our mental life. The deployment of language, and sometimes the deployment of silence, accomplishes these shifts in an elusive way.

Dialectic, as we saw, is concerned with the elimination of contradictions by suppressing them when they arise. Drama is concerned with the domestication of contraries to allow for their coexistence. Drama, by gradually voicing contradictions so that they can be retained as contraries, gathers up and disciplines the mind's centrifugal and disruptive tendencies. It saves us from contradiction while preserving those very impulses and emotions that tended, or actually gave rise, to the contradiction.

Contradictions and the manner in which they are handled are two different things. We sometimes criticize a philosopher by saying of him that his right hand doesn't know what his left hand is doing. But why *should* the one hand know what the other is doing so long as the philosopher knows what both are doing? No more than a pianist's right hand should know what his left hand is doing. If it did, it might not be able to move on its own, in independent counterpoint. It is enough that the pianist, or the philosopher, does the guiding and that he conveys his mastery. There is more virtuosity to be found in philosophy than is displayed in argument and analysis.

III

I want now to consider some of the devices and techniques that bring non-dialectical resolution to contradiction and drama to philosophy. I will comment on irony, dialogue, and soliloquy, though irony interests me most. It is, as I said, the paradigm case and represents drama at its greatest compression.

Irony has been "defined" in various ways: for example, the representation of something by its opposite (Freud); the description of a desirable state of things under the pretense of describing the real state of things (Bergson); and light sarcasm, the intended implication of the opposite of the literal sense of the words.

These definitions are fairly equivalent. In each instance two statements or opinions are somehow involved, and of the two, one is understood to represent the author or user of the irony. The other viewpoint, the one actually articulated, is ludicrous or absurd enough not to be seen as a real assertion. The technique of irony involves the establishment of a context or aura in which it will not be possible, or at least it will not be likely, that a statement will be taken simply and wholly at its face value. The contextual aura is established quickly; in the irony of the isolated statement, immediately.

In this special case of irony there is no doubt about the meaning intended, there is no ambiguity, and the implied view more or less obliterates the articulated view. But if irony were merely a way of meaning the opposite or the negative of what is literally said, there would never be any occasion for it. A straightforward statement would serve the purpose more clearly and directly. Something must be gained through irony that has no equivalent in any number of declarative statements.

What is gained, of course, is some voicing of the repudiated view and, in effect, a voicing of contradictions. By a deliberate display of inconsistency, by a deliberate juxtaposition of opposing attitudes, irony evades what would otherwise be dialectical vulnerability. Inconsistency ordinarily involves blindness, forgetfulness, an inadvertent assertion of something that was previously denied. When pro and con, A and not-A, are brought together in irony, the togetherness makes its own mischief and acquires special prerogatives. Irony, by silently voicing contradictions, invokes the principle of drama.

So far as the simple instance, the special case, of irony is concerned the drama is rather one-sided. What the ironist says is heavily outweighed by what he means. But in writing that is pervasively ironic, where the ironies accumulate and the mind behind them ranges, the dramatic scope is enlarged. Collectively these ironies do not constitute two distinct classes of statement, so that what is said can be distinguished from what is meant, or what the author asserts from what he denies. Rather, the emphasis varies. What is asserted here is discredited there. What is valued now is debunked later. This has been characterized by Barzun something that "must cut both ways and from a center which is itself ever-shifting."[9] In sustained irony these shifts of emphasis are often subtle, like modulations in music, and we may be uncertain as to which key we are in or what view is being foisted on us. But this is the characteristic uncertainty of drama, which deliberately causes our allegiance to waver and fluctuate and which avoids any singular and final triumph.

It should be noted that the experience of irony can neither be coerced by dialectic nor repudiated by it. The dialectician can always deny the presence of that silent aura that makes a statement function ironically. If he allows himself to be aware of it, he can still boorishly reject the intended irony on the grounds that it violates the theory of types. No matter how adamant he remains, he is not vulnerable to the charge of unreasonableness (that is, he is not vulnerable to dialectical repudiation), but only to the *ad hominem* charge of blindness or foolishness. Irony, in other words, is a psychological primitive; it can be pointed to, illustrated, circled, displayed—but not defined. And what applies in this respect to irony applies, *a fortiori*, to the experience of drama and, most generally, to the sense of beauty itself. These are human dimensions, states and attitudes; they can contest for the scene only by option, by persuasion, and force; they must counter dialectic as vital, and never merely as reasonable, alternatives.

To sum up, then, an instance of irony is drama at its greatest compression. The voice that speaks is contextually countered by a stronger, a more important and nearly obliterating voice. In sustained irony the drama can be enlarged. There is a wavering and a development of the respective voices. None is entirely demolished and none is entirely victorious.

If I seem too much enamored of the category of irony I would defend my interest in it by a quotation from Thomas Mann. This master ironist said of irony, and I presume in all seriousness, that it was "incomparably the most profound and alluring problem in the world."[10] Irony seems to be the nearest thing to a meeting ground between logic and art. It is a category and an experience that can be readily understood and felt, and the peculiar relationship between the understanding and the feeling can itself be easily understood—and felt. In the function of irony, in the challenge of it and to it, one gets to the crux of the relevance of both drama and dialectic in human experience.

Dialogue is the classical and typical dramatic technique. In irony, drama can be compressed to instantaneousness; but in dialogue, drama is measured out in time and the effect is quite different even from that of sustained irony. In dialogue the two countering voices must occur separately before the listener can rise to the dramatic awareness of their mutual relevance. Viewpoint A lasts as long as it takes character A to articulate it. Then viewpoint B supervenes, with character B's contradictions and alternatives. One knows as a consequence of the format that the philosophical statement is not contained within the voice one hears at the moment and that it will only arise as a result of later juxtapositions. In a word, the dialogue form requires us to be indulgent and to wait as long as is necessary for the completion of a speech. No matter how long it runs, we are attuned to it as a voice among voices, and we may not readily challenge or counter it until it has been heard in its own domain. (In a passage in Santayana's *Dialogues in Limbo* entitled "Normal Madness," Democritus launches the "exchange" with a fifteen-page soliloquy. Aristippus and Dionysius fall asleep during it, but the reader knows that others are listening and he expects they will have their say.)

The dialogue is a natural oscillation between viewpoints. There can be progress within the oscillation as each viewpoint provokes and develops the other. Together they move not to dialectical reconciliation or consistency but to dramatic resolution, an awareness that is "existential," felt but unspoken.

The soliloquy, as we have seen, is a special case of the dialogue. In soliloquy one speaks with one of several possible voices. The other voices are held entirely in abeyance, but there remains the clear implication that there are other voices.

There are more soliloquies in philosophy than are clearly tagged with the title. The philosopher is much inclined to voice, to apostrophize, to bracket what he is momentarily saying. It is a reminder to himself and to his reader that he carries with him a sense of the inadequacy and incompleteness of what he has set down and is aware of the unspoken exceptions and the ever-hovering alternatives.

It is for this reason, perhaps, that the piecemeal quality of philosophical production is different from the piecemeal quality of either scientific or purely literary production. The scientific paper is related to all other papers by a perpetually deferred hope for collective consistency and completeness. The literary work has its precisely contained aesthetic unity. But philosophy, in its every real instance or on its every real occasion, pleads for the display of an overarching vision that will unite that instance with everything that might have been or ought to have been said along with it. If, as Sartre says, every choice defines mankind, then, in some comparable way, every attempt to philosophize implicates and defines philosophy.

IV

I want now to get back to the problem of choice and to consider why some utterances are preserved and some discarded, why in fact we oscillate between the modes of drama and dialectic.

Some of our statements—not too many, really—are easily relinquished as soon as they are confronted by forceful contradictions. We all contain collections of utterance, or potential utterance, that represent so much historical and personal debris. These we can strip from ourselves without harm, and the stripping no doubt makes us clearer and more effective and better fit for action.

But other utterances are more entrenched. They are tied up in tangles of utterance and are deeply rooted in our affective natures. It is decision respecting these entrenched utterances—as between dialectical elimination and dramatic comprehension—that is most difficult. It is such decision that is the real measure of what we are and of how we philosophize. To eliminate by dialectic an utterance that craves to be heard and that is reluctant to be stilled, and that might have been saved by drama, is to diminish one's being. On the other hand, to perpetuate such an utterance and to fail in the attempt to contain and dramatize it properly is to confuse one's being.

Dialectic, though it is the tool by which philosophical systems are built and the world is controlled, can be and often is destructive. It is destructive for the same reason that any worthy ideal is destructive when one tries to live by it and cannot. A dedication to consistency, like any dedication to proud and puritanical virtue, does violence to our varied natures. Dialectic is too extravagant, visionary, and exclusive. It doesn't allow us to shore up—as we must during actual moments of life and reflection and evaluation—all the fragments that we have and all the arguments that we are. It would have us renounce too much. Such shoring is the function of drama. Drama is more modest, more practical, more compromising, more tentative—closer to the circumstances of who we are and what we might realistically hope to be.

Another weakness of dialectic, when it becomes an autonomous and exclusive interest, is its inability to provide a criterion of what to be dialectical about. While the method is foolproof, and reason can be nothing but reasonable, the topics upon which it is employed are often arbitrary, accidental, and extraneous to our real interests. Where shall we start? What shall we examine? Should we study the ideas of a famous philosopher? Should we try to define justice, virtue, irony, beauty? Should we consider the nature of an ideal state? Should we develop a strategy for destroying a neighboring state? Should we play a game of chess? Before proceeding dialectically we always have to be given, or to discover, or somehow to arrive at what to reason about. Without such prior wisdom, reason can become relentless and irrelevant.

In the light, perhaps, of some of these considerations Seneca called dialectic the Greek disease. But the cure can be worse than the malady, and there are sickly excesses in drama, too. One sees it, for example, in Kierkegaard's pseudonymous extravagance. One sees it whenever rhetoric overwhelms reason and wherever an indifference to the canons of argument is not tempered by irony or regret or a tragic sense of loss.

Human diminution and confusion are the respective pitfalls, the Scylla and Charybdis, between which we dangerously move. Too much attempted dramatic volume and variety can lead to irresolution, to will-lessness, to excessive chatter, and to ominous silence. But too much dialectical clarity can lead to tidiness at the price of largeness and to precision at the price of plenitude.

There are times when the Augean stables of intellect have to be cleaned and when wrong-headedness has to be chastised. But there are times— and politically and philosophically we are in them now—when the belligerence of reason might yield to a chivalry of coexistence and when a tower of Babel, standing erect, is better than methodical elimination and demolition, with little beauty, and even less love, to be found among the ruins.

There is a work by Santayana, one of the later dialogues in *Dialogues in Limbo*, that deals with the choices I have been speaking of and that might serve to wind up my own attempts to give them dramatic expression. That dialogue, "The Vortex of Dialectic," is a conversation between Socrates and The Stranger. The Stranger is always Santayana himself or, to be more exact, one of his deliberate voices. At one point in the dialogue, The Stranger remarks on "the profound ambiguity which I felt in the value of beauty, as it was possessed and exhibited in Greece. . . ."[11] This beauty, he says, "was a misfortune in some respects, though at the same time it was, I admit, a privilege and a dignity."[12] Socrates is no friend of ambiguity and is as much as ever an enemy of sentiments that are unresolved and opinions that are unexamined. He counters The Stranger and prepares to move in for the kill:

> *Socrates.* How many things you clever people manage to say at once, so that if any one of your observations proves false you may still pride yourselves on having been right in some one of the others, which has not yet been investigated. If you wish, as I do, to reach the truth on this subject . . . perhaps you will answer me a few questions on one point at a time; then, when we put your answers together, we may perhaps discover what you meant.[13]

This is the dialectical attitude in a nutshell—not to leave any statement in the form of a floating sentiment or a blurted opinion, not to come to conclusions without squaring them with each other, and never but never to remain of two minds about anything.

In the discussion that ensues, The Stranger attempts to hold to his equivocations and in effect to justify his dramatic comprehensions.

> *The Stranger.* It was because I felt this internal and intrinsic ambiguity in the cult of the beautiful that I expressed myself in the qualified way which you complained of as confusion of thought: since when things are hybrid and many-sided it is not easy for a judicious man to dispatch them simply and categorically.[14]

Socrates is not won over. "Things," he says, "are many-sided indeed . . . and if you piled up together all the qualifications and all the contradictions that language affords, you would fail, I fear, to express adequately the flux and self-contrariety of nature."[15]

The dialogue runs on for several pages and inevitably Socrates bests The Stranger. The latter has to concede that he was verbally in the wrong. What he calls the "vortex of dialectic" has swept him around from a statement to its contradictory. But he really had no inclination to pursue the argument and he does not wish, like Socrates, "to strain all [his] thoughts and affections through the sieve of reason."[16] He half believes he was right in the first place and is willing to let the examination lapse.

It is then that the "dialogue" takes a novel turn. Socrates, the embodiment of the sort of reason that is expressed as dialectical relentlessness, can do anything but cease being reasonable, and he is caught up in his own vortex. He is the bulldog who cannot let go. With nobody to argue with, he becomes his own interlocutor, assumes different positions on the "stage," and asks and answers his own questions. By enacting this little travesty of the Socratic method, and reducing it to absurdity, Santayana indicates his decidedly qualified regard for it. The argument that Socrates has with himself is—needless to say—fixed. The tightness of his definitions and the cogency of his proofs are gained as much by betraying The Stranger's meanings and sentiments as by clarifying them. The strands of a neat argument are not necessarily the voices of a real drama, which voices are not so easily disposed of, or heard, encompassed. And that, in effect, is what The Stranger says in his final speech. Beauty (and he might have said irony or drama) prescribed and defined is not the same as beauty experienced and felt and dialectic cannot dictate otherwise.

Though the subject here is beauty, the same problem of choice and direction obtains whatever the nominal subject, whenever our sentiments are so touched that comprehension vies with logic, or knowledge with feeling, or dialectic with drama.

Dialectical exploration easily becomes vertiginous. It produces a local rampaging of waters and tends to carry us down in a destructive whirl. But there are other vortices elsewhere, all of them clamorous and intriguing, threatening and revealing, and as urgent or as persuasive as we permit them to be. The trick is to touch them without being caught in them, to sense their diversity, to swirl and escape, and to find peace and safety in wider waters.

For Santayana, for Plato, for the philosopher worthy of the name, the many-faceted inner man is more important than those separate vortices, and no argument is worth pressing, no position is worth holding, which closes off the multiplicity of alternative sentiments that are always waiting in the wings. To interrupt an argument or to quail before its consequences is admittedly to sacrifice a significant fiber of one's humanity. But to withhold the promptings of those contrary sentiments, and to keep them in abeyance for the sake of that one strand, is to sacrifice the very fabric of one's humanity. Between these alternatives the choice for Santayana was as inevitable as can be for one not inclined to exclusive choices. "A man's life," he wrote, "as it flows is not a theorem to which there is any one rigid solution. It is composed of many strands and looks to diverse issues."[17]

To conclude, then, the choice between drama and dialectic is itself a drama that is always with us. At any moment we can try to clarify what we've got, secure what we are, put up boundaries, milestones, and markers. This is the role of dialectic. But contrariwise we can try to extend our domains, become more than we have been, and venture into incertitude and conflict. This is the role of drama.

Dialectic and drama might be regarded as polarities, as tensions between which philosophy properly moves. Because they are tensions they cause different philosophers to have different leanings, sometimes to the exclusion, or near exclusion, of either strain. Such exclusions are unfortunate and possibly a criterion for what might mark the abandonment of philosophy. The presence of both these strains, and responsiveness to the drama of choice, might serve as philosophy's hallmark.

This doesn't leave us with any rules for the guidance of the mind. If wise choices are sometimes the directives of reason, so do they sometimes come by luck, by grace, through venturesomeness and vitality. So far as philosophy is concerned, I have simply been opting for openness and a continued retention of the several strains of achievement that make up the tradition.

EIGHTEEN

ONTOLOGY AND MORALITY

Santayana on the "Really Real"

1980

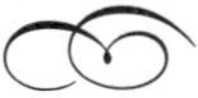

Santayana rejects the search for the most real and the highest good in attempting to avoid traditional philosophical errors due to undeclared moral biases. Rationalistic and theological philosophies elevate the human "power of generating and appreciating ideals into the conceit of attained cosmological discovery," which by turning attention away from facts of human suffering is ultimately dehumanizing. "By recognizing that the actual and the possible are neither of them ultimately privileged nor ultimately coincident . . . we can care about this tragic sundering in the primal order of things and act to undo it as far as" we are able. Santayana's ontology discriminates essence (being) and matter (existence) but gives moral priority to neither. He aims "both to create an ontology, . . . and also to hold it in abeyance as preferred or special. . . . Santayana's ontology is that choice which frames itself in an extended vision of the optionality and arbitrariness of all choice." This is Santayana's "double seriousness [or] controlled ambiguity" that embraces "optional imaginativeness" while also "employing his categories with an intended scope that should carry them, for those who shared his vision, to the steadiness and wholeness of all that there is."

Philosophy's search for the "really real" is gradually being abandoned. That search has repeatedly generated a metaphysical or ontological hierarchy in which the most real was dubiously assumed to be morally the best. Indeed, the search for the real and for the best was tacitly taken to be the same enterprise, often beginning and ending with God. The difficult abandonment of the search marks a doing away with those hidden and prior moral preferences that always undergirded the hierarchies of Western thought.

Why is the abandonment of the search for the "really real" desirable? Is it . . . really? Why is it so difficult? The things we most prefer in our human encounters with the world we naturally think of as the most important—to wit, the most real. Evidence to the contrary is resisted. The perennial human discovery that many of those best-liked things are transient, dream-like, fabricated, and evanescent undermines neither ancient metaphysical dogma nor, what is coequal with it, its parallel religious manifestations.

Santayana placed much blame on Plato for moralizing physics and contributing to the creation of false cosmology. But the moralizing and aesthetic impulses in us (in us, not in higher powers, though they sometimes seem to come from elsewhere) are ancient and noble. They are not easily dismissed because of their indifferences to truth. Dante, one of Santayana's "three philosophical poets," created a cosmology that is even more extravagant than Plato's.

Justus Buchler's concept of "ontological parity" is a profound formal attempt to get rid of ontological priority. Buchler says, "It is misleading to ask whether what is exhibited [in philosophy] is a structure of 'ideas' or a structure of 'existence.'"[1] It seems to me that Santayana's ontology represents the first major attempt in philosophy to depart from moral orders of reality. The following discussion seeks to show this and to vindicate the paradoxes and ambiguities that are associated with such an enterprise. For reasons of brevity and focus, I deal primarily with the realms of matter and essence.

The realm of matter, for Santayana, is the realm of existence or of existent things. The realm of essence is the realm of entities (we need such a substitute word here) that do not exist but that are real. Santayana's ontology embraces (or one might say oscillates dramatically between) the existent and the real. In encountering concepts like existence and reality, if we are to understand Santayana aright, we must guard against traditional responses to these words and discern the actual baggage with which Santayana weighs them. For in resting in these two primary— equally primary—ways of being, and in distinguishing between them,

Santayana deliberately evades any obvious linkage of splendor, importance, or moral authority with the one or the other. The reality of essence is not a greater reality than the reality of existence. This primal and ultimate neutrality with respect to the realms is philosophically the most significant element in the manner of their choice. Santayana was interested in how a philosopher grafted his moral onto his natural philosophy and sought, himself, to do it most subtly and carefully.

He attempts to avoid what he sees as the errors of traditional philosophy, that is, the making of distinctions and classifications on the basis of hidden moral or cosmological preferences rather than on the basis of human aesthetic choice. In making his own distinctions, in marking out his own realms, Santayana is not searching for the *ens realissimum* (the most real of things) or the *summum bonum* (the highest good). Neither of the realms can be so characterized. Santayana's ontology is designed to do away with the confusions of past philosophy—particularly the tendencies to assimilate the power of fact to the authority of value and to engage in categorical summitry.

Santayana had once hoped to write a book on the mistakes of philosophy, and among the earliest mistakes was Platonism. He sees in it the casuistry of a "moralistic physics,"[2] a false conjunction of excellence and existence, a misconstrual of the relationship between fact and value. Plato disliked sensuous and worldly things and he liked recondite intellectual ones. On this account (to put it a bit crudely), he attached higher being and existence to intellectual ones. Such projection or hypostatization of preference is what Santayana wishes to avoid, even (as we shall see) to the extent of conceding the tentativeness, even the human arbitrariness, of his own categories and realms.

In the Western tradition, theological philosophizing out-Platonized Plato in the tendency to identify all being, or the most real of being, with all power and goodness. The ontological argument so-called is based on the premise that other things being equal, to exist is better than not to exist. Even philosophical systems without central theological emphasis, like Spinoza's and Hegel's, tend to equate the highest being or existence with the highest value.

Santayana departs from traditional, rationalistic, and theological views of the universe. For him, such philosophies actually dehumanize man (and unwittingly humanize and falsify the universe) by elevating man's autonomous power of generating and appreciating ideals into the conceit of attained cosmological discovery. Such philosophies turn the wishable horse of the beggar into a proclaimed Pegasus. The world might have been a better place if fact and value were not rivals for our attention, if our hopes and ideals, well conceived, were provided us by an accommodating universe. But thinking that the universe is so, wanting it to be so when it is not, makes it appear a worse place than when we properly see the ambiguous conflicts and disparities between the is's and the ought's. By recognizing that the actual and the possible are neither of them ultimately privileged nor ultimately coincident—not mysteriously one in some reach of things we say we cannot fathom—we can care about this tragic sundering in the primal order of things and act to undo it as far as is in our power. It expresses a concern for modifying what needs modification by proposing a universe that is amenable to moral effort, not a universe that is perfect beyond our comprehensions. It could be perversely argued that picturing the universe in Santayana's fashion does indeed satisfy a moral desire—the desire to make moral effort significant and difficult and the desire to perpetuate righteousness and care. From this paradox, the paradox of firmly denying a primal order of reality and excellence, and yet imputing some reality to moral desire, there is no extrication apart from its articulated acceptance.

Let us get closer to Santayana's ontology in order to show just how moral concerns interweave with existential details. As we have indicated, there are two sorts of reality in Santayana's scheme, existence and being, matter and essence, but neither one *per se* is the lesser or the greater. Value does not belong univocally to either. Here Santayana departs from the Platonists and theologians at one extreme, and from coarse materialists (he was an ironic one, and only in a manner of speaking) at the other extreme. There is value in both existence (the realm of matter) and in being (the realm of essence) and also negative value or disvalue in both. The values of existence are associated with its irrationality, its surdness, its external relations, its fecundity, its awesome power of generation. But existence also generates wantonly; it produces tragic conflicts of purpose; it is indefinite, mindless, and irrational.[3] Santayana encounters matter with as much moral neutrality as he can muster. The identification of the realm of matter is not a projection of feelings of fear or admiration, nor an indication of unconditional approval or disapproval.

The realm of essence includes what are the best, even if still unwritten, masterpieces of art and philosophy. But the realm is not a limiting haven for the humanly or cosmically best. People live with the aid of hopes, ideals, values, logical constructs—and these are avenues to non-existent essences. But just as essences can be lovely and wonderful objects of intuition, they can be ugly and distasteful. The values and disvalues that apply to matter also apply to essences. The opera *Don Giovanni* has an essence, but so do hair, dirt, cruelty, and so forth (as Plato realized). Santayana feels none of the embarrassment that Socrates felt with respect to undesirable forms. Essences for Santayana are democratic, infinite, equal *qua* essences, and the superiority of *Don Giovanni* (or of God) to the essences of hair and dirt is a matter of human preference, not of cosmic status. Essences do not *do* things; they just *are*, definite and sometimes thinkable. Even the fact—if we can call it a fact—that they are timeless and powerless and infinite is morally neutral. Santayana's occasionally expressed fondness for contemplating essences is certainly not an unconditional partiality for all of them, and indeed it is not an unconditional partiality for any of them. Like matter, essences are not accorded any *a priori* fear or worship. Santayana somewhere says that it would be mad to worship essences. The realm of essence, rather than functioning as a hypostatization of some primal preference or aversion, is generated as a neutral moral backdrop, as a safeguard, to make clear that preferences and aversions are just that—not convenient accommodations by nature to our desires.

In naming the realms, and in making a choice of such high ontological generality, can one at the same time be free of the taint of human posturing and projection? The naming of the realm of essence as a category of thought, as a proclaimed reality, as a moral choice, is *that* moral choice that is completely transparent to its own arbitrariness. Or, it is the choice so designed as to free us of any illusions about choice. Or, it is the choice so exercised as to prevent its own hypostatization and the creation of a "moralistic physics." Santayana accomplishes this by attributing being to essences, but not existence to them, by making essences equal and infinite—and by not setting up any implicit or explicit moral hierarchy between being and existence. Santayana is profoundly impartial with respect to being and existence—this is perhaps his uniqueness as a philosopher—and the structure and definition of the realms is carefully designed to exhibit and celebrate such impartiality.

The function, then, of the realm of essence is to display ultimate impartiality even in the face of the paradox of the human partiality in bothering to discriminate it. Santayana does discriminate that realm and in doing so conveys by his performance, if not by overtly saying it, that he regards it as good to do so. And it is good, provided that it is good to care about ultimate detachment and to mark out the backdrop of undifferentiated indifference from which all preference and aversion must emerge. For in recognizing that our preferences and aversions have this enormous optionality, we might be freed of the tendency to give false import to our desires and fears and hence might relinquish our fanaticisms and dogmatisms about them.

It is a recurrent theme in Santayana that there is a need to make choices that are human, limited, bound to time and place, and that at the same time there is a need to extricate oneself from human partiality. But this must apply, self-reflexively and on a meta-level, even to the human impulse to discriminate realms of essence and matter in a certain way and to any tendency to attach great cosmological importance to such discrimination. This then is a part of the central drama of Santayana's life and enterprise: Santayana ventures both to create an ontology, a generalized system of metaphysics, and also to hold it in abeyance as preferred or special. We might say that Santayana's ontology is that choice that frames itself in an extended vision of the optionality and arbitrariness of all choice. (Understanding this might help us to understand what Santayana's struggles with "spirituality" were about, both dramatic and dialectical, as developed in "Spirited Spirituality," Chapter 19.)

A further point about the ambiguous self-reflexivity previously touched upon: The realm of matter is in one sense the class of all material and existing things in their elaborate external relations. The realm of essence is in one sense the class of infinite, non-existent, ideal, or possible objects of intuition and discourse. But we can also say that the realm of matter (or the "realm of matter"—though it is significant that Santayana himself did not clarify or do away with ambiguity with such quotation marks, and in fact constantly interlinked things like nature and the idea of nature, beauty and the sense of beauty) is a category in Santayana's philosophy, an essence, a member of a class of such categories. Likewise the realm of essence is another such category, an essence among essences, a member of itself. For some who don't like paradox it is even a philosophical no-no.

The categories or realms, taken as essences or logical constructs, provide Santayana with a convenient way to "shepherd . . . his thoughts,"[4] as he put it, and to discriminate, in ways congenial to him, the things he chose to discriminate. As categories of thought, as more or less definable essences, the "realm of matter" and the "realm of essence" are themselves essences and hence non-existent. In Santayana's words the contrast between essence and existence is not a division among existences, and so in that sense the realms can hardly be constitutive of an ontology. This is the stance that Santayana took in response to critics who did not find his categories congenial or satisfactory and who preferred their own. He simply relinquished the faith and intent with which he approached his realms, even the realm of matter.

Could Santayana be serious in such relinquishings and see the realms, to which he devoted so many years of effort, as optional and personal categories of thought? The answer is that Santayana could be serious in two ways: serious in acknowledging the optional imaginativeness of his philosophizing, and serious also in employing his categories with an intended scope that should carry them, for those who shared his vision, to the steadiness and wholeness of all that there is. This double seriousness, this controlled ambiguity, is at the heart of the smiling sadness of the entire Santayanian corpus. As has been suggested, only with his realms so chosen, and left so undefended against attack, could he have accomplished such remarkable duplicity (in the best sense) of ontological function. The realms are Santayana's synthetic *a priori*, the "true but necessary" that perhaps finds its way into every philosophy.

The two ways of seeing that we have been talking about are ubiquitous to Santayana and constitute what has been called his binary or dramatic vision. He could intend his realms to carry him to the "unvarnished truth" and he could also see his realms as congenial essences of his own devising. It might be helpful to draw on Santayana's own words as evidence of his capacity to renounce his own ontology. Such "renunciation," although always implicit, appears explicitly and poignantly in his concluding remarks at the end of *Realms of Being*. In this footnote to his long work, Santayana writes:

> In general, it would avoid misunderstanding to remember that essence, matter, truth and spirit are not, in my view, separate cosmological regions, separately substantial, and then juxtaposed. They are summary categories of logic, meant to describe a single natural dynamic process, and to dismiss from organized reflection all unnecessary objects of faith.[5]

That essence, truth, and spirit are not separate cosmological regions is fairly obvious, but that the realm of matter can be seen as a "summary category of logic" is, as it were, another matter. As we saw, what is said about matter in one sense is said about the existent; this belongs to cosmology and *a fortiori* is part of bona fide ontology. But we also saw, and now see again, the sense in which the discrimination of the realm of matter is the delineation of an essence, to wit, "the realm of matter." On this latter view, Santayana holds it to be the philosopher's business to articulate, so to speak, the essence or idea of existence, leaving it to scientists to get to matter more directly. So even the realm of matter, if you argue about it too much, can be airily dissolved into a category of logic. Santayana goes on to say in the section quoted:

> Essence is not an object of faith. . . . In regard to the realm of matter I propose no theories. . . . What I lay down about the realm of spirit involves no system of idealism . . . no eschatology . . . no . . . philosophy of history. . . . In reconstructing the *moral* history of spirit. . . . there is . . . the language of poetry and religion.[6]

Poetry and religion are at once the stuff of dreams, the stuff of philosophy, and all the "really real" in which we can rest secure. Santayana's summary dismissals of any residual dogmatic or hierarchical claims to his ontology are reminiscent of a statement that appears twice in the Santayana corpus, once in *Platonism and the Spiritual Life* and again as the closing words of *The Last Puritan*:

After life is over and the world has gone up in smoke, what realities might the spirit in us still call its own without illusion save the form of those very illusions which have made up our story?[7]

Like Prospero (or Shakespeare), who at the end relinquishes his powers of enchantment, Santayana, the artificer of an elaborate ontology, dispenses with his masterful artifice at the very moment of its completion.

NINETEEN

SPIRITED SPIRITUALITY

1996

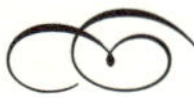

In Santayana's examination of spirit and spirituality, tension between his attempts to live the spiritual life and to define spirit reflects tension between drama and dialectic. Texts from all periods of Santayana's career dramatize the conflicting viewpoints. The spiritual life, "which as a life cannot be purely spiritual and, were it to attain purity, would no longer be a life. . . . is a life of difficult seeking, lighted by the vision of a goal but never attaining the precision of that vision." The essence of spirit appears to be its indefinability, and Santayana accepted "the paradoxes and the drama as over against a vacuous and nonhuman clarity." This did not entail the rejection of logic, but rather spurred reflection on logic's limits. Santayana realized the flaw in forcing an unsuitable clarity on what needed to be experienced in its imprecision. "Definitional clarity is not the same as moral accomplishment." It was important to define spirit in some way, but so was communicating and celebrating the "moral feel of spiritual effort"—both tasks had to be done together. Evidence suggests that Santayana was not logically impaired, but rather engaged in the dramatic struggle that marks good thinking.

It is said that Kurt Goedel, perhaps the greatest logician who ever lived, long refused to become an American citizen and pledge allegiance to the principles of [the Constitution] because it was, to his eye, so obviously internally inconsistent.[1]

The search for consistency and completeness in our vision of the nature of things, and in our lives, is at once heroic and pathetic. For what if such a laudable vision—sometimes called seeing life steady and seeing it whole—is not, in the nature of things, attainable? What to do then? It is possible to decry the Constitution and to refuse to be an American out of dissatisfaction with its inconsistencies. But is it possible to refuse to be human? Isn't some internal inconsistency inevitable? Indeed, would philosophy be at its best without some uncertainty, humanness, and incompleteness? Don't things have to end—papers, the Constitution, even life itself—before they are properly completed?

The noble demand for dialectical precision conflicts, then, with the human need for dramatic largeness and openness. In Santayana's examination of spirit and spirituality, the tensions between drama and dialectic are very keen.[2] What follows is a very brief, and certainly incomplete, look at the issues involved, with the help of some selected texts. My references are limited. Although it is good critical procedure to look at everything—usually a great variety of things—Santayana has said about any particular subject, I can only claim a fair sampling. My examples focus on the conflicts, indeed the ongoing drama, associated with the tasks of both defining spirit and living the spiritual life. They involve perspectives that cannot be molded into a consistent outlook, though there is an unspoken, behind-the-scenes perspective of perspectives. Santayana's occasional self-deprecatory remarks, that he momentarily took a transcendental point of view or that he "skirted psychologism,"[3] sound dismissive of himself but are themselves voices among a chorus of voices.

The tension between defining or clearly specifying what is meant by spirit on the one hand, and living the spiritual life on the other hand, led Santayana to puzzle over attributing existence to spirit. He confesses his perplexities in the frankest and most disarming fashion. One might say that the decision about attributing existence to spirit turned out to be, for Santayana, at once an intellectual puzzle and an agonizing "existential" dilemma.

As an intellectual problem it involved a search for the essence of spirit. But as an "existential" problem it had to do with moral claims and possibilities, with timeless and old-fashioned questions, such as "What is it to live life well?" and "What is it to convey effort and care?" There was the paradox, pervasive and for Santayana always tantalizing, that spirit ultimately perfected, accomplishes its own extinction, or nonexistence.[4] Spiritual effort might be furthered by logical clarity, but clarity, partially gained, never undid the need for further effort. The clarity and the effort were not the same, and clarity alone did not suffice. The spiritual life might involve the vision of seeing things under the form of eternity, but it was not a life that passed into eternity or that ceased its precarious existence. In one instance, Santayana says that the subtlest form of spirit's distraction is "when it torments itself about its own existence."[5] This is certainly autobiographical, and there is considerable evidence of such torment. In the Santayana manuscripts, his indecisions about attributing existence to spirit jump from the pages—with the word *exists*, on occasion, written and then crossed out. It is, for Santayana, a problem that must persist; its facile resolution, one way or another, would be an evasion of something important. It is as though Santayana could not, in good conscience, escape the horns of his own dilemma.

I propose that it is helpful, and appropriate, to see this Santayana problem as non-temporal and to look at the texts from different periods for what they have in common. For one cannot dispel the difficulties, even the contradictions, by careful attention to the chronology of various statements and by presuming, or claiming, that Santayana's views changed. It is not as though at one time he clearly said this and at another time he clearly said that. The myth of two Santayanas is indeed that, created by critics who (like Goedel) cannot accommodate to contradiction. So the dilemmas of the spirit are not limited to the elderly Santayana, the result (as has been suggested) of a geriatric transformation in his thinking. His reflections on consciousness, as early as *The Sense of Beauty*,[6] prepare for and parallel his later thoughts, dilemmas, and paradoxes.

That early work lays the groundwork for and anticipates, with a slightly different vocabulary, the writings that followed. In *The Sense of Beauty* there is the distinction between consciousness as purely intellectual (comparable to non-existing spirit) as opposed to "emotional consciousness" (comparable to existing spirit). This discussion long anteceded Santayana's eventual substitution of the word *spirit* for consciousness, but the words, and the problems associated with them, are essentially the same. Santayana's definition of beauty (as "pleasure objectified")[7] is an early attempt to deal with the two kinds of consciousness or spirit already alluded to, one emotional and human, the other a kind of transcendent consciousness. In *The Sense of Beauty* he attempts to imagine the transition from emotional consciousness (possessed of feeling, will, and change) to consciousness purified, in which pleasure is no longer felt but rather known and transcended. It is the spiritual life, seen in aesthetic terms. It is the move from passion felt to passion Platonically overcome, in the constant or modal refrain of Santayana's attempts, logical and moral, at a passionately passionless, or a spiritedly spiritual, life.

Indeed, the phrase "pleasure objectified," on the face of it, is an oxymoron. Pleasure, or emotion, is subjective. What can be seen in its objective clarity is a term or an essence, which is not the same as having a human emotion. (The essences of surprise and anger, for example, are not the same as being surprised and angry.) The only way to interpret the blatant contradiction of the phrase "pleasure objectified" (as with the phrase "spirited spirituality") is to see it as a depiction of an always imperfect and uncompleted process, a human happening that cannot be fully seized. The same with "spiritual life," which as a life cannot be purely spiritual and, were it to attain purity, would no longer be a life.

In his persistent quandary about the existence of spirit, and in the language that followed *The Sense of Beauty* (where "consciousness" eventually became "spirit"), Santayana wavered between denying the possibility of pure spirit on the one hand and affirming as a viable option an active furtherance of a spiritual life on the other. Thus, pure spirituality, godly omniscience, would preclude the actualities of spirit that occur as phases or moments of human life. Those actualities include intent, care, belief, surprise—in a word, the instabilities of existence.

Surprise, about which Santayana has some words, could not be known by an omniscient spirit. The definition could be known, but surprise as surprise could not be experienced by such a being. "To know surprise by experience is the only way of knowing its essence," Santayana writes.[8] Surprise can't be known by a spirit that sees all things under the form of eternity. Or, surprise defined is not the same as surprise experienced. And the same applies to spirit's existence. ("Knowing its essence" is the problematic phrase here, which is why, later, intuiting essences is not the same as knowledge.)

"The idea of final union with anything specific, even with omniscience or with pure Being, therefore contradicts the very nature of spirit."[9] Of course, what it contradicts is spirit seen as existing, as on the wing, as affiliated with psyche, as longing, as music felt. It does not contradict that other, that greater-than-human sense of spirit that can be defined, and that needs to be defined, but that cannot be achieved. Santayana's strategy (eventually, if not at the outset) is to deal with the interplay, dramatic and poignant, between these aspects of spirit.

Some further remarks might help us to get at the drama and the interplay.

> If spirit in us could be entirely dominant we should esteem everything in nature as if it were the inmost part of ourselves, and everything in ourselves as if it were the remotest and the least part of nature. But the actual life of spirit is all compromise, being continually stopped in its flights, and enslaved by some particular passion or illusion. To that extent spirit is not spiritual and exists only in a thwarted effort to be born.[10]

Spirit is known, then, by being imagined, by the thought or specification of its clearly defined termination. It has its essential nature. But it is also "known," or needs to be known, by the unclear actualities and experiences of pursuit and moral effort. The spiritual life is not a life of mere philosophical precision and consistency. It is a life of difficult seeking, lighted by the vision of a goal but never attaining the precision of that vision. Spirit is "known" the way existence is known, by the felt stress and distraction of it instead of by its perceived or intuited clarity. This gets at the winged evasiveness of spirit and at the logical futility of trying to capture it frozen and motionless. That effort will inevitably be thwarted. But the logical futility of a task (and it is time to say this) certainly does not rule out the desirability of logical effort—especially for a philosopher. To render that logic futile required a *failed logical effort as a phase of the larger task!* There's a difference between failing and not trying—also, between merely failing and stopping as opposed to failing and then reflecting constructively about why the failure occurs.[11]

Another passage about spirituality: "Such a triumph over nature and human nature can never be complete, and the moments in which it *almost* exists are rare."[12] Notice the "almost" in the above. Again, what is conveyed is a defeated movement. And it could only be conveyed by being defeated—that is, by being attempted *and* failing.

Santayana is Heraclitean in his constant insistence on two simultaneous phases. "Were there less change there would be no spiritual realization of repose; for eternity lies above or beneath life, and even to *pass* into eternity . . . is still an act and a transition. If time were ever arrested, the experience and the thought of eternity would be abolished."[13] So much for any practical claims about living in the eternal, which Santayana only proclaimed ironically. But living in pursuit of the eternal, and in changing approximation to it, is another matter and is always possible. Intellectually delineating that pursuit and humanly exemplifying the effort were what Santayana's career was about.

Again: "Spirit lives by transcendence from its center."[14] Note that what is meant here is not transcendence accomplished but, as I have been suggesting, transcendence ventured and imperfectly approached.

There are times when Santayana seemed to affirm a spiritual state, as though transcendence was arrived at and attained (though some irony in the claim is usually evident). But consider this spirited scolding of spirituality:

> Shall we detach our love altogether from existing beings and platonically worship only universal Ideas of the Beautiful and the Good? This might be wisdom or spiritual insight, but is it love? And can such sublimation really be professed without hypocrisy?[15]

In the above self-directed taunt, a bit surprising in isolation, we again see Santayana's rational naturalism in conflict with his other self and chiding the claims of spirituality. Hypocrisy is a strong accusation. At times he was more charitable toward himself—less Goedel-like and dialectical, may we say—about the inevitability of professing conflicting sentiments and needing to live with such professions.

Santayana bravely sought to define certain elusive things, like "feeling" and "existence," as clearly as he could. "Feeling" he called the intuition of the inarticulate, and "existence" was specified in terms of external relations. But there is something unsatisfactory—and Santayana knew or felt it—about bringing pseudo-precision, a clarificatory essence, to that which needed to be experienced in its imprecision and in its obscure movement. This caused the wavering and the drama. Definitional clarity is not the same as moral accomplishment. Giving spirit some definition was important, but doing something else—getting at, celebrating, and conveying the moral feel of spiritual effort—was also important. They had to be done together: each properly depended upon the other, though they pulled in different directions. "Logic and morals": this phrase, this juxtaposition, I believe, appears an astonishing number of times in the Santayana corpus—for reasons I hope I have been suggesting.

Once again: "Spirit is not a reality that can be observed. . . . Spirit can never be observed as an essence is observed, nor encountered as a thing is encountered. . . . The essence of it . . . can be described only circumstantially, and suggested pregnantly."[16]

Essences, ordinarily, are precisely what they are, unchangeable and definable. Is the essence of spirit different from all other essences? Is there an essence of spirit, in view of its recalcitrance to definition? As I have suggested, we need to note Santayana's ungainly attempts to define existence, motion, feeling. These attempts tend to be paradoxical and elusive. Some things are "essentially" defined as indefinable, as man's nature is, by existentialists.[17] This is especially so for existence, whose essence is to elude essential capture. "Existence itself is a surd. . . . Nothing accurate can be said of a thing supposed to bridge two moments of time. Yet to bridge two moments, in some sense, is indispensable to existence."[18] The same applies to spirit. Spirit eludes accurate description for the same reason that existence does. Santayana prefers to live with the paradoxes and the drama as over against a vacuous and nonhuman clarity.

"Spirit is a category, not an individual being."[19] But, of course, it only exists in its instances or individual occasions. "In intent, in belief, in emotion a given essence takes on a value which to pure spirit it could not have."[20] This is connected with Santayana's early thoughts about aesthetics and emotional consciousness. The notion of an essence "taking on a value," however, is clearly problematic. Essences don't change; even the essence of change undergoes no change.

> All this intuition of turbulence and vitality, which a cold immortal spirit could never know, fills the spirit of man, and renders any contemplation of essences in their own realm only an interlude for him or a sublimation or an incapacity. It also renders him more conscious than a purer spirit would be of his own spirit.[21]

It's like knowing surprise better than God knows surprise. The cold immortal spirit is the godlike idea of non-existing spirit. Existing spirit, in man, is precarious, on the move, with only intimations of pure spirit. Morally, *in this passage*, Santayana used derogatory words like "sublimation" and "incapacity" (not as derogatory as "hypocrisy") to characterize this impulse toward self-transcendence. *In this passage*, I noted. For on other occasions Santayana reverses his moral perspective and sees the impulse to transcendence not as a sublimation in any negative sense, nor as an incapacity, but as a mode of moral fulfillment—certainly one of life's greater moral options.

The evidence that Santayana is dramatizing conflicting viewpoints is overwhelming. To isolate one of Santayana's voices to the neglect of other voices, or to present one voice as contradicting another voice, is a failure of criticism. The textual evidence, in its fullness, should keep us from this. And if we still had any doubts about the matter, there are the frequent passages where Santayana does not hold a second voice in abeyance, or hidden from us, but he presents the voices juxtaposed, in a transparent rendering of them as dramatic alternatives. Consider the following:

> If I am spiritually proud and choose to identify myself with the spirit, I shall be compelled to regard my earthly person and my human thoughts as the most alien and the sorriest of accidents; and my surprise and mortification will never cease at the way in which my body and its world monopolise my attention. If on the contrary I modestly plead guilty to being the biped that I seem, I shall be obliged to take the spirit within me for a divine stranger, in whose heaven it is not given me to live, but who miraculously walks in my garden in the cool of the evening.[22]

Here, side by side, are existing and non-existing spirit. Given such passages, and there are many of them, how can Santayana be faulted for taking a dogmatic, or a spirited, stand in favor of spirituality? He displays the drama, and his spiritual detachment is ironically, and indirectly, revealed by his refusal overtly to opt for spirit in the very moment of that remarkable detachment.

Once more: "But the existence of spirit really demands an explanation; it is a tremendous paradox to itself, not to say a crying scandal. . . .

Spirit, since it *can* ask how it came to exist, has the right to put the question and to look for an answer. And it may perhaps find an answer of some sort, although not one which spirit, in all its moods, will think satisfactory."[23]

Santayana sometimes talks about taking the "point of view" of spirit, which would be different from the point of view of psyche. But there are large dramas and smaller ones, and here we see that even spirit has its moods and some varying moral propensities.

It sometimes passes as scholarship to go behind the backs, or into the unconscious, of philosophers and to presume to reveal them, as it were, to themselves. We are pleased if we can show that they missed some important implications of what they said, or indeed that what they said here was contradicted by what they said there. Such an approach is sometimes useful and sometimes even appreciated. I do not myself find many such opportunities in Santayana. What he said here might indeed contradict what he said there—but not for want of remembrance. As I have indicated, his repeated *deliberate* juxtapositions of conflicting viewpoints ought to remove all doubts about such viewpoints when they are spread out and not juxtaposed. They ought also to keep us from presuming logical carelessness on Santayana's part.

When they are juxtaposed, we can sense some element of pain and dilemma in the moral predicament. We can see greater and lesser success in dramatizing the viewpoints in question. But I know of no instance where what is at stake is logical failure, where Santayana could not see the internal inconsistency he was deploying.

Santayana had extraordinary self-knowledge. He was not at the mercy of, and there is little evidence of, logical or psychological perplexity. There is, however, much evidence of the kind of dramatic wrestling and rewriting that accompanies the effort of good thinking.

Consider the following, which might serve as a prime, and here a final, example of Santayana's overt grappling or wrestling with his dilemma:

> For a man, and especially for a philosopher, to suggest that spirit does not exist may accordingly pass for a delicious absurdity, and the best of unconscious comedy. If it had been some angel that denied it, because in his serenity and selflessness he could not discover that he

was alive, we might regard the denial of spirit as the highest proof of spirituality: but in a material culture struggling to see and to think, and tossed from one illusion and passion to another, such a denial seems not only stupid, but ungracious. . . . Nevertheless I think that those who deny the existence of spirit, although their language is rash and barbarous, are honestly facing the facts, and are on the trail of truth.[24]

So much for the "existence" of spirit (its precarious existence, one might say), which agonized Santayana and which involved him in so many richly dramatic affirmations and denials.

What more can one do with the paradoxes of spirit than display them? Even so, there are some (the earnest logicians, the Goedels) who will persist in missing the message. Santayana at one point made a remark, most unspiritual and unphilosophical, even with a touch of pique, about terminating his efforts. Although he did not adhere to his own declaration, let me use his words as an excuse to bring my own remarks to a close. "I will not pursue this topic: if the reader does not understand, he probably never will."[25]

INTERPRETING *INTERPRETATIONS*

1989

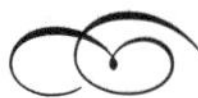

Despite the growing tendency toward literary interpretation of philosophy, Santayana scholars still approach him in a "traditional, orderly, sensible, analytic fashion." This demands an extreme ironic reading of Santayana that maintains "(1) There are no contradictions in Santayana" and "(2) Everything in Santayana is ironic or dramatic." These axioms are applied to Interpretations of Poetry and Religion *along with the assumption of "a double moral grid, a structure that is often hidden in Santayana" and that manifests in the shifting moral relations of, for example, work and play, supervening and intervening ideas, or imagination and truth. This interpretative approach aims to take Santayana whole, rather than focusing on one part and neglecting another for the sake of consistency. Santayana is a dramatic and ironic writer who sets contrary "concepts in motion, examines them, inverts them, and shows how each of the distinguished terms can be, indeed needs to be, further scrutinized." And this suggests "proper writing about Santayana needs itself to be appreciative and dynamic, sustained and developed. The arguments that merely uncover or underline certain arguments in Santayana, or that direct certain arguments at him, are necessarily threadbare and insufficient."*

When I first wrote about Santayana a long time ago, I assumed that I was working more with literary critical categories than strictly philosophical ones. My attempt to see Santayana stylistically, in terms of drama and irony, was different from other approaches at the time.

Literary interpretations have grown and even begun to prevail in philosophy. This is seen in the burgeoning of philosophy and literature enterprises, in deconstruction, and in the sometimes strange indiscernibility of texts with respect to whether they were written by professors of literature, professors of philosophy, or by some total interlopers from somewhere across the disciplines. There are now frequent literary and stylistic studies of poet-philosophers like Plato and Nietzsche, of barely poet-philosophers like Hobbes, Hegel, and Hume, and even of non-poet-philosophers like Kant and Peirce. For better or worse, philosophy as literary criticism, even philosophy as art, is staking out large claims and gaining wide recognition. And art as (a form of) philosophy is not far behind.

Remarkably (or ironically?), these newer stylistic approaches have been directed at philosophers for whom they are far less suitable than they would be for Santayana. Santayana scholars have tended to grapple with Santayana in traditional, orderly, sensible, analytic fashion. They think to disentangle the essential doctrines from the literary overlay; they even think to uncover serious arguments and moral claims that stand secure as Santayana's own—not to be confused with other arguments and claims that somehow got lodged in the texts in some insecure and potentially embarrassing way.

This inclined me, in a spirit of corrective misprisioning, to go to greater and greater lengths to see only irony and drama, more than I once saw, and to dismiss those arguments and doctrines that in the past I thought could be saved. I began by finding much irony and drama in Santayana, along with some argumentative seriousness and even some "positions." Now I find, or have decided to find, only irony and drama and literary art. Briefly then, if by argument one means anything like a serious development of a position that is then maintained univocally and securely, then there are no arguments or doctrines in Santayana as there are, indeed, no doctrines in Plato. There is an absence of religion and philosophy in Santayana in quite the same sense that he found such an absence in Shakespeare. This is not to detract from either of them. They were both too good, too aloof, and too remote to have to carry along that kind of baggage.

There is risk, I realize, in making irony ubiquitous and in not at least striking a balance between irony and seriousness. But I got consoling support from Richard Rorty,[1] who saw or located more irony among philosophers than anyone else would ever have dared. Of course there is something invulnerable about irony, and the discovery of endless irony can hardly be faulted or refuted in any ordinary way. For there is no avoiding the irony that finding irony in texts (as Rorty endlessly does) is simply the nether side of practicing irony in the interpretation of those texts.

At a conference I once heard Rorty scolded on the grounds that irony can be oppressive and also that irony was a form of self-therapy. Any way of doing philosophy is oppressive to someone doing it another way. Some of us find declarative sentences, mere assertive judgments, oppressive, particularly when a bit of interpretive acumen, or sleight of hand, or imagination, can turn them into something richer and more interesting. And if drama (of which irony is a form) is therapeutic, it only confirms what Aristotle said about drama a long time ago, without derogating it.

Ironists, according to Rorty, don't have to decide who is a poet and who is a philosopher. Only common sense metaphysicians worry about getting, as he puts it, "the genres right."[2] Rorty writes, "[Hegel] began a tradition of ironist philosophy which is continued in Nietzsche, Heidegger, and Derrida. . . . He helped turn [philosophy] into a literary genre."[3] "Hegel's so-called dialectical method is not an argumentative procedure . . . but simply a literary skill—skill at producing surprising gestalt switches by making smooth, rapid transitions from one terminology to another."[4] This last, it seems to me, can more exactly be said of Santayana than of Hegel. It is ironic that Santayana is not on Rorty's list of ironists, though Habermas and Foucault are. And how can Rorty forget the very beginnings of irony in Xenophanes, Heraclitus, and Plato? Rorty refers to "we ironists," but that has to be looked at cagily, coming from an ironist; Santayana, who at least on one occasion referred to his use of irony, would not have given it the central status of a philosophical attitude or genre.

In any case, I've veered to my extreme ironic interpretation of Santayana in part, perhaps, because no one else chooses to occupy this critical place. My rules, or axioms, are appallingly simple:

(1) There are no contradictions in Santayana.

(2) Everything in Santayana is ironic or dramatic.

If contradictions seem to be discovered in a text and (1) is threatened, use (2) to put things aright. Axioms, I think, should be like friends: not consistent, not independent, and willing on occasion to help each other out.

It should follow from the above, as surely as day follows night, that a capsulated account of a Santayana text, a univocal statement of its theme and its "argument," always misses the mark. Should we be surprised at the essential inadequacy of a summary statement when the object of it is a poetic essay or a prose poem? If the summary or argument could do the job, why does the author give detailed, complicated, challenging, poetic elaborations? Are the latter (recall Santayana) merely spread on the former like butter? Are they mere filler, to fatten otherwise slim volumes of clearly stated principles and truths? Such summaries are no more to be taken seriously, that is, unironically, than are Monarch notes, or thirty-minute papers read at conferences.

Summary fails whether we do it for Santayana or whether Santayana does it for us, though this latter case is interpretively more complicated. Santayana has, in fact, provided us with a number of neat summaries of himself, tempted at times by friends and correspondents who needed quick philosophical fixes, or perhaps provoked by publishers who wanted prefaces and introductions.

Santayana's "Preface" in *Interpretations of Poetry and Religion*[5] is a good case in point and allows me, for starters, to interpret his interpretation of *Interpretations*. Santayana on Santayana remains more interesting, though not more reliable, than anybody else on Santayana; if we could understand his comments about himself, usually part of a complicated internal drama, the rest would more easily fall into place.

In his "Preface," Santayana says that his essays are

> gathered together in the hope that they may lead the reader, from somewhat different points of approach, to a single idea. This idea is that religion and poetry are identical in essence, and differ merely in the way in which they are attached to practical affairs. Poetry is

called religion when it intervenes in life, and religion, when it merely supervenes upon life, is seen to be nothing but poetry.[6]

This is summarily provocative and neat, but there is no such single idea in the texts, no idea so coherent in its sharp boldness. Like the "argument" of a drama, it lays the groundwork for what is to be further explored, but it is not its substance and, indeed (unless taken ironically) betrays, rather than prepares for, the richness of what follows.

The same applies to the distinction between Don Quixote and Sancho Panza.

> The mass of mankind is divided into two classes, the Sancho Panzas who have a sense for reality, but no ideals, and the Don Quixotes with a sense for ideals, but mad. The expedient of recognizing facts as facts and accepting ideals as ideals—and this is all we propose— although apparently simple enough, seems to elude the normal human power of discrimination.[7]

This again is minimal and by no means all that Santayana proposes. It is merely the beginning of the drama, the cast of characters, and diminishes, by simplistic summary, the meaning and scope of what is to follow. Aren't such prefatory remarks, on the face of it, ironic or best to be seen as such?

Perhaps we can support this with Santayana's help. Joel Porte points to a passage on Browning where Santayana says that, "even in the poems where the effort at impersonality is most successful, the dramatic disguise is usually thrown off in a preface, epilogue or parenthesis."[8]

Could Santayana, knowing about throwing off dramatic disguises, fail us by actually throwing off his own dramatic disguise in his "Preface"? Hardly. To know you are throwing off a dramatic disguise is to engage in a dramatic disguise. So Santayana, we must conclude, only seems to say a few things that are straightforward, simple, compressed, and univocal. For Santayana without dramatic disguise is not Santayana. So much, then, about Santayana's "Preface," which we see now as an artful and ironic series of statements. Santayana would not inadvertently lapse into speaking in his own voice, that is to say, with summary simplistic directness.

Has the "Preface" perforce yielded to my interpretation? Is such procedure oppressive? Probably, but it cannot be helped. To interpret a worthy text in philosophy and literature is to show how much more complicated it is than it seems, not how much simpler. It is evident that my preferred interpretive way with Santayana would be to write little essays about sentences and paragraphs in the text, not to write summary sentences or paragraphs about entire essays.

I happened recently to read Carol Gilligan's *In a Different Voice*[9] while concurrently rereading the Santayana essay on Homeric Hymns.[10] They both deal with the story of Persephone and Demeter. It goes without saying that their interpretations are different, since Gilligan summarizes the myth from a feminist perspective. I do not wish to make invidious comparisons, since interpretations of myths are further myths, both true and imaginative. But what struck me was the greater detail and inventiveness in Santayana's account. He discusses relatively few lines at relatively great length. His interpretation is neither a summary of plot (though that is provided) nor a summary theory (though several hover in the background). His interpretation becomes, in effect, a poem about a poem.

II

To help understand the dramas and ironies that are my focus, I propose what I call a double moral grid, a structure that is often hidden in Santayana and hence not sufficiently taken into account in summary statements. It can be applied to much of Santayana, these essays as well as other writings. It connects with what Santayana says when he refers to the still non-existent "poet of . . . double insight."[11] Also to what has been called his own "binocular vision."[12]

Looking first at another book, consider the discussion of "work" and "play" in the opening of *The Sense of Beauty*.[13] Work and play are first distinguished in their conventional ways and in terms of common linguistic usage. But then Santayana sets the concepts in motion, examines them, inverts them, and shows how each of the distinguished terms can be, indeed needs to be, further scrutinized. Each term is shown to have two moral complexions, its morally good and bad sides. Obviously, seizing upon a part of the discussion, even a wonderfully quotable line, and neglecting the totality of the textual play will give a non-Santayanian, that is, a non-dramatic, glimpse of the issues at stake.

Consider intervening and supervening ideas. Men generate ideas; these ideas sometimes intervene in life and give it moral direction; such ideas, created by art, wit, and passion, modify how men live. This is good, and rational. Is it only that? No. Is there a bad side to it? Yes, because if ideals were merely practical, and never visionary and extravagant, there would be a paucity to them, and a diminution to life.

Some ideas intervene, however, in a derivative or secondary sense, and here there is an ambiguity, a double usage, that would not have been detected in the original distinction. Such ideas are entertained in imagination, do not modify actions, and seem merely to supervene. Nonetheless there is a difference, even imagining it, between imaginative actions and life actions. These ideas may express poetically, and even truly, the genuine needs of those who generated them, but they do not or cannot affect essential or motor behavior. They just "swim into our ken." Are they intervening or supervening? Are they good or bad? They are "bad" if imaginative extravagance, poetic decadence, and even religious mysticism turn attention away from right action; "good" if they enhance and supplement one's merely practical life by adding to it and enriching it in another dimension.

This double moral grid, as I have called it, here crudely set down, might help us to understand the groundwork of the complicated moral claims that Santayana variously develops. The distinction between poetry and religion, the definitions of "intervene" and "supervene," the characterizations of Don Quixote and Sancho Panza, do not begin to dramatize the larger issues, let alone even address them. They only start us off.

How sane ought the Don to become? If the change from madness were to bring him to dullness, should he make the move at all? Mightn't he be morally preferable as is? He is not entirely oblivious to facts. He recognizes a woman as a woman, even if he misses some of the finer points of her character. And windmills, especially in Spain, actually look a lot like giants. As for plodding, dull Sancho Panza—how much literary, religious, and philosophical education for him? Would we know the point at which we are no longer enriching his life but ruining it? Do we know these things for our students? For ourselves? The problem is not that the world is divided into Don Quixotes and Sancho Panzas. The problem is that we are so divided and are always facing the task of what to do about it. The characters and concepts aren't out there; they are us, and in constant dispute. The appropriate mix of truth and imagination awaits ongoing discovery; it cannot be blocked out or provided by prior definition; it is generated by the poetry of human self-creation, in the detailed words of uncertain effort. It always involves simultaneous attention both to who we are and who we ought to be.

Imagination and truth are another pairing, not unlike "supervene" and "intervene," each with its double set of moral inflections. Imagination has its rampant, extravagant, mad side, as with Don Quixote. Pressured by need, will, and desire, it generates the fantastic, the remote, the untrue. It sometimes moralizes physics, as in Platonism, and leads people to turn their desires of what ought to be into false claims about what is. Thus, even the greatest poets, Homer and Dante, distort. Imagination gives us the illusory and the false; it sometimes accompanies an unwillingness to face the world as it is.

But imagination has its wondrous, positive side. It enriches life. It generates poetry, religion, ideals. It is needed in order to discover truth. It also gives us something to envision that might be better to attend to than mere truth. In a word (though it takes more than a word to render the drama properly), some of Santayana's language lauds imagination, and some of it lauds facts and truth. Some of it deplores imaginativeness for its dangers, and some of it faults facts and truth for being dull and humanly incomplete.

Santayana's definitions do little for us, as little as do any summaries of his philosophical "positions." But the complicated dramas of moral choice he gives us, with momentous battles set upon a large and actively peopled stage, do a great deal. Santayana's plots, like Shakespeare's, are conventional and derivative. There is no sense in summarizing them. But the dramatic issues, sometimes in their carefully nuanced complications and sometimes in their unexpected and widely leaping moral modulations, are what his writing is significantly about.

If I had a central interpretive point to make, or an argument, it would be this. My delineation of this double moral grid, this oft-repeated Santayana structure, can at best be helpful in a negative way. Perhaps attention to it in reading a text could forestall hasty summary judgment. Too often, critics of Santayana focus on a part of him, to the exclusion or neglect of other parts. This makes him more coherent than he is and likeable in different ways to different people. In response to faulting critics, Santayana somewhere said that he was content, like the curate's egg, to be good in parts. My interpretation proposes that we try to understand and consume, sometimes with difficulty, the whole egg.

Here are a few samples of what happens when the egg is broken and scrambled, when parts are taken in isolation from the whole. I quote the part and then supply the dramatic context in which it is embedded.

"The ideal of mysticism is accordingly exactly contrary to the ideal of reason; instead of perfecting human nature it seeks to abolish it"[14] But we elsewhere learn that mysticism, spiritual life, and post-rational morality perfect a different way of being.

In evaluating those barbaric poets Browning and Whitman, Santayana suggests that they had "no grasp of the whole reality, and consequently no capacity for a sane and steady idealization."[15] Also, "The comparatively barbarous ages had a poetry of the ideal; they had visions of beauty, order, and perfection."[16] Sane idealization is at once an oxymoron and also the whole impossible art of life. Visions of beauty, order, and perfection risk departures from the truth. There is no way of having everything, both *"Dichtung und Wahrheit,"* other than by dramatizing the things that cannot be had together.

Santayana writes of "The silence of Shakespeare and his philosophical incoherence."[17] But one could speak of such incoherence in Santayana as well. In both men, a higher dramatic wisdom is predicated on the eschewal of a false coherence and orderliness.

The masterful skill with which Santayana regularly entered into conceptual and historical roles is evident in the way he vivifies pagan belief. He shows how it had a sense for "the real existence of religious objects" and knew that "god was not an invention but a fact."[18] But then decline and decadence came about. "Reflection . . . and desire for philosophical truth led inevitably to . . . the reduction of positive traditions to moral allegories."[19] "What an age of imagination had intuited as truth, an age of reflection could preserve only as fable."[20] So we see almost in process how that moral decline (from the perspective of enthusiasm and imagination) yields to moral advance (from the perspective of truth and philosophy). And conversely. It is the tragic recognition of that double moral insight that pervades Santayana.

Santayana ironically scolds "that zealous Protestant Xenophanes" for "decrying the fanciful polytheism of the poets."[21] And he says that Socrates, "invoking the local deities of brooks and meadows . . . is more reasonable and noble to our minds than are the hard denials of Xenophanes."[22] Reasonable and noble indeed! Is that what Socrates is about? Santayana will soon show us not the nether side of the argument, but a developed alternative argument that is the nether side of the drama.

Santayana himself sought in various ways to articulate a natural religion, a human orthodoxy that would be at once imaginatively poetic and philosophically true. In *Interpretations* he conveys the poignance of the conflict that he was never to resolve because there could be no resolution to it. Here, natural religion is seen as "most unnatural."[23] It has been "the appanage of a few philosophers in ages of religious disintegration. . . ." And it is the appanage of Santayana himself, who in many respects was at one with the Stoics whom he scolded, and who himself lived in an age of religious disintegration.

Joel Porte nicely gets to the essential psychological drama when he writes, "Santayana's critique of the [Catholic] modernist accordingly amounts to an oblique exercise in self-castigation, as if the believer in him needed to reprove the skeptic when he went too far and seemed about to commit spiritual suicide."[24]

Again, such squibs and summary judgments are interpretively insufficient. The structure of a drama does not give us the feel for what it celebrates, the moving intensity of certain oppositions, made to run their careful courses. Santayana characteristically gives us not arguments for viewpoints, which would be lean and insufficient, but intellectually passionate cases for them—as he also makes intellectually passionate cases for their opposites. To uncover the details, the inflections, the nuances of how he does this is beyond reductionist arguments or static interpretive schemes. Proper writing about Santayana needs itself to be appreciative and dynamic, sustained and developed. The arguments that merely uncover or underline certain arguments in Santayana, or that direct certain arguments at him, are necessarily threadbare and insufficient.

III

I venture some expanded attention, in closing, to the essay "The Absence of Religion in Shakespeare." It certainly dramatizes viewpoints and partakes of the uncertainties and problems that have already been sketched. Perhaps it tests to its very limits my critical approach of always attributing irony to Santayana.

"We might say," Santayana says, "that the absence of religion in Shakespeare was a sign of his good sense . . . and that he was in that respect superior to Homer and Dante."[25] And, "we might say," that the latter gave us a representation of life that was "indirect and partly unreal."[26] Earlier, Shakespeare's absence of religion was seen as a weakness. The two sets of claims build from different premises; we could easily detect, and indeed already have seen, what those premises are and why the arguments must clash. It is not too often that Santayana gives us a meta-comment on his method, a little postscript in his text that is a confirmation of his two viewpoints. But here he writes, "what I have treated as a limitation in him would, then, appear as the maturity of his strength."[27] The strengths and weaknesses of Shakespeare are explored, as are the strengths and weaknesses of the poets used for comparisons, Dante and Homer. Here quite clearly is that double moral grid to which I have alluded. The dramatizations, however, are not as finished and as settled as they might be, in full and detached equilibrium. Santayana here writes, "those who think it wise . . . to refrain from searching for general principles . . . may well see in Shakespeare their natural prophet."[28] He is giving us the perspective of "those who think . . ." in an essay that might well have been written as a dialogue between those who think "this" and those who think "that." A little further down, however, there is a twist. "Those of us, however, who believe in circumnavigation, and who think that both human reason and human imagination require a certain totality in our views . . . can hardly find in Shakespeare all that the highest poet could give."[29] "Those of us . . ." sounds like an authorial perspective, privileged above the first one.

These little phrases, "those who think," and "those of us," manage to entrap both Santayana and me in our mutual problem of getting him properly interpreted. If we can get out of this, other interpretive problems will seem easy and routine by comparison.

The problem is that we seem to find in Santayana's "those of us," a clear stance, a move away from Shakespeare as ultimate poet, a move to Dante and Homer as the likely exemplars of that superior person. Santayana even dares to say, and surely there is emerging irony here, that "what is required for theoretic wholeness is not this or that system but some system. Its value is not the value of truth, but that of victorious imagination."[30] Indeed! Santayana seems to be turning away from dramatization of his views to an unexpected univocacy; he seems to be replacing a preference for truth with a preference for imaginativeness. Has he momentarily forgotten that he has been concerned also about the falsenesses in Homer and Dante and the Christian tradition, memorably and imaginatively wonderful though they are? He was later to sustain the drama more fully and to acknowledge that Homer and Dante too, along with Shakespeare, Lucretius, and Goethe, are not the highest poets. They were all great, but in different ways and with respect to different values that needed to be argued and developed from different premises. The highest poet is merely imagined in *Three Philosophical Poets* and is yet to come.

Is there any other way of reading the move from "Those who think . . ." to "Those of us . . ."? I must make my own critical move here, summon up my axioms, and suggest that Santayana was being ironic against all appearances. Those who think that he was taking an unequivocal moral position might be right, merely right, but those of us who say he was ironic might be doing him a greater service.

What I really am proposing is that we had better see Santayana as ironic, and not as sincere, when he sides against Shakespeare and even against truth. We should do it for his own good and for a truth of sorts, our proper recognition of his ideal and profounder self. In a word, we would see Santayana in more moral fashion, and closer to the sources of his deepest inspiration, if we credit him here with irony rather than seriousness. Santayana himself will soon come to our rescue of him, to our ironic interpretation. In *Three Philosophical Poets* he will not take sides but give us, in purer fashion, the agonistic and unyielding drama of the claims of both truth and imagination.

It is necessary to be wary of labels. It does not suffice, as we all know, to see Santayana as a materialist, a moral relativist, a rational moralist, a post-rational moralist, a naturalist, a Christian, an anti-Semite, a Platonist—or anything else—"*simpliciter.*" Santayana is none of these things, and all of them.

The same applies to my drama-cum-irony approach. To deal with Santayana adequately and subtly, to interpret him effectively, is to bring some of his own splendidly interpretive skills to the task. Drama is trivialized if we do not search out its phases and its inflections and its waverings. Irony is trivialized if it is not dealt with ironically and if its moments and shifts are not imaginatively rendered. And irony becomes oppressive if it is only dealt with ironically; it can become as tiresome and as unsatisfying as uninterrupted seriousness and argument can become. The problem of philosophy, in this postmodernist age, is how to write philosophy.

Santayana's writing remains endlessly fascinating; how much of *Interpretations of Poetry and Religion* I marked for commentary, but here scanted. For me the book grows with rereadings, and if it can change, we can change.

The study of Santayana, then, like the new Santayana Edition, is still in the making. The proper interpretation of Santayana awaits the ultimate poet who cannot actually exist, but whose description Santayana prefigured and whose performance he sought mightily to emulate. Santayana quotes the poets in Dante's limbo greeting Virgil: "*Onorate l'altissimo poeta.*" "But the supreme poet," Santayana goes on to say, "is in limbo still."[31] By a strange confluence of truth and imagination, that is exactly where Santayana is, dialoguing with the other poets and philosophers, while the rest of us try to eavesdrop on them from a very great distance.

TWENTY-ONE

SANTAYANA'S AESTHETICS

1992

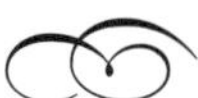

All of Santayana's works attempted aesthetic achievement, but his main work of aesthetic theory was The Sense of Beauty. *He claimed that "to feel beauty is a better thing than to understand how we came to feel it" and accordingly could regard distinctions quite blithely. But he did not court confusion and maintained that "the recognition of the superiority of aesthetics in experience to aesthetics in theory ought not to make us accept as an explanation of aesthetic feeling what is in truth only an expression of it." It is not distinctions but rather their dynamic making and unmaking that perhaps best exemplifies Santayana's efforts. He distinguished the moral and the aesthetic but was concerned to show that value theory needs to ambiguously embrace both sides. This ambiguity is apparent in his definition of beauty as "objectified pleasure," that is, feeling regarded as the quality of an object, which leaves the locus of beauty uncertain suggesting it resides in process.* The Sense of Beauty *is neither the direct descendent of any tradition of aesthetic writing nor the progenitor of any school, yet it is both conscious of historical antecedents and remarkably anticipatory of later theory and criticism.*

George Santayana somewhere notes that philosophers come to aesthetics through opposite routes—as metaphysicians who need to complete their systems and as artists who need to generalize about their experiences. He belonged in both camps, with emphasis on the latter. He was an obvious literary artist in his poetry and fiction, but he was a poet-philosopher all the time, even when he was a metaphysician. While he wrote *about* art intermittently, particularly in *The Sense of Beauty*[1] and *Reason in Art*,[2] he sought to be artful in all of his writings, including his "theoretical" ones.

His central work in aesthetics is that early and most remarkable book, *The Sense of Beauty*; its subtitle is *Being the Outlines of Aesthetic Theory*. Santayana reveals his hand, and his approach, when he says at the very outset: "The sense of beauty has a more important place in life than aesthetic theory has ever taken in philosophy."[3] And, indeed, the stylistic beauty of this treatise is as telling as its philosophical or theoretical side and must properly be seen as part of its "statement." Santayana also says: "To feel beauty is a better thing than to understand how we came to feel it."[4] He certainly feels it and might even be said to explain how he comes to feel it. But, as always, he explains it more as a literary critic than as a metaphysician. He addresses himself to the task of creating literary art as surely as he works at discovering any principles of art in a theoretical fashion.

Santayana is cavalier about distinctions, even the distinction between theory and art, between comprehension and inspiration: "But the recognition of the superiority of aesthetics in experience to aesthetics in theory ought not to make us accept as an explanation of aesthetic feeling what is in truth only an expression of it."[5] This might be seen as a form of self-scolding, or a way of guarding against the neglectful obliteration of an important distinction. But the distinction that he makes does not actually mark out different phases or moments of experience, or different sections of his own texts.

As further indication of his way with distinctions, Santayana objects, on theoretical grounds, to calling beauty a "manifestation of God to the senses."[6] Such an observation is obscure and beyond truth or falsehood, albeit high-minded. But then an analysis of what is meant by God, an unpacking of the metaphor, reveals how and why the attributes of God are indeed an appropriate way to reach an understanding of beauty. In a word, a good metaphor can give a scrawny theory some divine afflatus and some cognitive force. Art and philosophy always were one enterprise! The presumed structure of Santayana's "theoretical" work is the barest skeleton upon which various comments, or "little essays," are hung. The parts of the treatise, which *The Sense of Beauty* might be said to be, are quite incidental to a process that is fundamentally critical, literary, and ironic. The dynamic of making and unmaking distinctions, the play of perspectives—not the semblance of structure that these distinctions might have been thought to have created—constitute the essential quality of Santayana's presentation.

The organization of the book, such as it is, consists of part 1 on the nature of beauty and parts 2, 3, and 4 on matter, form, and expression. In part 1 Santayana distinguishes the moral and the aesthetic, or work and play. He teases out the distinction and accords it some initial and conventional deference. But then he undermines it and shows in effect how any adequate value theory must ambiguously embrace both the moral and the aesthetic.

Beauty is defined in part 1 as "objectified pleasure," or "pleasure regarded as the quality of an object." It suggests a psychological tendency or process in us whereby we attribute or affix our feelings to things. It is a provocative definition, but leaves the locus of beauty somewhat problematic. The lower senses, taste and touch, are mostly bodily and not objectifiable. Smell seems mildly but vaguely objectifiable. Hearing and seeing take us entirely from the organs whereby we perceive to the objects out there that we esteem and enjoy. Santayana was never entirely satisfied with this approach, and at a later date wrote self-critically of his tendency to skirt psychologism.[7]

Part 4, on the concept of expression, is most startling and unusual. Expression is an evocation of memory, the bringing of some association to mind, in the presence of sensed matter and form. The memory may be vague; some emotion may persist, with the details of its occasion forgotten. Indeed, vagueness sometimes helps make possible the fusion of present and past. Santayana's theory of expression, if it can be called a theory, undermines any clear and traditional notions about the fixity of the art object. In principle, any sensation or idea or concept can conjoin or fuse with any other, and this is what his "theory" asserts. But in practice, as we know from the associations we attempt in the making of metaphors, not everything tossed into the air can be said to fly. Theory cannot quite account for art or substitute for it.

Santayana's concept of expression, one might say, is the general case of which certain late-twentieth-century and radical views about art are so many special instances. Theories can attach to sensuous objects as surely as sentimental memories can. That an object is offered for appreciation by the art world demonstrates an "expressive value" in it. Expression allows any association—a previous sensuous memory, a mood, a thought, a theory—to attach itself to the presently perceived object. More exactly, Santayana's notion of expression allows this and our experience of art confirms that such things happen. But it is a question of sensibility, and criticism, as to whether an association "works" and whether or not it succeeds effectively in affiliating with a sensuous object.

Santayana's *The Sense of Beauty* fits into no clear tradition of aesthetic writing, yet is rich in historical antecedents. It has no clear influences and effects, yet shows remarkable anticipation of what is happening in aesthetic theory and criticism one hundred years after its appearance. It is at once *sui generis* yet full of perennial wisdom.

TWENTY-TWO

SANTAYANA'S *THE LAST PURITAN*

1995

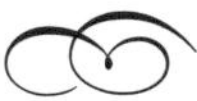

"Memory and imagination played out together intriguingly, pushing and pulling in both directions in Santayana's mercurial mind, and nowhere more than in" The Last Puritan (1936), subtitled A Memoir in the Form of a Novel. *It tells the story of the admirably gifted Oliver Alden, an imagined student of Santayana's, whose ideals were pure though tragically ill-suited to his times. The work "is a complicated interplay of biography and fiction" that is mirrored in the relation of the efforts of the editors of the 1994 Critical Edition to the spirit of the author. The critical edition shows a "relentless search for correctness down to proper hyphenations," while the work employs creative rememberings seeking "fidelity . . . to an absent ideal" as much as "verisimilitude to a supposed original." But the task of editing and the joy of thoughtful reading are not exclusive; The Critical Edition invites "ongoing and venturesome critical evaluation. . . . creating a Santayana the way characters are created in his novel." This requires willingness "to risk the mere facts, even to turn from them . . . and to indulge the artful process whereby we create both what we find and who we are."*

For a number of years, at used book sales, I was able to pick up copies of the original dark green edition of Santayana's *The Last Puritan.* Because the book became a best seller after its first publication in 1935, copies showed up in quantity at these sales, some perused, some in pristine condition with dust jackets. At fifty cents or a dollar apiece—and with such an enormous disparity between cost and value—they made choice gifts. Now the supply has dwindled and the books are much harder to find. So the new Critical Edition is not only excellent of its kind—definitive, accurate, thorough—but also very timely and sure to endure.

This edition of *The Last Puritan* is a major step in a long series and follows upon the publication of *Persons and Places*, *Interpretations of Poetry and Religion*, and *The Sense of Beauty*. Herman J. Saatkamp Jr. guides this huge project with the rarely combined skills of entrepreneur, fundraiser, and scholar. He has the help of a dedicated staff and has also been able to call upon a singularly talented editorial board. This polyglot band of Santayana enthusiasts has probably provided more ballast for the enterprise than actual help to Saatkamp in moving it along.

The new edition is dark blue, much longer, larger, and more readable than the original. It includes photographs of Beacon Hill in Boston, of Iffley Church in England, and of Santayana's sketch of his hero Oliver Alden—leaving us with the intriguing, perplexing, and thematic question as to whether it was done "from life." The scholarly apparatus is formidable. The editors summarize philosophical viewpoints for the less learned and there are many useful tidbits even for the well informed. In one instance, the full plot of Verdi's opera *Rigoletto* is provided so that the reader might be helped in interpreting one of Oliver's dreams—perhaps while simultaneously wondering whether it was one of Santayana's dreams. The notes are so finely detailed that they might serve as a Baedeker for anyone wishing to explore the places traversed by both Santayana and Oliver. They go well beyond Santayana's own considerable inclination to be specific and accurate about places. Beacon Street, for example, makes its move in the opening sentence of *The Last Puritan* when it "consents to bend slightly and begins to run down hill, and where across the Mall the grassy shoulder of the Common slopes most steeply down to the Frog Pond."[1] The notes elaborate on this and on many other locales, for example, London, Oxford, Paris, and New York. The Editorial Apparatus runs some 172 pages and includes Notes on the Text, Textual Commentary, List of Emendations, List of Variants, and Editorial Appendix.

The precision of this edition, and its relentless search for correctness down to proper hyphenations, might seem antithetical to the spirit of the author. But there was a side to Santayana that was thoroughly practical, even finicky in his concern about accuracy and detail. We learn from this edition a great deal about the nearly simultaneous publication of the original edition in both England and America. Santayana was attentive not only to places and place names but to matters like proofreading, typing arrangements, even publishers' libel fears, which required extensive letter writing and micromanaging. Persons, understandably, are less securely fixed than places, and the persons of *The Last Puritan* are evanescent indeed. The search for their sources, for their "originals" if they have any, has been widely undertaken—by Santayana among others. Indeed, the panoply of persons, at receding and uncertain distances, includes Santayana himself! He is a multivocal character among characters, as he is in all his writings. It is hardly the case that in *The Last Puritan* we get Santayana's viewpoints dramatized, while elsewhere we get them straight. The rendering of himself in his necessarily "transfiguring" memories is as problematic as his treatment of other "historical" personages.

The book is a complicated interplay between biography and fiction, and in *both directions* it is a move away from, and a recovery of, truth. Persons are recalled but are also created as characters, hence transformed into ideal and more appropriate versions of themselves than they otherwise ever could be. Thus Oliver and Mario Van de Weyer and even "Santayana" are elusive to the end. Santayana's subtitle, *A Memoir in the Form of a Novel* is daring for its time, long before the discovery (or was it the invention?) of factoids and other current fusions of fact and fancy. In his autobiography Santayana wrote that what we "think we remember will be remembered differently; so that a man's memory may almost become the art of continually varying and misrepresenting his past, according to his interests in the present."[2]

The mystery and strangeness of *The Last Puritan*, on a real-imaginary axis, are enhanced by a Prologue and an Epilogue that are at once part of and not part of the novel. They contain conversations between "Santayana" and Mario, first about whether the "biography" of Oliver should be written (both men "knew" Oliver, who was a "student" of Santayana) and finally about Mario's assessment of the "manuscript."

Santayana, as "Santayana," after Prologue and Epilogue, is mostly absent from *The Last Puritan*, though on one occasion he appears in a delightful Hitchcock-like vignette when some Harvard youngsters (overheard in Cambridge?) discuss the pros and cons of studying philosophy with him. This appearance has the same startling and uncanny effect—each philosopher making himself conspicuously minimal on the occasion—as does the appearance of "Plato" in the *Apology*. We all recall that Plato, along with others, wanting to be helpful to Socrates, upped the ante thirtyfold on the one mina fine that Socrates had proposed to his judges. For that matter, the multiple framings and ironic distancings employed by Santayana in *The Last Puritan* are not unlike those used by Plato in the *Symposium*, where we learn "what happened" during a long drinking party, with "real" people in it (a Memoir in the form of a Dialogue?), as it is told by Apollodorus, who checked some details with Socrates but who essentially got it from Aristodemus, who was there in person!

Santayana's Preface, written for the Triton Edition two years after the book's original publication, provides a further framing or distancing from *The Last Puritan* "proper." He offers some gentle rejoinders to criticisms of his work, along with reminders that he is not a definitive commentator: "Indeed, what I am now adding in this Preface, though an afterthought and spoken before the curtain, is also composed for the public, and is no innocent aside;"[3] and "who is man, especially histrionic rhetorical man, to see the truth of his own doings?"[4] There is no curtain, only a receding series of veils. We cannot quite agree with the editor that the Preface contains Santayana's "fundamental interpretation of the novel."[5]

Irving Singer, in his learned, sympathetic and extensive (36-page) Introduction, adds one more circle to these concentric circles of commentary. Though his is a non-Santayana framing, Singer is so finely attuned to Santayana, and to the dangers of dogmatic summary, that he continues in the spirit of Santayana's own explorative tentativeness. His own interpretation might indeed be as fundamental and reliable as Santayana's! His essay, a miniature "philosophy of love," provides a major review of the "originals" and sources of *The Last Puritan* and shows that they are more complicated than might seem to have been the case.

Singer elaborates on Platonic love and friendship, much misconstrued in this age, and deals with Santayana's homosexuality. Santayana's sexual orientation, partly concealed by Santayana from himself and from others, has surfaced in the recent attentions of scholars, with biographical questions as to whether he was a "practicing" homosexual and with literary questions as to the relevance of his sexual orientation to his writings.

Santayana would certainly have been sensitive to Christian strictures against homosexuality and somewhere refers to Michelangelo's "discreditable passions."[6] But the primary moral interest for Santayana, as for Plato, was not homosexuality versus heterosexuality but the overcoming of physical sensuality whatever its orientation. With respect to Santayana's sense of himself, Singer says, "I have no way of knowing whether Santayana thought that he himself approached the ideal he had in mind."[7] Of course Santayana, with his intense Spanish mix of pride and humility, his conceits and his modesties, his "passive passion," his pervasive ironies and dramatizations, would himself not have had a definitive answer to Singer's question.

Santayana's anti-Semitism, long evident in unpublished manuscripts and in the appearance in the Critical Edition of some previously suppressed texts, has been given detailed scrutiny by John McCormick in his ample biography. That prejudice derives much from Spanish (boyhood) and English literary (Trollope and Meredith) influences and enters at least obliquely into the fabric of *The Last Puritan*. Since I cannot imagine Santayana with an emotion, a love or a hate, he did not in part internalize, I venture the extravagant hypothesis that Santayana was a closet Marrano! In any case, while the distinction between "practicing and non-practicing" has in principle a clearer cusp with respect to homosexuality than to anti-Semitism, we are in areas of interpretive puzzlement with respect to both of them.

How are we helped by having before us, all in one place as it were, the entire apparatus of the Critical Edition, Singer's overview, references and cross references to Santayana's letters, to *Persons and Places*, to John McCormick's insights, to Daniel Cory's writings and conversations, to the recollections of other people who talked to Santayana or who imagined they did?

Scholars characteristically seek to resolve interpretive issues, to bring finality to their searches, by sufficient gatherings of material. Such searches are necessary and commendable, and this edition helps enormously in doing them for us. It surely adds richness to our sense of Santayana, a deeper awareness of his multi-voiced elusiveness, and brings us closer to one kind of comprehensive truth.

But it also serves as a reminder, by indirection and by what is absent from it, that issues of interpretation cannot be resolved by endless compilations of information, however vast. The interpretive process is as important as the truth-gathering one—endlessly layered and quite as interminable. There is never a last rung to the ladders of descent into a world or of ascent into a soul.

What the Critical Edition invites then, because of what is inherently absent from its purpose, is ongoing and venturesome critical evaluation. This means creating a Santayana the way characters are created in his novel—not merely for the sake of some verisimilitude to a supposed original, but for some fidelity or appropriateness to an absent ideal. This requires of the critic attention not only to what Santayana said but also some imaginative recreation of how he said it and what he might have said. It takes as much careful looking to see what is absent in an author as to see what is there. An absence can be a special kind of presence, and the implicit direction, or potentiality, of a person or of a tree, a book or a divinity, is part of the truth about it. Recall the "absence of religion" that Santayana saw in Shakespeare, or all the absences he saw in the friends he recalled and the characters he drew. This sense of absence, of something unreachable and unknowable that he yearned for, is a pervasive and haunting presence in Santayana himself—albeit with a vagueness that left him uncomfortable, and that spurred him to ongoing pursuits and clarifications.

Criticism requires us to be willing to risk the mere facts, even to turn from them—especially now that the Critical Edition brings them so fully before us—and to indulge the artful process whereby we create both what we find and who we are. It is what Santayana did when he wrote about Shakespeare, Browning, Whitman, Emerson, James, Christ, Lucretius, Lucifer, Dante, Oliver, anyone—when he created all those portraits of others that are simultaneous self-discoveries. There is still much to explore in Santayana's manner of writing, which needs to go well beyond crude summary judgments about irony, drama, and ambivalence. For example, there is Santayana's tendency to "flame" (as in his anti-Semitic remarks), to begin with moments of explosive bitterness and mockery, and then, after venturing his particularized and uncharitable resentments, to achieve, after real effort, some balance and constraint.

Santayana, we learn from the Critical Edition, not infrequently "misremembered" names and texts, including his own texts. But he did not always like to be corrected, and his errors could be part of his fun, his mischievous inventiveness, and make their own points. When Santayana remembers Emerson's phrase "slow but sure reclining" as "true and sure declining" there could be something deliberate, impish, and playful in the lapse.[8] According to Santayana, so-called misremembering "when it is not intentional or dishonest, involves no deception. . . . A point of view and a special lighting are not distortions. They are conditions of vision, and spirit can see nothing not focussed in some living eye."[9]

It has been said that Alzheimer's patients have one advantage over most of the rest of us—they keep meeting new and interesting people. Remembering is an endless affront to imagining, as possessing is to desiring, or as sleeping is to dreaming. Memory and imagination played out together intriguingly, pushing and pulling in both directions in Santayana's mercurial mind, and nowhere more than in his novel—though elsewhere quite as much.

What has happened to *The Last Puritan* between its first and latest appearances? Would it now even be considered for the Pulitzer Prize, as it was then? We learn that Santayana would have received it but for his lack of U.S. citizenship (late in life he refused to give up his prized Spanish citizenship for the honor of being made a citizen of Rome). So the Prize went to Margaret Mitchell for *Gone with the Wind*. Frankly, Santayana didn't give a damn. But, given the chance, he would have deferred to Miss Mitchell and gallantly credited her novel with being the superior accomplishment for having better love scenes!

Meanwhile we await the time when another Santayana letter might turn up, or another conversation be recalled, in which he *did* say the above. In fact, that is to say in fancy, it is what he told me in Rome, where I imagined visiting him, but didn't. Or was it said in one of the mislaid letters I received from Cory? Conversations in Limbo, we might have learned from Santayana, elsewhere as well as in *The Last Puritan*, are no less real than other conversations, and we *separate* the real from the imagined, essence from existence, at the peril of both.

Those of us old enough to straddle the publication dates of the original and current editions of *The Last Puritan* will note that the work has become more insistently cerebral, leisurely, literate, and learned. By chance and by choice, Santayana was remote even from his contemporaries. Nonetheless, he shone as an idiosyncratic light, a beacon that was much admired and that could inspire. But when the ambiance changes, so must everything else. The Western canon, in which Santayana was deeply immersed and which he uniquely rendered, has dimmed in sixty years. It is now defended mostly by quaint mugwumps and Quixotic old-timers, who still think it matters whether we can tell a hawk from a handsaw!

The fate of *The Last Puritan* is no longer in the hands of the general public, nor even in the custody of philosophy professors. Isolated young scholars in English departments are giving it the best and most thorough scrutiny it currently receives. Christopher Morley, when *The Last Puritan* appeared as a Book-of-the-Month selection, said "it must have close attention or none."[10] That is perhaps too much, or too little, to ask of it at any time. At least the book is now fully and finely available for whatever degrees of attention we can muster and it can attract, and for whatever light it still sheds. Santayana is surely an "ultimate" like his hero, the last philosophical poet of the classical tradition.

TWENTY-THREE

SANTAYANA IN CALIFORNIA

The Environment, Transcendentalism, and Nature

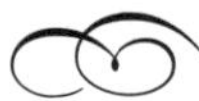

Some environmentalists have read Santayana as a comrade in their cause. They often cite his essay "The Genteel Tradition in American Philosophy," in which he criticizes Transcendentalism and praises the California landscape for its potential influence on thinkers who would free themselves from distorted philosophical traditions. But this neglects vital aspects of Santayana's thinking about nature and misidentifies him as an environmentalist. For Santayana, nature is neither "man-made garden [nor] distant fixed landscape," rather, following the ancients, "nature is remote, tragic, indifferent, an object of thought—inspiring awe and even worship but not pleasing or accessible in the usual aesthetic or sensory way." These three views of nature make for Santayana a kind of Platonic ascent: nature "is revealed, or understood, not by looking and listening but by intellectual reflection." But on this topic as on others Santayana exhibits "the ongoing play of [his] contradictory or dramatic attitudes:" Substance, claims Santayana, "must remain unconceived and inconceivable." He is no traditional Platonist and acknowledges the necessity of the aesthetic. Santayana's view of nature reveals his deep desire for an "Ultimate, named and intimated in various ways, and valued for being unavailable and beyond value."

Some writers, passionately devoted to ecologism or environmentalism (George Sessions and Kevin Starr, among others)[1] have sought to find support in Santayana and even to see him as a precursor of their own concerns. They pay particular attention to his criticism of Transcendentalism in his August 25, 1911, address in California, which became known as "The Genteel Tradition in American Philosophy."[2]

The following barely touches on the scope of "The Genteel Tradition." Perhaps wisely so. That essay ranges over the bulk of Santayana's achievement and pursues problems that would require assessments of him as broad as his own comprehensive assessments of Calvinism, Nature, Transcendentalism, Emerson, the Jameses, and Whitman. Putting the matter here summarily, the subjectivism in philosophy of which Santayana is so pervasively and repeatedly critical is a subjectivism he sought to escape but knew that he could only keep grappling with.

The following focuses on such grappling and scoffs at the notion that Santayana had environmentalist concerns. It is limited to a few aspects of Santayana's pursuit of nature, or of his idea of nature, for which his visit to California served as an energizing excuse. His references to California were politely deferential, but actually minimal.

Environmentalists want to keep nature from being ruined by man and to honor and preserve it as much as possible. To be sure, Santayana would not want the natural glories of California to be destroyed and he paid passing tribute to them. But unlike Marx, Santayana found philosophers too interested in changing (or preserving) the world and not sufficiently interested in interpreting and understanding it. Santayana had his own ways of thinking about nature. With ambiguous and sometimes changing perspectives, Santayana sought to get beyond landscapes, beauty, or any aesthetic delight.

Santayana's address is not without perfunctory respect for unchanging nature—nature as mountains and forests—which remarks might have pleased ecologists and the Californians he was visiting. He credits them with having the opportunity to free themselves of the distortions of European and "Eastern" (Eastern United States, that is) philosophy. Because of their remarkable macro environment, Californians could develop, like the Greeks, an "honest cosmology." Their notion of nature need not be subjectivist, egotistic, and conceited as the later European tradition had become. Californians were in a position to understand their own place in the scheme of things and to accord to nature the hands-off recognition and distant respect it deserved.

But what is that ultimate respect, and what is nature? The larger environment, of course, includes the part of nature that is fashioned by man and the part that isn't insofar as we can keep those parts distinct. The part that isn't fashioned by man is the glory of California, especially to a first-time visitor. But there is a *tertium quid*, something more to Nature than either changeable or changeless landscapes. There is Nature in the aforementioned classical sense.

Several times in Santayana's texts he distinguishes the English sense of nature from the ancient one. In the former or English view, nature is landscape, mountains, birds, people, animals, gardens. These things can be pleasingly visual and audible, whether man-made or not. In the latter or classic view, nature is *physis*, remote workings of hidden parts, not visible or audible at all, but minimally conceptual.

Looking at nature either as a man-made garden or as distant fixed landscape is still to see it as other than in the classical sense. For the ancients as Santayana understands them, and as he himself variously sought to interpret *physis*, nature is remote, tragic, indifferent, an object of thought—inspiring awe and even worship but not pleasing or accessible in the usual aesthetic or sensory way, whether close up or distant.

Beauty, Santayana has told us, is pleasure regarded as the quality of an object.[3] But can the profoundly or purely conceptual have a knowledgeable object that could be pleasurable or worthy of worship?

The classical view of nature understands it neither as man-made, as gardens are, nor even as more remote Sierras or redwood forests, which though not man-made can be aesthetic or pleasing to the eye. Though those glorious and distant landscapes might modify a Californian's philosophy by taking him from his conceits and anthropocentrisms, let alone from his gardens and flowers, even they are not yet *physis*, a vision or a theory of a thoroughly hidden and non-human universe. *Physis* is revealed, or understood, not by looking and listening but by intellectual reflection, as was done by pre-Socratic philosophers and as continued by modern physicists.

The persistent philosophical problem is that even nature in its classic sense, *physis*, cannot escape human terms in the description of it—and Santayana is aware of the paradoxes in his attempts. He encounters substance, the realm of matter, interpretively, at a great distance. Calling nature absolutely remote and inaccessible, like calling God unknowable, have been inevitable ways of "effing" or taming the ineffable. Santayana grappled long with the "Unknowable," sometimes finding Herbert Spencer's word romantic and unsatisfactory, sometimes workable if much qualified.[4] The distinction between nature as (1) man-made, as (2) non-man-made yet distantly visible and audible, and finally as (3) hidden, remote, and even less than conceptual, becomes Santayana's intimation of a Platonic ascent.

It might be entertaining, or even amusing (if not vulgar), to look at some of the frailer human impulses in the stages of this ascent or descent. The first distinction between (1) and (2), the man-made and the non-man-made, is suggested by the following. "Paris, the capital of food, fashion and fragrance . . . has joined the ranks of the polluted cities."[5] The French apparently give little, or belated, attention to the ozone and garbage that other nations are concerned about. Why is this so? One M. Jean Felix Bernards, of the Green Party, says, "The French are not very interested in the natural state of things. They love the arts, literature, human creativity. But nature is not human creation. Nature becomes beautiful when it is transformed."[6] The French, we are told, like formal gardens, trees lined in a row, not "natural" wilderness. The Pyrenees are not, as it were, the French Sierras, worth a lot of beholding. The French do not like what nature is and was before it was transformed—preferably by them. If they are sometimes negative or careless with nature, the garbage and the smells (we might conclude) can be ignored or covered up with their perfumes.

The ways of ignoring or transforming nature are surely multifarious. A positive and more subtle way of thinking about the matter might even get us to the Transcendentalists. A review by Richard Bernstein deals with "the proper relationship between human culture and the natural world"[7]—which of course is the great ongoing concern of the environmentalists. Bernstein writes, "John Muir's most famous epigram has to do with the inherent value of untouched nature, 'the great fresh unblighted, unredeemed wilderness.'"[8] But there is some wavering on his part, and Bernstein refers to writers Richard White and Daniel B. Botkin (academics greatly interested in the environment) as sharing "Ralph Waldo Emerson's notion of nature as receptive to human transformation."[9]

Can nature be both magnificently untouched and yet transformed by humans? Are there different ways of human transformation? Can there possibly be something betwixt and between ecological and interpretive transformation? The phrase "receptive to human transformation" suggests that nature, because receptive, is sometimes physically untransformed and that we might yet be transforming it even before, or without, laying hands on it. Isn't nature like Michelangelo's marble before it became David? Yet the marble was transformed, at least interpretively, when it existed unquarried and when, at least for Michelangelo, it was a vague vision of its possibilities. This can run a wide gamut of endeavor beyond marble for a sculptor: it could be a person for a lover, a music score for a pianist, a patient for a surgeon, a cosmos for a physicist or realms of being for a philosopher. The world could be far more transformed than we usually "realize" or readily acknowledge. Overt activity or physical encounter might not be at all to the point.

As we said, when engaged in his Platonic ascent to nature proper, Santayana wants to get away from landscape and the aesthetic, and indeed any other merely pleasant, evasive, or subjective versions of nature. He wants to repudiate the Transcendentalists and other romantics, though it is hard to evade their methods. In an aside, bluntly disparaging but surely deliberate, he lumps together landscape and music! "In the presence of music or landscape human experience eludes itself."[10] Whatever their wonders and joys, anything we see, hear, or create does not get us to the nature of things, more specifically, the nature of Nature. So the philosopher, *qua* philosopher, should banish the poets along with the Sierras! Perhaps he should allow only the ultimate philosophical poet, a being as remote and as unknowable as nature itself, to interpret without distorting, intruding, or changing. True Olympian heights, Plato must surely have said many times (possibly even to the Stranger in Limbo), cannot be reached by visiting or climbing Mount Olympus.

This just might get us back to the spirit of Santayana! What he says about the California landscape is old-fashioned and quaint. It is hardly relevant to the place of a hundred years ago, or of now. California has long been a pretext for good and bad dreams of all kinds, even the hopes and failed dreams of environmentalists. Yet whatever its persistent glories and scenic survivals, and whatever its spoilage and decrepitude,

California will still partake of the nature that Santayana could envisage even without a visit. California's passing value for Santayana was as an occasion for his philosophizing; it served to measure his Platonic impulses and his skill in articulating them. He was after an interpretation of *physis*, not to find and finally unfurl it but to imaginatively intimate it. He was a forty-niner of the mind, and so did not locate or lay up his treasure where others did. The resultant dream is Santayana's very real intellectual and spiritual journey. It might perdure as long or longer than California, though in a very different place.

Some remarks years later on substance, in *Scepticism and Animal Faith*, might further reveal the ongoing play of Santayana's contradictory or dramatic attitudes. He responds to those who object that substance, "because it is not an appearance represented exhaustively, must remain unconceived and inconceivable."[11] The "intrinsic essence [of substance]" Santayana assures us, "must always remain problematical." Further, "to pure spirit substance and all its ways must remain always dark, alien and impertinent."[12] The word "impertinent" here is itself almost impertinent and mocking. Perhaps his manuscript said "imperturbable." (Finding impertinence in the universe is as problematic as finding pleasure in objects of beauty, as Santayana did when, by his own admission in describing *The Sense of Beauty*, he "skirted psychologism.")[13]

Santayana had a deep hankering for ultimates, or one Ultimate, named and intimated in various ways and valued for being unavailable and beyond value. One sees it in "The Philosophy of Thule": Thule "is the mind of all tomorrows desired, but never experienced."[14] "Thule must be ultimate in an absolute sense, that however far we travel we shall never reach it, nor even [ever][15] approach it . . . yet beckoning us eternally Thule gives secret force and inward meaning to our whole pilgrimage."[16]

Santayana did his best to avoid what he saw as the subjectivism of the idealists and transcendentalists and to turn his deepest feelings (like Spinoza) into an impersonal or intellectual love. Perhaps it is even possible, with suitable spiritual effort and advancing physical fatigue (the two might have a post-rational symbiosis) to become indifferent to glorious mountains, to be unperturbed by the harmony of the spheres, and even, finally, to be unmoved by the music of Mozart.

TWENTY-FOUR

ULTIMATE SANTAYANA

1992

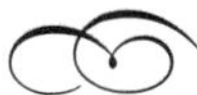

An aspect of Santayana's concern with ultimate meaning and reality is his attempt to situate his moral outlook in a thoroughly natural context. "One way of doing it would be simply to equate the moral with the natural," but Santayana opts for no such thoroughgoing solution. His approach is indicated in his ontology—his Realms of Being, in which his "artful structuring of the realms is such as to convey that excellence and existence are not necessarily linked; indeed they are largely disparate, though they are bonded and 'grafted' to each other." In his essay on Spinoza, "Ultimate Religion," Santayana seems to both embrace Spinoza's identification with the universe and distrust the inhumanity of such a view. Santayana's dramatic and ironic approach allows him to dramatize his different views. "Santayana's sense of an 'Ultimate Religion' is something he attempts to arrive at not miraculously but meditatively, not by some declared faith in the unknown or even by poetic presumptions about it. His effort is a disciplined examination of conscience, which examination is both a sustained dialectic and an exalted art. It is, like any great art, a miracle and revelation of sorts, both worshipful and cognitive."

Introduction

Santayana lived in many countries—Spain, America, England, France, Italy. He also dwelled in the realm of matter and the realm of spirit. He was at home in these different physical and intellectual places and also a stranger to them. This profound and tension-filled double locus of his affiliations is the story of his life and of his work. He was variously a foreigner among natives, a European among Americans, a Catholic among Protestants, an ancient among moderns, a Tory among democrats, a materialist among idealists, a poet among philosophers (and a philosopher among poets), and vis-à-vis some of his family, a full-blooded Spaniard among half-breeds!

People sometimes forget that Santayana was born in Spain of Spanish parents and might have become, under "ordinary" circumstances, a minor soldier or a minor architect. If not for his mother's earlier marriage and the untimely death of her Sturgis husband, if not for various chance-like events in the realm of matter, and if not (as it can appropriately be summed up) for God's will, Santayana would hardly have become both an exile from his deepest roots and a philosopher to the world. It was a burden to come to the United States as a boy, to leave his father in Spain and join his mother and half-siblings in Boston. That burden, with its pains, ambivalences, and opportunities, determined the person that he became.

His life and thought straddled a sense of something permanently lost and of something permanently hoped for, both of them of a dreamlike quality. His life also entailed the wonderfully accompanying insight about what it was—as he himself put it—to dream awake, with one eye open.[1] His philosophy in large part is the dramatization of diverse perspectives.

Every philosopher worthy of the name is interested in ultimates—particularly ultimate meaning and reality. Else why be a philosopher? Particular things and problems are nicely handled by plumbers and doctors, biologists and historians, maybe even by physicists and theologians.

Generality admits of degrees, and when we get to the interests of physicists and theologians, we at least begin to veer toward the ultimate. Physicists now, like the very earliest ones, are cosmologists and they address the total order and even the origin of the physical world. Theologians, who justify the ways of God to man, have always, and variously, addressed issues of ultimate meaning.

It has been the aim of philosophers to go beyond the interests of cosmologists and theologians, to bring those interests together, to combine and relate them, and to look at them in comprehensive and unique ways. They not only explore being and value but ponder the connections between the two. Santayana somewhere suggests that the hallmark of a philosopher is how he grafts his moral onto his natural philosophy—and he himself clearly gave much thought to this grafting. One way of doing it would be simply to equate the moral and the natural, perhaps by proposing that "whatever is, is right," or else by saying that the most real of beings is the most perfect of beings, or by identifying God with Nature as Spinoza does.

Such thoroughgoing grafting, where root and branch practically fuse, is hardly what Santayana proposes, and in what follows I show how he addresses the issue. While there are endless Santayana texts to choose from, I turn in detail only to his essay "Ultimate Religion" (1936), a commentary on Spinoza that is naturally appropriate to matters of ultimacy and that reveals Santayana as much as it reveals Spinoza. Otherwise, I make some general, and necessarily abbreviated, observations about *Realms of Being* (1942).

Santayana has properly enough been called the *Mona Lisa* among philosophers. But it is not the case that he merely smiles and is inscrutable. He can also be very earnest and precise. What is not available to the hasty glance is the complicated interplay of the multiple perspectives of his tragicomic vision. In that sense he is indeed elusive, and to know him at all is to trace, perhaps only here and there, his artful and serious way of envisioning the sundry components of his character.

The Realm of Matter and the Importance of Physics

Philosophy has sometimes, and paradoxically, been hostile to the mistakes and dangers of generalization. Whitehead called philosophy "a critique of abstractions," and many contemporary philosophers are contemptuous of attempts to address anything but specific and clearly defined problems; they tend to see anything else as hopeless vagueness or "literature."

Santayana is hardly of this particularist temper and he avowedly philosophizes in the manner of the ancients. The very idea of creating a "system" of philosophy (despite Santayana's ironies about building systems) and his scheme of four all-inclusive realms confirm his own impulse to generalize. Nonetheless, Santayana often honors the concrete details of proper wisdom, certainly with respect to physics, without partaking in them.

His approach to the realms, particularly the realm of matter, is evidence of this. Santayana salutes the specifics, the elaborations of the realm of matter that physicists might supply, not what the philosopher might dwell on in an *a priori* fashion. These details are given their due but they are fitted only obliquely, as it were, into his philosophy. Such work in physical theory is not Santayana's métier, and he knows it. Still, he acknowledges the importance of physics; it is luggage that he carries even though others have done the packing for him.

The importance of the realm of matter, and the physics that studies it, is evidenced in Santayana's avowal of materialism. While there is some irony in this, Santayana goes so far as to identify considerably with Democritus and Epicurus. But whereas the latter were indeed physicists and natural philosophers, and devoted much effort to an elaboration of their physical theories, Santayana, living in a later age, refers the changing details of physical theory to those who might be called physicists-as-such. His sketch of the material universe is minimal; the moral lessons he draws from that sketch are considerable.

Epicurus, for Santayana, is a philosopher who carefully grafted his moral onto his natural philosophy. To say this is to note that Epicurus's physics was a necessary and prior effort to provide a base for his ethics. He couldn't properly deal with the gods, and the fears associated with them, and the task of living with equanimity in a puzzling universe until he explained the workings of that universe, and indeed of the gods, in physical terms. The explanations were directly connected with, and gave rise to, the moral lessons.

Santayana's rendering of the realm of matter, at once laudatory and dismissive, implies (one might say) an unusual taunt at traditional philosophy. Philosophers of the West have been addicted mostly to ontological priorities—assumptions to the effect that reality, existence, power are necessarily wedded to value, importance, divinity.

Santayana radically departs from such notions. The realm of matter is the primary realm of existence. While the intuitions of the realm of spirit also exist, in ways that Santayana had some difficulty in acknowledging, that existence of spirit is a clear consequence of local flurries and organizations, as it were, in the underlying realm of matter. Matter makes consciousness possible, and makes values possible, but the realm of matter, the universe in its existential ordering, is not an object of un-equivocal value or worship. The value of the realm of matter is not in-trinsic; its value is not in its wholeness; its value is in making specific and limited things possible.

There are some waverings and qualifications here, which pervade Santayana's writings and enter into his Spinoza essay. Briefly, matter is a source of value and consciousness, and the realm of matter is therefore worthy of a sort of awe and reverence. It is a pietistic reverence, an hon-oring of sources and origins; but for Santayana it would veer toward superstition to bring any sense of divine worship to the realm of matter. Its excellence is implicit and potential, not explicit and actual. So that which is, that which exists, that which is the entire subject of physics and cosmology is, strangely enough, given peripheral and not central atten-tion in Santayana's scheme. Or perhaps more accurately, it is given central existential importance but peripheral human and moral importance. The human and morally important, again strangely enough, frequently involve the non-existent.

The Realms of Spirit and of Truth, the Non-Existent Realm of Essence

If existence, or the realm of matter, is not central, or morally central, then what is? It is the realm of essence, which Santayana tells us does not exist. It is also the realm of spirit, the existing moments of consciousness or intuition that focus on the non-existent essences. Santayana confers reality or being on essences, but denies them existence. In doing this, Santayana is saying that power and might are not the be-all and end-all of that which is valuable in the scheme of things and, indeed, that existence and power might sometimes be indifferent or irrelevant to the valuable. Value is a precarious and local thing in the universe, generated in much isolation among thinking minds who often differ radically from other thinking minds.

In Santayana's naturalism, consciousness, the human values it looks to, the psyche itself, are small and minor incidents in the large existential scheme. Santayana is profoundly sympathetic to the human impulse to generate ideals and to intuit essences, and is accordingly also sympathetic to the impulse to create religions and even supernaturalistic worlds. What he wants to avoid—and what the structure of his ontology helps him to avoid—is a confusing of the human impulse to idealize with the hard, unfriendly, painstaking search for the uncooperative facts. The faults of traditional religion, as Santayana occasionally sees them, are not that they generate ideals and even a supernatural world; the faults are faults of physics, for example, seeing the supernatural, heaven and hell, say, as a continuation of a natural order rather than as non-existent essences invented by imagination. Santayana's artful structuring of the realms is such as to convey that excellence and existence are not necessarily linked; indeed, they are largely disparate, though they are bonded and "grafted" to each other. Morality requires that we reckon with the existent, but there are different ways of making the connections, which can range from the casual and remote to the intimate and the preoccupied.

Santayana's avowed naturalism and materialism are a puzzle to many critics. How could anyone who lives so much in the imagination, whose philosophy in such large part is literary and dramatic invention, who dwells so happily among non-existent essences and who hardly ever enters, in any detailed way, the world of physical theory—how could such a person, at least in many asides, proclaim a materialism and give such centrality to the realm of matter?

It is part of Santayana's intellectual courage and heroism to do this, akin (though not identical, as we shall see) to the courage and heroism that he attributes to Spinoza. Power needs to be honored and reckoned with, but it would be a moralism of a dangerous and inhuman kind merely to honor power and never to question or challenge it. Material power and human virtue are in persistent contestation.

I will not dwell on the realm of spirit—it involves its own considerable problems. But briefly, consciousness, "the light of actuality," is of supreme moral (but not physical) importance in the universe, akin perhaps to Pascal's thinking reed, small and weak in itself but capable of the large survey. Consciousness, though it could conceivably arise out of organized matter elsewhere, belongs only to humans. Santayana is not dogmatic about this but he sees no evidence of consciousness or spirit in the universe at large, and this view squares with his naturalism and his general skepticism about religions.

Though Santayana provides us with an ontology, with a total scheme of ways of being, his attention to spirit is largely an attention to spiritual life—to the moral issues faced by humans in the distracting and difficult task of trying to live well. Santayana somewhere says that moral philosophy is his chosen subject. In a sense it is, but his natural philosophy, his comments on the powerful and purposeless existential framework, underlie and give a needed setting to his moral concerns. The grafting of the moral onto the natural is an ongoing agon, what spiritual life is about.

Santayana nowhere proposes a solution to the origin of consciousness (or spirit), which leaves his system with some of the traditional problems of any dualism. Santayana would perhaps see the problem of origins as resolvable not by abstract speculation but possibly in the technical details of advancing physical theory. He likely would have been interested in some of the recent converging of computer theory, brain study, and artificial intelligence. One could argue that Santayana's system is monistic, not dualistic, since only matter exists. But spirit exists too in some problematic way, and in any case the realm of essence, infinite in scope but non-existent, needs to be reckoned as being in some way "part" of Santayana's philosophy.

Calling essences non-existent but real, proclaiming their infinity, giving them much detailed attention, is an ironic bit of self-abnegation on Santayana's part. Again, what is selectively and morally important to him, what receives his extensive attentions and definitions, by no means coincides with the power and obscurities of nature, with its executive ordering or mere "truth." This philosophical modesty, this absence of dogmatism on Santayana's part, is clearly and neatly a consequence of the very structuring of his system and goes well beyond any mere denials of dogmatism or any avowals of modesty and tentativeness.

The realm of truth, though terribly important to philosophy (some might argue), can mostly be left out of my sketch of what is meaningful and ultimate in Santayana. For the realm of truth is part of the realm of essence, likewise non-existent but obliquely connected with existence. Santayana actually calls it a tragic segment of the realm of essence[2]—

perhaps recalling the weighty burden of thinking, the connections between knowledge and sorrow, and maybe even the overall unpleasantness of so much of the realm of matter that intrudes, destroys, or is irrelevant to the needs and hopes of men. It would be very much in the spirit of Santayana to see the realm of truth as the comic segment of the realm of essence, for the facts of the world (as both Shakespeare and Santayana tell us) are neither comic nor tragic except as we see them as such or as thinking makes them so. They can be seen either way or both ways at once. The laughing and the weeping philosophers, Santayana somewhere tells us, encounter the same facts.[3]

Making truth but a part of the realm of essence implies, again, a kind of modesty and an equivocation—a modesty and equivocation that arise from the structure of Santayana's system. We esteem truth and aspire to it. Many of the values we conceive, the plans and aspirations we articulate, are non-existent essences that we hope we can get the material world to exemplify by our efforts. We hope that our wishes will eventually obtain in the "real world." But Santayana is not devoted only to the truth—only to what exists, has existed, or will exist. There are essences worth dwelling on, worth intuiting, that will not and cannot be accommodated by the realm of matter. Santayana at times is critical of moralists who are merely practical and rational, for whom, as he once put it, "nothing counts but realization." He leaves room for post-rational sentiment, for essences that are congenial but that are thoroughly remote from the practical, as works of art and of the religious imagination sometimes are.

Distinction between What Is (the Universe) and What (the Universe) Ought to Be (Wish-Fulfillment, Mystical and Imaginative Yearnings)

Santayana's essay on Spinoza, "Ultimate Religion," is a good summary revelation of Santayana's own views. Santayana constantly sounded out other philosophers to discover both differences and affinities between himself and them. Santayana's strong attachment to Spinoza, his tributes and his approvals, along with his qualifications and modifications of that approval, help us to understand Santayana at least as much as they help us to understand Spinoza.

Santayana's tribute begins with his reference to the *Domus Spinozana* at The Hague, where he gave his lecture, as a "consecrated place." He admires Spinoza's "courage, firmness and sincerity." Spinoza "did not ask God to meet him half way: he did not whitewash the facts, as the facts appear to clear reason, or as they appeared to the science of his day."[4]

Santayana's devotion to and confidence in reason were not as great as Spinoza's. For Spinoza, reason could comprehend and master the universe, that is, master it in thought, whereas for Santayana, "reason in us may be imperfectly adapted to the understanding of nature."[5] So, for Santayana the task of living well required not only the acknowledgement of an unfriendly universe, as Spinoza acknowledged it, but also of an elusive and mysterious universe that had limited accessibility to human reason and that was often alien to human needs and desires.

The moral task, for Spinoza, for Santayana, perhaps for anyone alive to the miracle and elusiveness of existence, is to recognize that spirit in man, his consciousness, "though it is living it is powerless to live; that though it may die it is powerless to die; and that altogether, at every instant and in every particular, it is in the hands of some alien and inscrutable power."[6] The moral task, the grafting of the moral onto the natural, seems to require both an acknowledgement of an alien power that can and will destroy us, along with a simultaneously difficult reverence for that power.

This "moral presence of power" can be transformed into a belief in, and dogmatic recognition of, the omnipotence of God. Santayana is ambiguous about such transformation. While at times he approaches the realm of matter with a sense of awe, or piety, or worship, he more usually refrains from the risk of attributing or imposing perfection on a universe where such perfection is not what is actually encountered. That would not be grafting the moral on the natural but uprooting the supporting tree—the very tree that is the source of knowledge of good and evil—and declaring that it is good *simpliciter*. What is directly felt vis-à-vis the realm of matter, what it directly conveys, is "the unfathomableness of the world" prior to the subsequent judgments that might be made about it. But there *are* subsequent judgments, and the unfriendly and misunderstood world that will eventually destroy us can become, to the disciplined will, a delight to the understanding for the temporary gifts and insights it allows us.

The realm of matter can become even more for a stoic temperament like Spinoza's—it can become quite all that the universe, or God, should be. It was Spinoza's achievement to profess a heroic affiliation with the universe, to proclaim a coincidence of will and intellect, to aver, indeed, that what is is what ought to be. In Spinoza's intellectual love of God, as Santayana puts it, "spirit was to be ultimately reconciled with universal power and universal truth."[7]

Is this Santayana's view and stance? It is a crucial and difficult question. I must waver in my answer because Santayana wavered in his. Declaring oneself reconciled to the universe, and affirming an unconditional admiration of it, runs the risk of superstition and pretense. Did Spinoza engage in the pretense and make-believe of traditional religion? Did he invent and proclaim a reality that was wonderful but did not exist, or did he do something else? Santayana's naturalism is hard put to deal with Spinoza's heroism. There are different inflections in the two. At times Santayana is disposed to equate himself with Spinoza, to identify spiritually and charitably with the infinite and varied dispositions of the existing universe, to worship it as God. There are other times when Santayana sees the danger in the pretense and recognizes that it is inhuman (in an undesirable sense of inhuman) not to see the disparity between who we are in our moral and human specificities and what the universe is in its remote workings and its mysterious indifference.

Santayana indicates his difference with Spinoza, particularly the latter's "intellectual love of God,'" in the following lines: "if we wish to make a religion of love . . . we must take universal good, not universal power, for the object of our religion. This religion would need to be more imaginative, more poetical, than that of Spinoza, and the word God, if we still used it, would have to mean for us not the universe, but the good of the universe."[8]

This is an apparent departure from Spinoza. The distinction between the universe and the good of the universe (like comparable distinctions Santayana makes, for example, between beauty and the sense of beauty, Christ and the idea of Christ) leads to some pervasive interpretive difficulties that arise repeatedly in the texts. The universe (the realm of matter) exists but the good of the universe is, or seems to be, a non-existent essence—what the universe ought to be as *distinct* from what it is.

Let us elaborate. The good of a man, like the good of an acorn, is a vision or description of what he or it not yet is. To love a person is to love what he or she may become. A man may envision not only goods for himself that do not yet exist and will not ever exist, but even "goods" that ought never to exist. His vision of himself as the ruler of the universe would be an essentially clear idea but existentially neither possible nor desirable. And yet—and this creates the difficulty—some goods, envisioned in essence but as yet non-existent, are goods that would be true (or "true") fulfillments of the man (or the acorn). For us to love, or to be charitable, is not to wish to change something, or someone, in a direction that would be congenial to us, but to change something in a direction that would be fitting, and appropriate, to *it* or them. Can "the good of the universe" be approached with the kind of dialectic that one uses for "the good of a man"? Can "the good of the universe" include the concern for, and prospect of, its improvement? Perhaps the universe admits of no such clarification, and perhaps its good is linked to what it always is and was—powerful, mysterious, unaccommodating or hurtful to man at times, unyielding to reason at times. This for man, given man's nature and needs, is not what a universe ought to be in the usual understanding of these matters. A "good" universe (like a beneficent deity) would provide ultimate succor and safety, would reward the just and punish the wicked, and make itself truly comprehensible.

To worship, then, the universe as it is, and as it seems continuously to have been out of an unknown past and into an unknown future, is somehow inappropriate—and Santayana often enough indicates this inappropriateness. And yet, a possible heroism in man, a courage, a rare stoicism, an unusual regimen, a special discipline, a dedicated intelligence might enable such a man indeed to worship the universe as it is, and see in what it is, without distortion or pretense, the "good" of it and indeed its ultimate and final appropriateness.

Spinoza, apparently for Santayana, and perhaps in actuality, was such a person and I think it is safe to say, by way of summary, that Santayana, in his dramatic and ironic fashion, and in his various comments on Spinoza, both identifies with, and keeps some distance from, his admired master.

It is possible to take different passages in Santayana and to show (as is my wont) the way he dramatizes his different views. With respect to

Spinoza, Santayana writes: "For there is a mystery here, the mystery of seeming to attain emotionally the logically unattainable."[9] To attain emotionally the logically unattainable smacks of wish-fulfillment, of projecting our desires, our mystical and imaginative yearnings, to where intelligence and cognitive scruples cannot reach or give us what we want. Hence the "seeming" in the quotation above. Santayana goes on to say: "Universal good is something dispersed, varied, contrary to itself in its opposite embodiments; nevertheless, to the mystic, it seems a single living object, the One Beloved, a good to be embraced all at once, finally and forever, leaving not the least shred of anything good outside."[10]

Santayana seems to suggest, on the one hand, that the moralizing and inventive impulse in man is not cognitively reliable. And yet, on the other hand, the aspiration for acceptance and wholeness, of the need to approve of all that there is, of regarding the realm of matter as ultimately worthy, is so powerful that Santayana also sees it (for the mind that is severely dedicated) as a cognitively right judgment. So Santayana too, in his more glowingly poetic, that is, religious, moments, collapses the distinction between God and Nature in the large sphere even as Spinoza does, as he collapses the distinction between will and intellect in his own heroically disciplined meditations.

Santayana says, at the end of *Realms of Being*, "Theology could not possibly be true unless revealed miraculously; and I presume that most of my readers would agree that miraculous revelations are creatures of the heart. Religion itself sometimes calls its dogmas mysteries and its creeds symbols, as if admitting the difference in kind between imagination and truth."[11] Santayana's sense of an "Ultimate Religion" is something he attempts to arrive at not miraculously but meditatively, not by some declared faith in the unknown or even by poetic presumptions about it. His effort is a disciplined examination of conscience, which examination is both a sustained dialectic and an exalted art. It is, like any great art, a miracle and revelation of sorts, both worshipful and cognitive.

Note again that the collapsing of what ought to be into what is, is perhaps the mystic's privilege but not the rational philosopher's, or maybe the privilege of both at once in a rare person like Spinoza. Santayana goes on to say, perhaps with some rational glibness, "Yet I think this mystery may be easily solved. Spirit is essentially synthetic; and just as all the known and unknown forces of nature make, in relation to experience and destiny, one single omnificent power; and just as all facts and all the relations between facts compose for the historical and prophetic mind one unalterable realm of truth; so exactly, for the lover, all objects of love form a single ineffable good."[12]

Yes, spirit is synthetic, but spirit is not the consciousness of the realm of matter, or of nature. There is no such pervasive consciousness, no spirit to bring unity to the universe the way the spirit in man might be said to bring unity to him, or to his specific art works. Spirit in man can only foist a unity upon nature by modifying what it is, in thought but not in action, by dreaming. An artist can foist a unity on his materials by modifying in thought how they come to him and then by actively changing them. In a word, if we press Santayana's naturalistic presumptions there is no way of arriving at a nature that is a worthy object of worship, no more (but also no less) than any great imaginative object is, or ought to be, an object of worship. On the other hand, if we stay with Santayana's inspirational and Platonic impulses, we can acknowledge that, for the rare individual, nature might come to be seen as an object of worship—even indeed as great works of art and the imagination sometimes are.

Spirit Is Essentially Synthetic by Modifying What It Is in Thought by Artistic "Dreaming"

Santayana, at the end of *Realms of Being*, draws a broad analogy between his realms and the Christian Trinity (recalling that the realm of truth is part of the realm of essence, so the four can be turned into three). But his qualifications and hesitations, his recognition of his own artistic play with metaphors, precludes any residual dogma that might be implied in his comparisons.

We have already seen how and why the realm of matter has a somewhat precarious link to divinity. As for the realm of essence (the second person of the Trinity), it is honored but declared to be non-existent, a deliberate fabrication, one might say, of the philosopher who wants his legerdemain to be entirely visible. Its moral importance is completely opposite to its existential importance, which is an inversion of the traditional way of looking upon divinity. The realm of essence is an infinite backdrop to all human choice and even to the contingent choices that emerge in the obscure operations of the realm of matter. It functions (for Santayana) as a tremendous expression of modesty in the face of the unknown, not as an expression of faith in what must be. He is, in fact, dramatizing the ultimately awesome outlooks of belief and unbelief.

Overall, the realms provide us not with ultimate religion but with ultimate art, or else the place where the two ultimates come closest to each other. Surely Santayana creates and envisions his scheme in the manner of any other great artist who addresses ultimate issues, issues (might we say) that *matter*. His work has all the seriousness, passion, dedication, and purpose of religious art, but presented with human modesty, and detached and disinfected of all dogma and theological conceit.

Notes

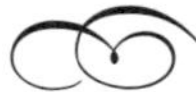

INTRODUCTION

1. William Safire, "Vitiate: Senate's Word a White House Mystery," On Language, *New York Times Magazine*, 16 May 2004, 28.

2. Valerie Peterson and Emmanuel Pierre, "A Drop of Cream, A Good Scream," *New York Times*, 1 January 2009.

3. The text occurs in *Winds of Doctrine* (New York: Charles Scribners' Sons, 1913), 77; *Scepticism and Animal Faith* (New York: Charles Scribners' Sons, 1923), 247; *Realms of Being* (New York: Charles Scribners' Sons, 1942), 141; and *The Letters of George Santayana*, Book 6 (Cambridge, MA: MIT Press, 2004), 58, 187. Santayana's reference is to Spinoza's *Ethics*, Part II, Prop. XVII, Scholium: "Moreover . . . we clearly understand what is the difference between, *e.g.*, the idea of Peter which constitutes the essence of the mind of Peter, and the idea of Peter as it exists in the mind of another, say, Paul. The first directly explains the essence of the body of Peter, nor does it involve existence save as long as Peter exists; but the second idea indicates rather the disposition of Paul than the nature of Peter, and so as long as this disposition of Paul's lasts his mind will regard Peter though he no longer exists as if he were nevertheless present to him" (trans. A. Boyle [New York: E. P. Dutton & Co. Inc., 1910], 54–55).

4. Quoted in Anton Felix Schindler, *Beethoven as I Knew Him: A Biography*, ed. Donald W. MacArdle, trans. Constance S. Jolly (Chapel Hill: University of North Carolina Press, 1966), 474.

5. Charles S. Peirce, "How to Make Our Ideas Clear," *Writings of Charles S. Peirce: A Chronological Edition*, vol. 3, 1872–1878 (Bloomington: Indiana University Press, 1986), 261.

1. ART AND MORALITY: ON THE AMBIGUITY OF A DISTINCTION

Originally published in *The Journal of Aesthetics and Art Criticism* 32, no. 1 (Autumn 1973): 103–6.

1. Dionne Warwick, "Loneliness Remembers What Happiness Forgets," written by Burt Bacharach, 1970.

2. Quoted by Robert Hughes in "Art: An Obsession with Seeing," *Time* (8 April 1974).

3. William Butler Yeats, *The Collected Works of W. B. Yeats*, vol. 1, 2d ed., ed. Richard J. Finneran (New York: Scribner, 1997), 251.

2. MORALITY BOUND AND UNBOUND: SOME PARAMETERS OF LITERARY ART

Originally published in *Actes Du VIIe Congrès International D'esthétique* [Proceedings of the Seventh International Congress of Aesthetics], Bucarest, August 28–September 2, 1972, Part I (Academiei Republicii Socialiste Romañia, 1977).

1. Although some form of this quotation has been attributed to Samuel Goldwyn at least since 1949 (George E. Sokolsky, "These Days: Visit to Hollywood," *Owosso Argus-Press*, March 19, 1949, page 4), the original source cannot be verified. One of Goldwyn's biographers says it had long been the attitude among Hollywood filmmakers and is falsely attributed to Goldwyn (A. Scott Berg, *Goldwyn: A Biography* [New York: Riverhead Books, 1998], 219); another biographer calls the saying a Hollywood cliché (Arthur Marx, *Goldwyn: A Biography of the Man Behind the Myth* [New York: Norton, 1976], 175).

2. Charles Marowitz, "If a House Is on Fire and I Cry Fire . . . ," *New York Times*, 2 January 1972, Sec. 2, 5.

3. H. Osborne, "General Report," in in *Actes Du VIIe Congrès International D'esthétique* [Proceedings of the Seventh International Congress of Aesthetics], Bucarest, August 28–September 2, 1972, Part I, (Academiei Republicii Socialiste România, 1977), 68.

3. MUSIC, MODULATION, AND METAPHOR

Originally presented as "Music, Modulation, and Time," at the International Congress of Aesthetics, Dubrovnik, Yugoslavia, August 1980.

1. *The Sense of Beauty* (Cambridge, MA: MIT Press, 1988), 64–74.

2. "April is the cruelest month, breeding / Lilacs out of the dead land, mixing / Memory and desire, stirring / Dull roots with spring rain" (T.S. Eliot, "The Waste Land," in *Collected Poems: 1909–1962* [London: Faber and Faber, 1963]).

3. John Murdock Tarrh, "Gustav Mahler's *Das Lied von der Erde*" (master's thesis, New England Conservatory of Music, 2006), 34.

4. As spoken by Hamlet. Shakespeare, *Hamlet*, 5.2.363.

4. PERFORMANCE AND OBLIGATION: MUSICAL VARIATIONS ON ART AND MORALITY

Originally published as "Performance and Obligation," in *What Is Music?: An Introduction to the Philosophy of Music*, ed. Philip Alperson (University Park: Pennsylvania State University Press, 1987), 255–81.

1. Francis Sparshott, "Aesthetics of Music: Limits and Grounds," in Alperson, *What Is Music?*, 82.

2. Some of the material in this essay was drawn from "Is There an Obligation to Accuracy in the Performing Arts," a paper I read at the 1980 meeting of the American Society for Aesthetics in Milwaukee, Wisconsin.

3. Nelson Goodman, *The Languages of Art: An Approach to a Theory of Symbols* (Indianapolis, IN: Bobbs-Merrill Company, Inc., 1968), 186.

4. Sparshott, "Aesthetics of Music," in Alperson, *What Is Music?*, 82.

5. Sparshott, "Aesthetics of Music," in Alperson, *What Is Music?*, 82.

6. Sparshott, "Aesthetics of Music," in Alperson, *What Is Music?*, 82.

7. Sparshott, "Aesthetics of Music," in Alperson, *What Is Music?*, 83.

8. Sparshott, "Aesthetics of Music," in Alperson, *What Is Music?*, 82.

9. Sparshott, "Aesthetics of Music," in Alperson, *What Is Music?*, 82.

10. In an American Society for Aesthetics conference city, so it invited reflections on interpretation.

11. Sparshott, "Aesthetics of Music," in Alperson, *What Is Music?*, 47.

12. Sparshott, "Aesthetics of Music," in Alperson, *What Is Music?*, 46.

13. Sparshott, "Aesthetics of Music," in Alperson, *What Is Music?*, 46.

14. Sparshott, "Aesthetics of Music," in Alperson, *What Is Music?*, 37.

15. Cf. *Encyclopedia Britannica*, 14th ed., s.v. "harmony," by D. F. Tovey: "The contrast between major and minor keys acquires a high emotional value" (207); "The loss of modal subtleties is more than compensated by the powerful dramatic and architectonic values of clearly-established keys with a capacity for modulation to similar keys in relations of clear significance" (206).

16. David Carrier, "Interpreting Musical Performances," *The Monist* 66, no. 2 (April 1983): 205.

17. *Principles of Psychology* (New York: Henry Holt and Company, 1890), 243.

18. Fred Hoyle, *The Black Cloud* (New York: Harper & Brothers, 1957), 159.

19. Hoyle, *The Black Cloud*, 158.

20. Hoyle, *The Black Cloud*, 158.

21. Goodman, *Languages of Art*, 185.

22. Sparshott, "Aesthetics of Music," in Alperson, *What Is Music?*, 89.

23. Edward Strickland, "Moralist at the Keyboard," review of *The Glenn Gould Reader*, ed. Tim Page, and *Reflections from the Keyboard: The World of the Concert Pianist*, by David Dubal, *New York Times*, 30 December 1984, Sunday Book Review.

24. Strickland, "Moralist at the Keyboard."

25. Michiko Kakutani, "Do Facts and Fiction Mix?" *New York Times*, 27 January 1980, Sunday Book Review.

26. Susan Sontag, "Remembering Barthes," *New York Review of Books*, 15 May 1980.

27. George Stade, "A Luminous Parable," review of *Man in the Holocene*, by Max Frisch, *New York Times*, 22 June 1980, Sunday Book Review.

28. Harold C. Schonberg, "A Critic Reflects on 44 Years in the Business," Music View, *New York Times*, 6 July 1980.

5. A MOZARTIAN RECOGNITION SCENE

Originally presented as "A Mozartian Recognition Scene, or, Some Notes on Knowledge and Art," at the International Congress of Aesthetics, Darmstadt, West Germany, August 1976.

1. *Poetics*, XI, 1451a30–36. This particular phrasing is from the translation by Samuel Henry Butcher, *Aristotle's Theory of Poetry and Fine Art* (London: Macmillan and Co., 1895), 39.

6. A NOTE ON ECONOMY AND ART

Originally presented at the 32nd annual meeting of The American Society for Aesthetics, University of Minnesota, Minneapolis, 24 October 1974. It was part of the session on Art, Craft, and Morality.

1. "Poetry in Concrete," Art, *Time*, 11 November 1957, 104.

2. "Spectacular Structures for Olympic Games," *Life*, 15 August 1960, 56.

3. One critic of this essay thought it should be much longer. If it were less succinct and economical, it would not illustrate its own point.

7. AN AESTHETIC GLANCE AT THE CONSTITUTION: STYLE, INTENTION, PERFORMANCE

Originally published in *Philosophical Reflections on the United States Constitution: A Collection of Bicentennial Essays*, Studies in Social and Political Theory, vol. 4, ed. Christopher B. Gray (Lewiston, NY: Edwin Mellen Press, 1989), 98–107. Ideas for this essay grew out of a Symposium on Art and Law at Fairfield University (Fairfield, Connecticut), 4 April 1975.

1. Aesthetic approaches in these areas are not unusual. For example, Albert Furtwangler, *The Authority of Publius: A Reading of the Federalist Papers* (Ithaca, NY: Cornell University Press, 1984), applies literacy and stylistic considerations to the Federalist Papers. The Declaration of Independence has been studied stylistically in great detail.

2. Cf. Ferdinand Lundberg, *Cracks in the Constitution* (Secaucus, NJ: Lyle Stuart, 1980), 128.

3. Edward Dumbauld, *The Constitution of the United States* (Norman: University of Oklahoma Press, 1964), 160–61.

4. Dumbauld, *The Constitution*, 56n103.

5. William K. Wimsatt and Monroe C. Beardsley, "The Intentional Fallacy," in *Problems in Aesthetics: An Introductory Book of Readings*, 2nd ed., ed. Morris Weitz (New York: Macmillan, 1970), 347–60.

6. Frank Donovan, *Mr. Madison's Constitution: The Story behind the Constitutional Convention* (New York: Dodd, Mead, 1965), 69–70.

7. See also Chapter 4, "Performance and Obligation."

8. *Hearings before the Senate Committee on the Judiciary on the Nomination of Judge Antonin Scalia to Be Associate Justice of the Supreme Court of the United States*, S. Hrg. 99–1064 (1982), 32 (statement of Antonin Scalia, nominee for the Supreme Court).

9. Faculty who have ever worked on Handbooks and Grievance Procedure documents have sometimes discovered that loose structure leaves free what wordiness binds.

10. I would no more want radical restagings of the Constitution than I would of Mozart's *Don Giovanni*, which was fashioned concurrently with the Constitution in 1787.

8. HUMAN RIGHTS AND ARTISTIC APPRECIATIONS

Originally published in *Essays in Arts & Sciences* 8 (May 1979): 1–6.

1. George Santayana, *The Sense of Beauty*, vol. 2 of *The Works of George Santayana*, eds. William G. Holzberger and Herman J. Saatkamp Jr. (Cambridge, MA: MIT Press, 1988), 33.

2. See particularly Arnold Isenberg, "Critical Communication," *The Philosophical Review* 58, no. 4 (1949): 330–44.

3. By "articulate" and "articulation" I obviously mean communications of different kinds. The wail of a baby is an articulation, as is, under certain circumstances, the movement of a fetus. It has been argued that Indians had no right to their lands on the grounds that they did not articulate such rights in deeds of possession. Yet they certainly articulated their angers and frustrations in their attempts to regain the traditional use of their lands. Part of the point of this paper is to get away from the notion of rights as having to do merely with abstract claims and precise, legalistic utterance.

4. My characterization of human rights comes close to what Hegel has written about honor: "honour is not only a semblance in me myself, but must also exist in the mind and recognition of *another*, which again on its part makes a claim to a similar honourable recognition" (G. W. F. Hegel, *The Philosophy of Fine Art*, trans. F. P. B. Osmaston, vol. 2 [London: G. Bell and Sons, 1920; New York: Hacker Art Books, 1975], 335). Hegel goes on to say, "it is purely a matter of personal caprice how far I choose to extend the claim and to what material I care to relate it" (335). I would grant a *measure* of caprice—which is why claims

are not rationally resolvable. But the capacity for caprice belongs to all of us, and we can warm to the quaintness of another's claim in the light of the recognition of our own uniqueness and capriciousness.

5. Quoted in Edward S. Shapiro, "Right Turn? Jews and the American Conservative Movement," in *Jews in American Politics: Essays*, rev. ed., ed. Louis Sandy Maisel and Ira N. Forman (Lanham, MD: Rowman and Littlefield, 2004), 202.

9. INTERPRETING PEIRCE

Originally published in *Transactions of the Charles S. Peirce Society* 21, no. 1 (1985): 109–19. I hold in deliberate abeyance whether I am interpreting (1) Peirce the man, (2) the argument of "The Fixation of Belief," (3) the literary status of "The Fixation of Belief," or (4) all of the above.

1. References are to *The Writings of Charles S. Peirce: A Chronological Edition*, ed. Christian J. Kloesel, vol. 3, 1872–1878 (Bloomington: Indiana University Press, 1986).

2. *Writings of Peirce*, 257.

3. *Writings of Peirce*, 253.

4. *Compact Edition of the Oxford English Dictionary*, s.v. "bride."

5. Elizabeth Flower and Murray G. Murphey, *A History of Philosophy in America*, vol. 2 (New York: Capricorn Books, 1977), 592.

6. *Writings of Peirce*, 256.

7. *Writings of Peirce*, 249–50.

8. *Writings of Peirce*, 257.

9. Max Fisch was kind enough to read my paper and to give me some useful suggestions. I draw here on some of the detailed information about Peirce that he supplied to me. Peirce was not divorced in 1877, as I might have implied. He was separated from Harriet Melusina ("Zina") Fay Peirce but did not divorce her until 1883, when he chose another bride, Juliette Froissy Pourtalai.

I should have mentioned the "Melusina" paragraph "How to Make Our Ideas Clear." Those lines are similar in spirit to the ones I reflected upon. If anything, they are more direct, personal, poignant, ironic, and moving than those at the end of "The Fixation of Belief":

Many a man has cherished for years as his hobby some vague shadow of an idea, too meaningless to be positively false; he has, nevertheless, passionately loved it, has made it his companion by day and by night, and has given to it his strength and his life, leaving all other occupations for its sake, and in short has lived with it and for it, until it has become, as it were flesh of his flesh and bone of his bone; and then he has waked up some bright morning to find it gone, clean vanished away like the beautiful Melusina of the fable, and the essence of his life gone with it. I have myself known such a man; and who can tell how many histories of circle-squarers, metaphysicians, astrologers, and what not, may not be told in the old German [French!] story? (*Writings of Peirce*, 261)

A word about closing paragraphs: Peirce decided to delete the ending of "The Fixation of Belief" when he edited it in 1893. So the occasion for my piece, in a manner of speaking (but only in a manner of speaking), is gone. My own closing paragraph, a friendly critic pointed out to me, is stylistically wrong and inappropriate. In modest imitation of the irony of the master, I too will request its deletion after it has been published.

10. ON RUF'S *THE CREATION OF CHAOS: WILLIAM JAMES AND THE STYLISTIC MAKING OF A DISORDERLY WORLD*

Originally published as a review of Frederick J. Ruf, *The Creation of Chaos: William James and the Stylistic Making of a Disorderly World*, in *Transactions of the Charles S. Peirce Society* 28, no. 4 (1992): 888–93.

1. Frederick J. Ruf, *The Creation of Chaos: William James and the Stylistic Making of a Disorderly World* (Albany: State University of New York Press, 1991), 115.

2. Ruf, *Creation of Chaos*, 69.

3. Ruf, *Creation of Chaos*, xvi.

4. Ruf, *Creation of Chaos*, xv.

5. Ruf, *Creation of Chaos*, xv.

6. Ruf, *Creation of Chaos*, 135.

7. Ruf, *Creation of Chaos*, 80.

8. Ruf, *Creation of Chaos*, 77.

9. Ruf, *Creation of Chaos*, 46.

10. Ruf, *Creation of Chaos*, 17.

11. Ruf, *Creation of Chaos*, 123.

12. Ruf, *Creation of Chaos*, 136.

13. Ruf, *Creation of Chaos*, 137.

14. Ruf, *Creation of Chaos*, 138.

15. Ruf, *Creation of Chaos*, 9, 130.

16. Ruf, *Creation of Chaos*, 140.

17. Ruf, *Creation of Chaos*, 67.

11. HOW SARTRE MUST BE READ: AN EXAMINATION OF A PHILOSOPHIC METHOD

Originally published in *Bucknell Review* 16, no. 1 (March 1968): 18–29.

1. Jean-Paul Sartre, *Literature and Existentialism*, trans. Bernard Frechtman (New York: Citadel Press, 1962), 7–37.

2. Sartre, *Literature and Existentialism*, 8.

3. Sartre, *Literature and Existentialism*, 8.

4. Sartre, *Literature and Existentialism*, 8.

5. Sartre, *Literature and Existentialism*, 9.

6. Sartre, *Literature and Existentialism*, 10.

7. Sartre, *Literature and Existentialism*, 11.

8. Sartre, *Literature and Existentialism*, 12.

9. Sartre, *Literature and Existentialism*, 13.

10. Sartre, *Literature and Existentialism*, 13.

11. Sartre, *Literature and Existentialism*, 13.

12. Sartre, *Literature and Existentialism*, 14.

13. I have avoided any appeal to Sartre's own discussion of method in the presentation here, but various suggestions and turns of phrase, particularly in *Critique de la raison dialectique* (Paris: Gallimard, 1960), could have been called upon. For example, there is Sartre's distinction between "analytic reason" and "dialectical reason" (perhaps the distinction between what has also been called "essential analysis" and "existential analysis," cf. Peter Fransen, "Three Ways of Dogmatic Thought," *Cross Currents* 13 [Spring 1963]: 142–44), the former getting us into the contradictions we have dealt with, the latter getting us out of them, or at least beyond them. Further, Sartre's discussion of a series and a group is comparable to our distinction between items taken in isolation and items constituting an array. What Sartre does in his "existential analysis" is to show how a series turns into a group; or, less crudely, he displays the complicated and dynamic interplay between them, the "double reciprocal relationship."

14. Sartre, *Literature and Existentialism*, 37n5.

15. Sartre, *Literature and Existentialism*, 10.

16. Sartre, *Literature and Existentialism*, 8.

17. Sartre, *Literature and Existentialism*, 36.

18. George Santayana, *Winds of Doctrine* (London: J. M. Dent & Sons, 1913), 115.

12. ON BEARDSLEY'S "AN AESTHETIC DEFINITION OF ART"

Originally published in *What Is Art?*, ed. Hugh Curtler (New York: Haven Publications, 1983), 33–47.

1. Arthur C. Danto, "Artworks and Real Things," *Theoria* 39 (1973): 17.

2. Joseph Margolis, "An Autobiographical Sketch of a Philosophy of Art" (presentation, annual meeting of the American Society for Aesthetics, Milwaukee, Wisconsin, 1980).

3. Monroe Beardsley, "An Aesthetic Definition of Art," in *What Is Art?*, ed. Hugh Curtler (New York: Haven Publications, Inc., 1983), 15.

4. Beardsley, "An Aesthetic Definition," 15.

5. Beardsley, "An Aesthetic Definition," 16.

6. Beardsley, "An Aesthetic Definition," 16.

7. Beardsley, "An Aesthetic Definition," 16.

8. Beardsley, "An Aesthetic Definition," 16.

9. Beardsley, "An Aesthetic Definition," 17.

10. Beardsley, "An Aesthetic Definition," 16.

11. Beardsley, "An Aesthetic Definition," 24.

12. Beardsley, "An Aesthetic Definition," 25.

13. Beardsley, "An Aesthetic Definition," 27.

14. As quoted in *What Is Art?*, 32. Originally published by Joseph Margolis in "An Autobiographical Sketch of a Philosophy of Art."

15. Beardsley, "An Aesthetic Definition," 27.

16. Beardsley, "An Aesthetic Definition," 17.

17. Beardsley, "An Aesthetic Definition," 28.

18. *Parmenides*, 130c–d.

19. *What Is Art?* ed. Hugh Curtler (New York: Haven Publications, 1983).

20. Beardsley, "An Aesthetic Definition," 20.

21. Beardsley, "An Aesthetic Definition," 18.

22. Beardsley, "An Aesthetic Definition," 18.

23. Beardsley, "An Aesthetic Definition," 22.

24. Beardsley, "An Aesthetic Definition," 18.

25. Beardsley, "An Aesthetic Definition," 18.

26. Beardsley, "An Aesthetic Definition," 18.

27. Beardsley, "An Aesthetic Definition," 18.

28. Beardsley, "An Aesthetic Definition," 18.

29. Beardsley, "An Aesthetic Definition," 16.

30. Beardsley, "An Aesthetic Definition," 21.

31. Monroe Beardsley, "The Philosophy of Literature," in *Aesthetics*, ed. George Dickie and R. J. Sclafani (New York: St. Martins, 1977), 326–27.

32. Beardsley, "An Aesthetic Definition," 23.

33. *The Sense of Beauty*, vol. 2 of *The Works of George Santayana*, eds. William G. Holzberger and Herman J. Saatkamp Jr. (Cambridge, MA: MIT Press, 1988), 33.

34. See Aldous Huxley, "Young Archimedes," in *Young Archimedes and Other Stories* (New York: George H. Doran, 1924), 250–312, for a literary exploration of this connection between logic and art.

13. LESSING AS PHILOSOPHICAL DRAMATIST:
ON *NATHAN THE WISE*

1. Gotthold Ephraim Lessing, *Nathan the Wise*, trans. Bayard Quincy Morgan (New York: Frederick Ungar Publishing Co., 1983).

2. Act 3, Scene 2, lines 17–18.

3. Daniel Mendelsohn, "The Bad Boy of Athens," in *How Beautiful It Is and How Easily It Can Be Broken* (New York: HarperCollins, 2008), 409.

4. Lessing, *Nathan*, 118, lines 144–45.

5. Lessing, *Nathan*, 118, lines 146–47.

6. Lessing, *Nathan*, 97–98, lines 36–62.

7. Lessing, *Nathan*, vi.

8. Henry B. Allison, *Lessing and the Enlightenment* (Ann Arbor: University of Michigan Press, 1966).

9. Allison, *Lessing*, 60.

10. Allison, *Lessing*, 117.

11. Allison, *Lessing*, 121.

12. Allison, *Lessing*, 132.

13. George Santayana, *Realms of Being* (New York: Charles Scribner's Sons, 1942), 853.

14. LEWIS CARROLL: PEDOPHILE AND/OR PLATONIST?

Originally published in modified form as "Carroll's Platonic Love," *Knight Letter* 75 (Summer 2005): 11–14. An earlier version was presented at the spring 2005 meeting of the Lewis Carroll Society of North America, New York, 30 April 2005.

1. Kenneth Baker, "In the Eye of the Beholder: Lewis Carroll Photography Show Raises Difficult Aesthetic Questions," *San Francisco Chronicle*, 5 August 2002.

2. I deliberately conjoin the words attribution and creation, since they are part of my theme.

3. Arthur Danto, "Body and Soul," *The Nation*, 19 July 2004, 41.

4. Anthony Lane, Books, "Art for Love's Sake," *New Yorker*, 14 August 2000, 80.

5. E. Fuller Torrey, M.D., and Judy Miller, "The Capture of the Snark," *Knight Letter* 73 (Spring 2004): 21–25.

6. Henry Holiday, "The Snark's Significance," *Academy* (29 January 1898), reprinted in *Lewis Carroll and His Illustrators: Collaborations and Correspondence, 1865–1898*, ed. Morton N. Cohen and Edward Wakeling (New York: Cornell University Press, 2003), 33. Quoted in Torrey and Miller, "The Capture of the Snark," 24.

7. George Santayana, *Interpretations of Poetry and Religion*, vol. 3 of *The Works of George Santayana*, ed. William G. Holzberger and Herman J. Saatkamp Jr. (Cambridge, MA: MIT Press, 1989), 74.

8. Santayana, *Interpretations*, 74.

9. Santayana, *Interpretations*, 74.

10. Santayana, *Interpretations*, 75.

11. Santayana, *Interpretations*, 76.

12. Stephen Greenblatt, *Will in the World* (New York: Norton, 2004), 75.

13. Santayana, *Interpretations*, 75.

14. See Justus Buchler, *The Metaphysics of Natural Complexes*, 2nd ed., ed. Kathleen Wallace, Armen Marsoobian, and Robert S. Corrington (Albany: State University of New York Press, 1990).

15. *Egotism and German Philosophy* (London: J. M. Dent & Sons, 1916), 116.

15. ART AND DEATH: A SERMON
IN THE FORM OF AN ESSAY

Originally published in *Philosophical Aspects of Thanatology*, vol. 1, ed. Florence M. Hetzler and Austin H. Kutscher (New York: Arno Press, 1978), 77–81.

1. Leo Tolstoy, *Tolstoy's Short Fiction*, second edition, edited and with revised translations by Michael R. Katz (New York: Norton, 2008), 85.

2. Leo Tolstoy, *Tolstoy's Short Fiction*, second edition, edited and with revised translations by Michael R. Katz (New York: Norton, 2008), 128.

3. L. N. Tolstoy, *Complete Works* in 90 vols., Vol. 22 (Moscow, 1936), 508. The accuracy of this English translation has been verified by the editors, but its source remains unidentified.

4. George Santayana, *The Sense of Beauty*, vol. 2 of *The Works of George Santayana*, ed. William G. Holzberger and Herman J. Saatkamp Jr. (Cambridge, MA: MIT Press, 1988), 141.

5. Santayana, *Sense of Beauty*, 141.

6. Charles Hartshorne, The Zero Fallacy and Other Essays in Neoclassical Philosophy (Chicago: Open Court, 1997), 206.

16. BRANCUSI: SOME CHANGING
AND CHANGELESS PERSPECTIVES

Originally presented at the Brancusi Colloquium, Fordham University, Bronx, New York, 9 April 1976.

1. Sidney Geist, *Brancusi: A Study of the Sculpture* (New York: Grossman Publishers, 1968), 146.

2. Justus Buchler, *The Main of Light* (Oxford: Oxford University Press, 1974), 171.

3. "2 Sculptors Seek to Withdraw Work From Whitney Show," *New York Times*, 31 March 1976.

4. Andre Malraux, "As Picasso Said, Why Assume that to Look Is to See? A Talk between Malraux and the Master," *The New York Times Magazine*, 2 November 1975, 260.

5. Geist, *Brancusi*, 64.

6. Geist, *Brancusi*, 177.

17. DRAMA AND DIALECTIC: WAYS OF PHILOSOPHIZING

Originally published in *The Southern Journal of Philosophy* 10, no. 2 (Summer 1972): 137–47.

1. George Santayana, *The Idler and His Works*, ed. Daniel Cory (New York: George Braziller, 1957), 56.

2. Santayana, *Idler and His Works*, 53.

3. Santayana, *Idler and His Works*, 60.

4. George Santayana, "Apologia Pro Mente Sua," in *The Philosophy of George Santayana*, vol. 2 of *The Library of Living Philosophers*, ed. Paul Arthur Schilpp (Evanston, IL, and Chicago: Northwestern University Press, 1940), 604.

5. George Santayana Collection, Miscellaneous Notebook, IX: 14:4, Special Collections, Columbia University. Reprinted in Morris Grossman, "Santayana as Dramatist and Dialectician: A Critical Estimate Made with the Help of Unpublished Manuscripts" (PhD diss., Columbia University, 1960), 181.

6. George Santayana, *The Letters of George Santayana*, Book 6: 1937–1940, vol. 5 of *The Works of George Santayana*, ed. William G. Holzberger and Herman J. Saatkamp Jr. (Cambridge, MA: MIT Press, 2004), 190.

7. George Santayana, *Winds of Doctrine* (London: J. M. Dent & Sons, 1913), 115.

8. Santayana, "Apologia," 569.

9. Jacques Barzun, *The Energies of Art* (New York: Vintage Books, 1962), 94.

10. Thomas Mann, quoted in Paul Friedlander, *Plato*, trans. Hans Meyerhoff (New York: Pantheon Books, 1958), 137.

11. George Santayana, *Dialogues in Limbo*, rev. ed. (New York: Charles Scribner's Sons, 1948), 192.

12. Santayana, *Dialogues in Limbo*, 190.

13. Santayana, *Dialogues in Limbo*, 190.

14. Santayana, *Dialogues in Limbo*, 193.

15. Santayana, *Dialogues in Limbo*, 193.

16. Santayana, *Dialogues in Limbo*, 210.

17. George Santayana, *Soliloquies in England and Later Soliloquies* (New York: Charles Scribner's Sons, 1922), 83.

18. ONTOLOGY AND MORALITY: SANTAYANA ON THE "REALLY REAL"

Originally published as "Reality Revisited: The Controlled Ambiguity of Santayana's Realms," in *Two Centuries of American Philosophy*, ed. Peter Caws (Totowa, NJ: Rowman and Littlefield, 1980), 128–34.

1. Justus Buchler, *The Concept of Method* (New York: Columbia University Press, 1961), 166.

2. George Santayana, *Realms of Being* (New York: Charles Scribner's Sons, 1942), 323.

3. Note that we can use some of the same terms to describe the good and evil aspects of existence.

4. Santayana, *Realms of Being*, xvi.

5. Santayana, *Realms of Being*, 831.

6. Santayana, *Realms of Being*, 831–32.

7. George Santayana, *The Last Puritan: A Memoir in the Form of a Novel*, vol. 4 of *The Works of George Santayana*, eds. William G. Holzberger and Herman J. Saatkamp Jr. (Cambridge, MA: MIT Press, 1994), 572. In Santayana's earlier work, *Platonism and the Spiritual Life*, the text reads "for after life is done, and the world is gone up in smoke, what realities may the spirit of a man boast to have embraced without illusion, save the very forms of those illusions by which he has been deceived?" ([New York: Charles Scribner's Sons, 1927], 89).

19. SPIRITED SPIRITUALITY

Originally published as "Santayana: Spirited Spirituality," *Frontiers in American Philosophy*, vol. 2 (College Station: Texas A&M University Press, 1996), 127–32. Some ideas for this paper were generated by reflections on Victorino Tejera's paper, "Spirituality in Santayana, and the Critique of Calculative Reason" (which later appeared as "Spirituality in Santayana," *Transactions of the Charles S. Peirce Society* 25 [1989]: 503–29). I commented on that paper at the annual meeting of the Society for the Advancement of American Philosophy, at Pennsylvania State University, 4 March 1988. My title, "Spirited Spirituality," is an oxymoron, and it is intended to be in the spirit (may I say) of Santayana's awareness of the ambiguous and even contradictory senses of "spirit" in his philosophy.

1. Kenneth McKenna, letter to the editor, *New York Times*, 25 April 1988.

2. These categories, I have argued elsewhere, are particularly useful in studying all aspects of Santayana's achievement. See Chapter 17, "Drama and Dialectic: Ways of Philosophizing."

3. George Santayana, "Apologia Pro Mente Sua," in *The Philosophy of George Santayana*, vol. 2 of *The Library of Living Philosophers*, ed. Paul Arthur Schilpp (Evanston, IL, and Chicago: Northwestern University Press, 1940), 554.

4. Santayana saw that this was the case in Indian philosophy, which intrigued him endlessly, and against which he bounced off his own reflections.

5. George Santayana, *Realms of Being* (New York: Charles Scribner's Sons, 1942), 742.

6. George Santayana, *The Sense of Beauty*, vol. 2 of *The Works of George Santayana*, ed. William G. Holzberger and Herman J. Saatkamp Jr. (Cambridge, MA: The MIT Press, 1988).

7. *Sense of Beauty*, 35.

8. George Santayana, *Scepticism and Animal Faith* (New York: Charles Scribner's Sons, 1923), 276.

9. Santayana, *Realms of Being*, 817.

10. Santayana, *Realms of Being*, 612.

11. Some would see this approach to dialectic as the pervasively hidden, and at times not so hidden, Platonic refrain and message. Santayana, as we know, constantly disparaged logic while never relinquishing the search for logical clarity. In the dialogue "The Vortex of Dialectic" (George Santayana, *Dialogues in Limbo*, rev. ed. [New York: Charles Scribner's Sons, 1948], 189–217), he dealt in specific fashion with the thwarting, albeit necessary, futility of logic.

12. Santayana, *Realms of Being*, 647 (italics added).

13. Santayana, *Realms of Being*, 694.

14. Santayana, *Realms of Being*, 696.

15. Santayana, *Realms of Being*, 782.

16. Santayana, *Scepticism and Animal Faith*, 274.

17. Though I have been suggesting connections with the existentialist tradition, there is no evidence that Santayana cared much for the writers in this tradition.

18. Santayana, *Realms of Being*, 109–10.

19. Santayana, *Scepticism and Animal Faith*, 275.

20. Santayana, *Scepticism and Animal Faith*, 276.

21. Santayana, *Scepticism and Animal Faith*, 277.

22. Santayana, *Scepticism and Animal Faith*, 278.

23. Santayana, *Scepticism and Animal Faith*, 284.

24. Santayana, *Scepticism and Animal Faith*, 286.

25. Santayana, *Scepticism and Animal Faith*, 280.

20. INTERPRETING *INTERPRETATIONS*

Originally presented at the annual meeting of the Santayana Society, Atlanta, Georgia, 28 December 1989. Subsequently published in *Overheard in Seville: Bulletin of the Santayana Society* 8 (1990): 18–28.

1. Richard Rorty, *Contingency, Irony and Solidarity* (Cambridge, UK: Cambridge University Press, 1989).

2. Rorty, *Contingency*, 76.

3. Rorty, *Contingency*, 79.

4. Rorty, *Contingency*, 78.

5. "Preface," *Interpretations of Poetry and Religion*, ed. William G. Holzberger and Herman J. Saatkamp Jr. (Cambridge, MA: The MIT Press, 1989), 3–5.

6. Santayana, *Interpretations*, 3.

7. Santayana, *Interpretations*, 4.

8. Santayana, *Interpretations*, 127; quoted in Joel Porte, "Santayana's *Interpretations of Poetry and Religion*: An Introduction," in *Interpretations*, xxi.

9. Carol Gilligan, *In a Different Voice* (Cambridge, MA: Harvard University Press, 1982).

10. Santayana, "The Homeric Hymns," in *Interpretations*, 19–34.

11. George Santayana, *Three Philosophical Poets: Lucretius, Dante, and Goethe* (Cambridge, MA: Harvard University Press, 1910), 214.

12. George Santayana, *Winds of Doctrine* (London: J. M. Dent & Sons, 1913), 115.

13. George Santayana, *The Sense of Beauty*, ed. William G. Holzberger and Herman J. Saatkamp Jr. (Cambridge, MA: The MIT Press, 1988), 19–21.

14. Santayana, *Interpretations*, 14.

15. Santayana, *Interpretations*, 104.

16. Santayana, *Interpretations*, 104.

17. Santayana, *Interpretations*, 96.

18. Santayana, *Interpretations*, 38.

19. Santayana, *Interpretations*, 38–39.

20. Santayana, *Interpretations*, 39.

21. Santayana, *Interpretations*, 39.

22. Santayana, *Interpretations*, 39.

23. Santayana, *Interpretations*, 43.

24. Santayana, *Interpretations*, xxviii.

25. Santayana, *Interpretations*, 99.

26. Santayana, *Interpretations*, 99.

27. Santayana, *Interpretations*, 99.

28. Santayana, *Interpretations*, 100.

29. Santayana, *Interpretations*, 100.

30. Santayana, *Interpretations*, 100.

31. Santayana, *Three Philosophical Poets*, 215.

21. SANTAYANA'S AESTHETICS

Originally published as "George Santayana," in *A Companion to Aesthetics*, ed. David Cooper (Oxford, UK: Blackwell, 1992), 375–76.

1. George Santayana, *The Sense of Beauty: Being the Outlines of Aesthetic Theory*, vol. 2 of *The Works of George Santayana*, ed. William G. Holzberger and Herman J. Saatkamp Jr. (Cambridge, MA: The MIT Press, 1989).

2. George Santayana, *Reason in Art*, vol. 4 of *The Life of Reason* (New York: Charles Scribner's Sons, 1905).

3. Santayana, *Sense of Beauty*, 5.

4. Santayana, *Sense of Beauty*, 11.

5. Santayana, *Sense of Beauty*, 11.

6. Santayana, *Sense of Beauty*, 10.

7. George Santayana, "Apologia Pro Mente Sua," in *The Philosophy of George Santayana*, vol. 2 of *The Library of Living Philosophers*, ed. Paul Arthur Schilpp (Evanston, IL, and Chicago: Northwestern University Press, 1940), 554.

22. SANTAYANA'S *THE LAST PURITAN*

Originally published as a review of George Santayana, *The Last Puritan: A Memoir in the Form of a Novel*, vol. 4 of *The Works of George Santayana*, in *Transactions of the Charles S. Peirce Society* 31, no. 2 (1995): 437–44.

1. George Santayana, *The Last Puritan: A Memoir in the Form of a Novel*, vol. 4 of *The Works of George Santayana*, ed. William G. Holzberger and Herman J. Saatkamp Jr. (Cambridge, MA: The MIT Press, 1994), 21.

2. George Santayana, *Persons and Places*, vol. 1 of *The Works of George Santayana*, ed. William G. Holzberger and Herman J. Saatkamp Jr. (Cambridge, MA: The MIT Press, 1986), 145.

3. Santayana, *The Last Puritan*, 3–4.

4. Santayana, *The Last Puritan*, 3.

5. Holzberger and Saatkamp, "Textual Commentary," in Santayana, *The Last Puritan*, 651.

6. George Santayana, *Interpretation of Poetry and Religion*, vol. 3 of *The Works of George Santayana*, ed. William G. Holzberger and Herman J. Saatkamp Jr. (Cambridge, MA: The MIT Press, 1986), 81.

7. Irving Singer, "An Introduction to *The Last Puritan*," in Santayana, *The Last Puritan*, xli.

8. See Holzberger and Saatkamp, "Discussions of Adopted Readings," in Santayana, *Persons and Places*, 627n427.30, for a discussion of the misquotation and the justification for emending it in the critical edition.

9. Santayana, *Persons and Places*, 145–46.

10. Christopher Morley, review of *The Last Puritan: A Memoir in the Form of a Novel*, by George Santayana, *Book-of-the-Month Club News*, January 1936.

23. SANTAYANA IN CALIFORNIA: THE ENVIRONMENT, TRANSCENDENTALISM, AND NATURE

1. See George Sessions, "Ecocentrism and the Anthropocentric Detour," in *Deep Ecology for the 21st Century*, ed. George Sessions (Boston: Shambala, 1995), 156–83; and Kevin Starr, *Americans and the California Dream 1850–1915* (New York: Oxford University Press, 1973), 419–25.

2. *University of California Chronicle* 13 (1991): 357–80; reprinted in *Winds of Doctrine: Studies in Contemporary Opinion* (New York: Charles Scribner's Sons, 1926), 186–215.

3. *The Sense of Beauty*, ed. William Holzberger and Herman Saatkamp Jr. (Cambridge, MA: MIT Press, 1988), 33.

4. See George Santayana, "The Unknowable," in *Obiter Scripta*, ed Justus Buchler and Benjamin Schwartz (New York: Charles Scribner's Sons, 1936), 162–88.

5. Marlise Simons, "A Breath of Fresh Air? Don't Stroll by the Seine," *New York Times*, 14 July 1995.

6. Simons, "A Breath of Fresh Air?"

7. Richard Bernstein, "Hauling Nature Back Down to Earth," review of Richard White, *The Organic Machine: The Remaking of the Columbia River*, and Daniel B. Botkin, *Our Natural History: The Lessons of Lewis and Clark*, in *New York Times*, 28 July 1995.

8. Bernstein, "Hauling Nature Back Down to Earth."

9. Bernstein, "Hauling Nature Back Down to Earth."

10. Santayana, *Winds of Doctrine*, 200.

11. George Santayana, *Scepticism and Animal Faith: Introduction to a System of Philosophy* (New York: Charles Scribner's Sons, 1923), 205.

12. Santayana, *Scepticism and Animal Faith*, 205.

13. George Santayana, "Apologia Pro Mente Sua," in *The Philosophy of George Santayana*, vol. 2 of *The Library of Living Philosophers*, ed. Paul Arthur Schilpp (Evanston, IL, and Chicago: Northwestern University Press, 1940), 554.

14. Morris Grossman, "Santayana as Dramatist and Dialectician: A Critical Estimate Made with the Help of Unpublished Manuscripts" (PhD diss., Columbia University, 1960), 184.

15. The quotation is from an unpublished manuscript in which it is unclear whether the author wrote "even" or "ever."

16. Morris Grossman, "Santayana as Dramatist and Dialectician," 183.

24. ULTIMATE SANTAYANA

Originally published as "Santayana's Idea of Ultimate Reality and Meaning: Material Universe Making Specific and Limited Things Possible, the Realm of the Spirit Included," in *Ultimate Reality and Meaning: Interdisciplinary Studies in the Philosophy of Understanding* 16, nos. 1–2 (March–June 1993): 87–96.

1. "Nature denies at every moment, not indeed that I am troubled and dreaming, but that there are any natural units like my visions, or anything anomalous in what I hate, or final in what I love. Under these circumstances, what is the part of wisdom? To dream with one eye open; to be detached from the world without hostility to it; to welcome fugitive beauties and pity fugitive sufferings without forgetting for a moment how fugitive they are; and not to lay up treasures, except in heaven" (George Santayana, *Soliloquies in England* [New York: Charles Scribner's Sons, 1922], 96–97).

See also George Santayana, *Realms of Being* (New York: Charles Scribner's Sons, 1942), viii–x; and George Santayana, *Interpretations of Poetry and Religion*, vol. 3 of *The Works of George Santayana*, ed. William G. Holzberger and Herman J. Saatkamp Jr. (Cambridge, MA: The MIT Press, 1989), 156.

2. George Santayana, *The Realms of Being* (New York: Charles Scribner's Sons, 1942), xv.

3. "Between the laughing and the weeping philosopher there is no opposition: *the same* facts that make one laugh make one weep" (George Santayana, *Persons and Places*, vol. 1 of *The Works of George Santayana*, ed. William G. Holzberger and Herman J. Saatkamp Jr. [Cambridge, MA: The MIT Press, 1986], 156).

4. George Santayana, "Ultimate Religion," in *Obiter Scripta*, ed. Justus Buchler and Benjamin Schwartz (New York: Charles Scribner's Sons, 1936), 281.

5. Santayana, "Ultimate Religion," 283.

6. Santayana, "Ultimate Religion," 284.

7. Santayana, "Ultimate Religion," 288.

8. Santayana, "Ultimate Religion," 293.

9. Santayana, "Ultimate Religion," 293.

10. Santayana, "Ultimate Religion," 293.

11. George Santayana, *The Realms of Being* (New York: Charles Scribner's Sons, 1942), 853.

12. Santayana, "Ultimate Religion," 293–94.

Index

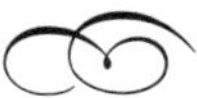

aestheticism, 10, 12, 23, 98

aesthetics, 35, 59, 69, 76, 101, 146–47, 160, 263–66

Alice (*Alice in Wonderland*), 40, 178–89

ambiguity and vagueness, 7–8, 23–24, 29, 31–32, 42–43, 45, 52, 76–79, 95–96, 99–101, 102–3, 107–10, 122, 128, 130, 159, 188–89, 213, 220, 225–26, 230, 232, 234–35, 255, 265, 276, 283

Aristotle: on drama, 251; on knowledge, 169; on life as art, 20; on mental activity, 182; recognition and reversal, 86–87, 89, 217; on sensation, 149; and the State, 3; on tragedy, 193

art: and life, 19–25, 28, 30–32, 35, 41–42, 59, 64, 72, 81, 192, 194–95; and morality, 2–12, 19–25; and nature, 111; and philosophy, 145, 148, 157; and religion, 157, 198, 292; and rights, 109, 111–13; and scarcity, 95; and urgency, 93–96

Beardsley, Monroe, 101, 145–60

Beethoven, Ludwig van, 11, 30, 41–43, 46–47, 50–51, 69, 71, 75–76, 83–84, 193

belief, 242, 245, 294; and desire, 150, 159; determining, 117–26

Bernstein, Leonard, 75

bird song, 37, 50, 67–68, 70, 71

Bond, Edward, 29

Brancusi, Constantin, 199–207

Brecht, Bertolt, 28, 89

Buchler, Justus, 200, 230

Carrier, David, 73–74

Carroll, Lewis, 40, 177–89

castrati, 66

chaos, 127–31

Constitution, U.S., 97–105, 239–40

constellations, 36–37, 49, 50

criticism, 82–83, 272–73; artistic, 94, 109–13, 152, 265–66; literary, 98, 103, 119, 126, 178–79, 188, 249–50, 250; philosophical, 119, 213–14, 240, 246, 275–76

Dante Alighieri, 185–87, 230, 256, 259–61, 272

Danto, Arthur, 146, 159, 181

death, 191–98

The Death of Ivan Ilyich, 191–98

Dewey, John, 23

dialectic, 211–27

distinction(s), 23, 133–34, 138, 157–58, 231, 264–65; aesthetic and erotic, 181, 183, 186; aesthetic and moral, 98; art and morality, 1, 2, 7–8, 9, 11, 14, 19–25, 31, 44, 53; betrayal and expression of emotion, 141; boundness and unboundness, 27–32; on the dominant and in the dominant, 44–45, 55; Don Quixote and Sancho Panza, 253–56; fact and fiction, 81–82; feminine and masculine, 130; intellectual and sensuous, 177–89; internal and external, 130; "is" and "ought," 288–93; life and art, 20, 23; live and recorded performances, 81–82; making and undermining, 134; making and unmaking, 265; making or not making, 158; Nature as man-made or as *physis*, 277–79; newly felt appropriateness and established form, 52; part and the whole, 20–21, 25, 156, 256–57; philosophy and art, 145, 148, 157; practicing and non-practicing, 271; real and unreal, 13; Santayana's making and unmaking, 263–66; Sartre's method, 133–43; sensuous and intellectual, 180–81, 185, 202, 231; speech and song, 67–68; tonic and dominant chords, 38, 45–46, 52, 54–55; work and play, 14, 93, 254–55, 265

Dwayne A. Tunstall, *Yes, But Not Quite: Encountering Josiah Royce's Ethico-Religious Insight*.

Josiah Royce, *Race Questions, Provincialism, and Other American Problems, expanded edition*. Edited by Scott L. Pratt and Shannon Sullivan.

Lara Trout, *The Politics of Survival: Peirce, Affectivity, and Social Criticism*.

John R. Shook and James A. Good, *John Dewey's Philosophy of Spirit, with the 1897 Lecture on Hegel*.

Josiah Warren, *The Practical Anarchist: Writings of Josiah Warren*. Edited and with an Introduction by Crispin Sartwell.

Naoko Saito and Paul Standish, eds., *Stanley Cavell and the Education of Grownups*.

Douglas R. Anderson and Carl R. Hausman, *Conversations on Peirce: Reals and Ideals*.

Rick Anthony Furtak, Jonathan Ellsworth, and James D. Reid, eds., *Thoreau's Importance for Philosophy*.

James M. Albrecht, *Reconstructing Individualism: A Pragmatic Tradition from Emerson to Ellison*.

Mathew A. Foust, *Loyalty to Loyalty: Josiah Royce and the Genuine Moral Life*.

Cornelis de Waal and Krysztof Piotr Skowroński (eds.), *The Normative Thought of Charles S. Peirce*.

Dwayne A. Tunstall, *Doing Philosophy Personally: Thinking about Metaphysics, Theism, and Antiblack Racism*.

Erin McKenna, *Pets, People, and Pragmatism*.

Sami Pihlström, *Pragmatic Pluralism and the Problem of God*.

Thomas M. Alexander, *The Human Eros: Eco-ontology and the Aesthetics of Existence*.

Nahum Dimitri Chandler, *X—The Problem of the Negro as a Problem for Thought*.

John Kaag, *Thinking Through the Imagination: Aesthetics in Human Cognition*.

Kelly A. Parker and Jason Bell (eds.), *The Relevance of Royce*.

W. E. B. Du Bois, *The Problem of the Color Line at the Turn of the Twentieth Century: The Essential Early Essays*. Edited by Nahum Dimitri Chandler.

John Lachs, *Freedom and Limits*. Edited by Patrick Shade.

Morris Grossman, *Art and Morality: Essays in the Spirit of George Santayana*. Edited by Martin A. Coleman.